Spinoza has been called both a 'God-intoxicated man' and an atheist, both a pioneer of secular Judaism and a bitter critic of religion. This study brings together his fundamental philosophical thinking with his conclusions about God and religion. Spinoza was born a Jew but chose to live outside any religious community. He was deeply engaged both in traditional Hebrew learning and in contemporary physical science. He identified God with nature or substance: a theme which runs through his work, enabling him to naturalise religion but – equally important – to divinise nature. He emerges not as a rationalist precursor of the Enlightenment but as a thinker of the highest importance in his own right, both in philosophy and in religion. This book is the fullest study in English for many years on the rôle of God in Spinoza's philosophy.

THE GOD OF SPINOZA

THE GOD OF SPINOZA

A philosophical study

RICHARD MASON

University of Cambridge

CAMBRIDGE
UNIVERSITY PRESS

PUBLISHED BY THE PRESS SYNDICATE OF THE UNIVERSITY OF CAMBRIDGE
The Pitt Building, Trumpington Street, Cambridge CB2 1RP, United Kingdom

CAMBRIDGE UNIVERSITY PRESS
The Edinburgh Building, Cambridge CB2 2RU, United Kingdom
40 West 20th Street, New York, NY 10011–4211, USA
10 Stamford Road, Oakleigh, Melbourne 3166, Australia

© Cambridge 1997

First published 1997

Printed in Great Britain at the University Press, Cambridge

Typeset in 11/12½ Monotype Baskerville

A catalogue record for this book is available from the British Library

Library of Congress cataloguing in publication data

Mason, Richard.
The God of Spinoza: a philosophical study / Richard Mason.
p.   cm.
Includes bibliographical references and index.
ISBN 0 521 58162 1 (hardback)
1. Spinoza, Benedictus de, 1632–1677 – Views on God.   2. God –
History of doctrines – 17th century.   3. Philosophical theology.
1. Title.
B3999.R4M385   1997
210.92–dc20   96–29112   CIP

ISBN 0 521 58162 1 hardback

SE

for Margie

Contents

Preface

This is a study of Spinoza's philosophy seen through his views about the existence, nature and rôle of God.

The titles of Parts I and II derive from the memorial written by Pascal in 1654: Dieu d'Abraham, Dieu d'Isaac, Dieu de Jacob, non des Philosophes et des Savants.

Part I looks at the God of the Philosophers: at God's existence and nature – at how God relates to us and to the rest of the world in terms of causality – at how a knowledge of God is supposed to fit in with other sorts of knowledge.

Part II looks at what Spinoza tells us about religion – its origins, history and practice.

Part III considers his own positive approach to God and religion: his views on religious freedom, his understanding of eternity and his puzzling use of the figure of Christ. The book ends with an assessment of Spinoza on God and religion.

Part I of the study is, of necessity, more philosophically technical, because the logical and metaphysical machinery requires close attention if the force of Spinoza's case is to be appreciated (in some ways, its general outline is misleadingly simple and clear). My interpretation will be controversial. A few people know a great deal about Spinoza and his work. Many people know a little, but would like to know more. This book is meant for the many as well as the few. I have tried not to slow down the discussion by including too much debate with other writers. The conclusions should be of interest to theologians and philosophers of religion as well as to philosophers. The sense of the subject dictates the order of the book; but readers with more interest in religion than in philosophy might prefer to start with Parts II and III and to return afterwards to Part I.

Spinoza's thinking about God and religion occupies an awkward intellectual location. It cannot be understood without a grasp of the central parts of his philosophical work. Conversely, many elements in his central philosophy cannot be understood fully without some grasp of his religious thinking. But those who have been interested in religion have seldom been willing to do justice to the metaphysical foundations of his work; and philosophers – at least in the English-speaking world – have paid too little attention to his religious position. They order this matter better in France; but the works of the best French commentators – Alexandre Matheron, Pierre-François Moreau and Henri Laux – have not yet been translated into English.

Material in Chapters 2, 3 and 8 has appeared in earlier forms in papers in *The Philosophical Quarterly*, *Philosophy*, the *Journal of the History of Philosophy*, *Studia Leibnitiana* and *Metaphilosophy*. These are listed in the bibliography.

I am glad to express my gratitude to Gerard Hughes, Howard Mayled-Porter, Harry Parkinson and Piet Steenbakkers for their advice and help. My interest in Spinoza as a serious philosopher, rather than a historical curiosity, was fired by reading Edwin Curley's *Spinoza's Metaphysics* as an undergraduate. Since Curley is often cited in these pages only to indicate my disagreement with him, it is a pleasure to record my initial, and continuing, debt to his work. It has been an example of what Spinoza deserves.

Abbreviations

For Spinoza:

G I–G IV   *Spinoza Opera*, ed. C. Gebhardt, 4 vols.
Heidelberg: Carl Winter, 1925 (reprinted 1972 vols. I to IV, with a supplement, vol. V, 1987). References to this are given as G I to G IV = vols. I to IV, with page and, where necessary, line. So G III 25/12 = volume III, page 25, line 12.

S   *Tractatus Theologico-Politicus*, trans. S. Shirley, with an introduction by B. S. Gregory, Leiden: Brill, 1989.

Ethics; Treatise on the Emendation of the Intellect

trans. S. Shirley, Indianapolis: Hackett, 1992. References to the *Ethics* are given to the geometrical sections, except where they are very long, where page numbers are used.

Curley   *Short Treatise* and *Descartes' Principles of Philosophy Demonstrated in the Geometric Manner*, from *Collected Works of Spinoza*, trans. and ed. E. M. Curley, vol. I, Princeton University Press, 1985.

L   *Spinoza: The Letters*, trans. S. Shirley, with an introduction and notes by S. Barbone, L. Rice and J. Adler, Indianapolis: Hackett, 1995.

For other writers:

CSMK   *The Philosophical Writings of Descartes*, trans. and ed. J. Cottingham, R. Stoothoff, D. Murdoch, and A. Kenny, 3 vols., Cambridge University Press, 1985 and 1991.

AT   *Œuvres de Descartes*, ed. C. Adam and P. Tannery, revised edn., 11 vols., Paris: Vrin, 1996.

Leibniz   *Philosophical Papers and Letters*, trans. and ed. L. E. Loemker, 2nd edn., Dordrecht: Reidel, 1976.

JPS   *Tanakh: The Holy Scriptures*, Philadelphia: The Jewish Publication Society, 1985.

Any unattributed translations are by the author.

Introduction: Spinoza's many contexts

Baruch or Bento Despinoza was born in Amsterdam on 11 Kislev 5393. Benedictus de Spinoza died forty-four years later at the Hague on 21 February 1677.

A few other clear facts are known about his life. He was born into the Portuguese-Jewish community of Amsterdam. His father was a merchant. His mother died while he was a child. His upbringing, it is believed, was conventionally Jewish.

By 1656, when he was 23, he had already become an anomaly. He was expelled from his synagogue for reasons which remain uncertain, despite much scholarly labour and conjecture.[1] From then onwards he was never a member or adherent of any religious group or community. He used a non-Jewish version of his name. For the rest of his life he studied and wrote, living partly from lens-grinding, and also from the generosity of his friends.

During his lifetime he published, in 1663, a volume on the work of Descartes and, in 1670, anonymously and under a disguised publisher's name, the *Theological-Political Treatise*. Soon after his death his friends brought to publication his posthumous works, including the *Ethics*, presumed to be the perfected expression of his thinking. There were also a number of minor early works and a body of correspondence with many of the leading scholars in Northern Europe.

The outward simplicity of Spinoza's biography, and the bareness of our factual knowledge about him,[2] is greatly misleading. In fact, one of the many problems that surround the interpretation of his work lies in the richness and multiplicity of its contexts. He lived in many worlds. He can be seen and understood from many directions.

---

[1] The fullest discussion is in A. Kasher and S. Biderman, 'Why was Baruch de Spinoza Excommunicated?', in D. Katz and J. Israel (eds.), *Sceptics, Millenarians and Jews* (Leiden: Brill, 1990).

[2] The only comprehensive modern work is K. O. Meinsma, *Spinoza et son cercle* (revised H. Méchoulan, *et al.* and translated from the 1896 edition), ed. S. Roosenburg and J.-P. Osier (Paris: Vrin, 1983). A clear, brief guide to Spinoza's life is given by Brad S. Gregory in his introduction to S.

The best introduction to his thinking about God and religion is to look at
the contexts in which it developed. To distil at least a dozen of these is
not difficult. Almost all of them are the subject of continuing scholarly
controversy:
(a) Spinoza was born and brought up as a Jew. Whatever he may have
wished himself, and regardless of his expulsion from his native community, it was as a Jew that he was widely known in his time – 'How goes it
with our Jew from Voorburg?'[3] What this meant positively – in terms of
what it brought him from Jewish life and tradition – and negatively – in
terms of any difference or separation from the society where he lived is
impossible to estimate.

Despite the ferocity of the wording of his *herem*, or excommunication,[4]
he could have chosen to return to his synagogue at any time in his life
but, for reasons we do not know, he did not make that choice.
(b) His education, at first, was wholly Jewish. He learned Hebrew as a
child. The text of the Hebrew Bible must have been the bedrock of his
imagination. He came not only from a Jewish family in a Jewish community, but from a grounding in Jewish scholarship which must have been
the most advanced of its time. His teachers, Saul Levi Morteira and
Manasseh ben Israel, were international figures. His work shows that he
had been in touch not only with rabbinic scholarship but with the Jewish
philosophers of the Middle Ages. Maimonides and Crescas could be his
points of comparison at crucial steps in his arguments. Ibn Ezra was his
benchmark in biblical scholarship. He started to write a *Compendium of
Hebrew Grammar*, in the hope of improving the understanding of scripture. Some commentators[5] have seen this as a measure of return to his
native background, though there is no support for that view in his writings.

The traces of Jewish philosophy in Spinoza's work are as obvious as
the traces of a Jesuit education in the work of Descartes. Yet, equally, in
his writing he takes us to Jewish philosophy to show us how he differs
from it, not to say what he has taken from it. His attitude towards
Maimonides, though carefully argued – most notably, in Chapter vii of
the *Theological-Political Treatise* – shows a frank brutality which may
explain how he managed to antagonise so many people so violently. Any

---

[3] Quoted from a letter of Huygens in Yirmiyahu Yovel, *Spinoza and Other Heretics*, vol. 1 (Princeton
University Press, 1989), p. 172.
[4] Henri Méchoulan argues some significant differences from Christian excommunication in 'Le
herem à Amsterdam et «d'excommunication» de Spinoza', *Cahiers Spinoza*, 3, 1980.
[5] e.g. Geneviève Brykman, *La Judéité de Spinoza* (Paris: Vrin, 1972), Ch. vii.

attentive reader, he tells us, will see that one opinion of Maimonides consists only of 'mere figments of imagination, unsupported by rational argument or Scriptural authority. To state this view is sufficient to refute it . . .'[6]

The same familiarity combined with the same studied distance can be seen in Spinoza's relationship with Jewish mystical or esoteric philosophy. Commentators have found in his work echoes from the Cabbala,[7] as well as structural patterns of esoteric significance and even traces of numerology.[8] Any philosopher who tells us that all individuals in different degrees are animate, that 'we feel and experience that we are eternal' or that an intuitive intellectual love of God arises from an eternal form of knowledge[9] has to be open to mystical readings, justifiably or not. But any mysticism is held in a firm grip. It is not mystical vision but logical proofs that are said to be the eyes of the mind. The love of God is to hold chief place in the mind; but it is clear and distinct understanding, not mystical illumination, which is to be the route to that love.[10]

Although Spinoza is an intensely difficult philosopher, and although the competing strains in his work create great difficulties in interpretation, his difficulties never derive from the obscurities of mystical traditions. Ineffability has no place in his thinking. Not only *can* we understand God but – surely in contradiction not only to most mystical writing but to almost all Christian and Jewish thinking – we *must* be able to understand God. One of his most extraordinary claims is that 'God's infinite essence and his eternity are known to all':[11] nature is open and transparent to us. Nothing can be esoteric.

(c) Spinoza was not only Jewish and educated as Jewish, he came from a quite specific Jewish background which lent an entirely specific colour to his thought – a colour which some, inevitably, have seen as a key to its interpretation.[12]

His family were marranos:[13] Sephardic Jews exiled first from Spain,

---

[6] S 123 = G III 80/14–17.

[7] e.g. H. W. Brann, 'Spinoza and the Kabbalah' in S. Hessing (ed.), *Speculum Spinozanum* (London: Routledge & Kegan Paul, 1977); or A. Matheron, *Individu et communauté chez Spinoza* (revised from 1969) (Paris: Editions de Minuit, 1988), pp. 30, 620. Spinoza's own judgment was harsh: S 180 = G III 135–6.

[8] e.g. Fokke Akkerman, 'Le caractère rhétorique du *Traité théologico-politique*', *Spinoza entre Lumière et Romantisme* (Les Cahiers de Fontenay, 1985), pp. 387–8, where the significance of any numerology might be rhetorical as much as mystical.   [9] *Ethics* II, 13, Scholium; V, 23, Scholium; V, 33.

[10] *Ethics* V, 23, Scholium; V, 16; V, 15.   [11] *Ethics* II, 47, Scholium.

[12] Notably Yovel, in *Spinoza and Other Heretics*.

[13] The term is supposed to come from a Castilian word for pig, and that in turn from an Arabic word meaning forbidden (Brykman, *La Judéité de Spinoza*, p. 16).

then from Portugal then – in the case of Spinoza's father – perhaps from France. The hallmark of their community after the expulsion of the Jews from Spain in 1492 had been the secret practice of their religious life, often masked by pretended conversion or outward conformity. This was a world of double meanings, careful expression and obliqueness. Like the world of much Jewish history, it was only one step away from a past of intolerance and persecution. The experience of a hidden religious life had its effect on the fabric of marrano life during the sixteenth century. When the Jewish community achieved reasonable tranquillity in Amsterdam – where, in effect, they were able to practise their religion as they wished by the late seventeenth century – there may have been attempts to rebuild a damaged orthodoxy. One reason for Spinoza's expulsion from his synagogue may have come from a wish by its members to show to themselves – and to their Christian neighbours – that they had drawn clear limits to what they could stand. Spinoza may have exceeded those limits.

The marrano world was one of ambivalence and insecurity. Any reader of the *Theological-Political Treatise* will be puzzled in trying to locate its religious position. Some respect and care towards Christianity, for example, would have been negated in the minds of Christian contemporaries by biblical interpretations that remain stunning in their insouciant insensitivity. A precept straight from the gospel, for example – 'whosoever shall smite thee on thy right cheek, turn to him the other also'[14] – is subjected to an unapologetically historicised interpretation. Christ spoke these words 'to men suffering under oppression, living in a corrupt commonwealth where justice was utterly disregarded'; this teaching could not apply in a 'just commonwealth'.[15] Where Spinoza stands may seem puzzling, but puzzling too is the attitude of critics[16] who have seen betrayal to Judaism and insincerity to Christianity, rather than the context of persecution from which his rather unsuccessful efforts at caution may have sprung.

One of the most striking passages in his correspondence is in a letter to a young friend, Albert Burgh, who had converted to Roman Catholicism and who not merely imagined that he might win over Spinoza, but who hoped that an appeal to the merits of Roman martyrs might reinforce his point. The response was characteristic in its detach-

---

[14] Matthew 5: 39 (AV).   [15] S 146 = G III 103. This passage will be discussed in Chapter 7.
[16] Most forcefully Leo Strauss, in 'How to Study Spinoza's Theologico-Political Treatise', in *Persecution and the Art of Writing* (New York: Free Press, 1948) and *Spinoza's Critique of Religion*, trans. E. M. Sinclair (revised from 1930) (New York: Schocken, 1965).

ment: yes, the Jews too have been arrogant and stubborn, claiming antiquity and exclusivity. But Spinoza's pride in his own background is devastating:

> I myself know among others of a certain Judah called 'the faithful' who, in the midst of flames when he was already believed dead, started to sing the hymn which begins *To Thee, O God, I commit my soul*, and so singing, died.[17]

(d) Although Spinoza ceased to live in a Jewish community he did not join a Christian one. He was uninterested in Protestant–Catholic polemics, but there seems to be no doubt where his mentality and sympathies lay. The milieu of his friends and contemporaries was almost entirely Protestant. This was not so much a matter of theological location. His standpoints on well-trampled post-Tridentine polarities such as 'faith' versus 'reason' or 'good works' versus 'faith' might seem nearer to the Catholic than to the Protestant platform.[18] But his frame of mind was undeniably Protestant. Ritual, sacrament and external observance might all have had intelligible places for him, in terms of confirming or perpetuating beliefs or social conformity, but what mattered was the 'true life'.[19] Some of his sympathies, we shall see, went further than his own philosophy could justify. His personal inclinations surely led him to say that the 'inward worship of God' could be distinguished from 'outward forms of religion', where religion consisted in 'honesty and sincerity of heart rather than in outward actions',[20] since a separation of the 'inner' from the 'outer' was opposed to the whole picture of the personality presented in Parts I and II of the *Ethics*.

He seems to have assumed a negative characterisation of Protestantism: it was seen in terms of Roman doctrines *not* believed. In the *Theological-Political Treatise*, he tried to argue for a religion with minimal dogmas: 'a catholic or universal faith must not contain any dogmas that good men may regard as controversial . . .'.[21] Since religion was better with as few doctrines as possible, this may have leant him towards what may seem a Protestant direction. But this was taste or temperament, not logic.

(e) Spinoza never allied himself to any religious group, but he did live for a time in the company of Protestants – Lutherans, Mennonites and

---

[17] Letter 76; L 343 = G IV 321–2. The story is an odd one, because it seems unlikely that Spinoza could have known personally about this: see Yovel, *Spinoza and Other Heretics*, pp. 187–8.
[18] '. . . faith does not bring salvation through itself, but only by reason of obedience; or, as James says (2, xvii), faith in itself without works is dead'; S 222 = G III 175/18–20. [19] S 218 = G III 171/22.
[20] S 280, 159 = G III 229/5, 116/29–31. [21] S 224 = G III 177/4–6.

Collegiants – who located themselves outside the Calvinist Dutch Reformed Church. 'The free character of their services and extreme flexibility on confessional matters remained their hallmark.'[22] The exact religious position of these people, and the origin of their views, has been the subject of massive scholarly labours, pioneered by Richard Popkin, who has written at length on the millenarian and messianic atmosphere of the 1650s which formed the background to Spinoza's development.[23] This was a period in which the self-proclamation of a Jewish messiah – Sabbatai Zevi – seemed of significance to millenarians in the more imaginatively enthusiastic fringes of the Protestant world. Spinoza may have had some contact with all this.[24] His 'dogmas of the universal faith' can be read without difficulty in a pietistic, quakerish sense – 'Worship of God and obedience to him consists solely in justice and charity, or love towards one's neighbour',[25] for example. His expressed distaste for partisan religious polemics and his liking for a peaceful life must have given quakerish company an obvious appeal to him.

This is an area where doctrinaire clarity is out of place, but it does seem clear enough that – despite his choice of company – Spinoza would not have been regarded as a Christian by even the most liberally minded of his Christian friends. Whatever it is, his moral philosophy is hardly a Christian moral philosophy, and could only be made to seem Christian with the most strenuous reinterpretation. Repentance and humility cannot be virtues. Pity is evil. We should seek not to live in hope.[26] His idiosyncratic use of the figure of Christ will be the subject of Chapter 9. For now, it should be enough to note that Spinoza did place himself, for a time, near to a particular and particularly fervent religious context. This must have affected him, but he did not choose to become part of it.

(f) Spinoza was a citizen of the United Provinces of the Netherlands, and he well understood the value of that. He was able to live and work – though not publish – in a condition of freedom unique in seventeenth-century Europe. The evasive life of Descartes, about forty years his

[22] J. Israel, *The Dutch Republic: Its Rise, Greatness, and Fall 1477–1806* (Oxford: Clarendon Press, 1995), p. 395; also see pp. 912–14.

[23] e.g., in summary, 'The Religious Background of Seventeenth Century Philosophy', *Journal of the History of Philosophy*, 25, 1987 or, in detail, 'Spinoza's Earliest Philosophical Years, 1655–61', *Studia Spinozana*, 4, 1988.

[24] And it has even been argued that his first published work may have related to it – see R. H. Popkin and M. A. Signer (eds.), *Spinoza's Earliest Publication? 'A Loving Salutation' by Margaret Fell* (Assen: Van Gorcum, 1987) – though this is highly controversial.   [25] S 224 = G III 177/33–35.

[26] *Ethics* IV, 54, 53; IV, 50; IV, 47.

senior, the Thirty Years War and the successive show trials of scientific and religious dissenters over the previous century would have been ground into his consciousness. The fact that he himself was never himself persecuted was not due to any particular sense of Dutch warm-heartedness, or to some anachronistically liberal sense of tolerance among the Calvinist majority. It was rather the outcome of a temporary stalemate in theological politics which opened a short interlude when the *Theological-Political Treatise* had a case to argue, and when it was not too dangerous for his book to appear in disguise.[27]

The *Theological-Political Treatise* was written in Latin, like all of Spinoza's work for publication.[28] He held the surprisingly optimistic view that the learned could be more sensible about religious matters than readers of the vernacular.[29] He forbade translation of the work into Dutch. That still did not prevent a huge uproar when the work came out, and a censure on it in 1674, together with Hobbes's *Leviathan*, by the States-General.[30] 'Wild animals, if they were capable of theological argument, would use the words which the adversaries of Spinoza liked to employ to refute him.'[31]

Dutch politics was one of the inescapable contexts for his thinking. This can be seen at points in his writing which can now only seem provincial and bathetic, as where he leaps from the presumed constitution appointed by Moses in ancient Israel to compare it – 'disregarding the common temple' – to the position in the High Confederated Estates of the Netherlands.[32] But there were far more important effects. In part, the *Theological-Political Treatise* is about the place to be given to religious thought and practice in society. The exemplars in Spinoza's mind were mainly the Netherlands, England and biblical Israel. His preference – to see control of religion in the hands of the state rather than a church – certainly derived from his experience of the indifference of the fragmentary Dutch state compared with the zealotry of the Reformed Church.

The extent of his links with real politics is debatable. It must be wrong

---

[27] See Israel, *The Dutch Republic*, p. 787 on the timing of the publication and pp. 660–73 on the politics of toleration.

[28] His native language is assumed to be Portuguese, though this has been debated.

[29] See S 56 = G III 12.

[30] Spinoza was placed on the Index in 1679, apparently a rare mark of recognition for a non-Catholic author whose writings were not directed specifically against Catholicism: see J. Orcibal, 'Les Jansénistes face à Spinoza', *Revue de Littérature Comparée*, 23, 1949, p. 454.

[31] J. Freudenthal, *Spinoza* (Stuttgart: Frommanns, 1904), p. 222.

[32] S 259 = G III 210, a type of contrast maybe taken from Grotius: see Israel, *The Dutch Republic*, p. 422.

to see him as an isolated scholar, cut off from the practical world. One recent historian has gone as far as to say that 'his whole strategy, in his writing and publications, was geared to the contemporary Dutch scene'.[33] His thinking at the end of his life, when he is presumed to have been working on his unfinished *Political Treatise*, darkened markedly after the murder and partial cannibalism of the de Witt brothers near his house in the Hague in 1672.

This book is not about Spinoza's politics. But we cannot forget that his understanding of religion had an unavoidably political context. His main work on it, after all, was entitled the *Theological-Political Treatise*. Even to assume that we can discuss his religious thinking without reference to politics is to take much of his argument for granted. It is to make an assumption that would have seemed bizarre in the seventeenth century. In his politics, the state is necessary, not optional.[34] We are not isolated rationalisers: we have to live, as natural beings, in society. This view is crucial to his understanding of religious ritual and practice – his natural history of religions, to be discussed here in Chapter 7. Religion in social practice – presumably or implicitly as opposed to 'personal religion' – is unavoidable, not incidental, and thus the political framework for religion becomes unavoidable as well.

(g) It is not known where he acquired the knowledge – possibly at the University of Leiden – but Spinoza was a scientist. He worked as a lens-grinder, but the current view is that this may have been more a matter of research in optics than of commercial manufacturing. He conducted a correspondence with some of the leading scientists of his time. His long correspondence with Henry Oldenburg, Secretary to the Royal Society, must have been shared with members of the Society. His opinion must have mattered. Again, this fact must undermine any preconception we may have about his personal isolation.

His originality and expertise in mathematics and physics have been debated.[35] Anyway, whatever the detail, it is not as a creative scientist that he deserves to be remembered. The scientific context to his thinking is enormously more important than any contribution he may have made to what we now see as the physical sciences. Whether or not he was a

---

[33] Israel, *The Dutch Republic*, p. 917.

[34] *Ethics* IV, 37, Scholium 2. For a short discussion of Spinoza's political position see Noel Malcolm's entry on Spinoza in J. H. Burns (ed.), *The Cambridge History of Political Thought 1450–1700* (Cambridge University Press, 1991).

[35] For a full assessment: D. Savan, 'Spinoza: Scientist and Theorist of Scientific Method', in M. Grene and D. Nails, (eds.), *Spinoza and the Sciences* (Dordrecht: Reidel, 1986).

scientist to be placed alongside Huygens or Boyle, he certainly grasped what they were doing, and he grasped what it implied for previous ways of seeing and controlling the world. In his thinking about religion, the opposition he discussed for the most part was not between 'faith' and 'reason', but between 'faith' and 'philosophy', where philosophy for him, as for all his contemporaries, included equally metaphysics – the 'first philosophy' familiar from Descartes – *and* physics. For Spinoza, claims about religious faith or knowledge had to be brought into some relationship with claims about physical activity. Claims about nature, necessity, essence and natural law were continuous with (or identical to) claims about bodies, space and time. The accommodation between the presence of religion and the development of workable scientific knowledge is of central importance to the understanding of his views on religion.

We shall see that Part I of the *Ethics* is where God's place in relation to the world was redrawn. The seventeenth century was a period when the judgment of science by theology shifted to a judgment of theology by the sciences; and there is a good case for saying that the balance can be seen best in the work of Spinoza.

(h) Some way down this list of contexts for Spinoza's work comes the overtly philosophical context. The only work published under his own name in his lifetime was his *Principles of the Philosophy of Descartes Demonstrated in the Geometric Manner* together with his associated *Metaphysical Thoughts*. The Preface by Lewis Meyer explains that the book does not represent the author's own opinions, but contains his understanding of Descartes. That may have been so, but the philosophical reader is likely to adopt a rather different perspective. Descartes is not, on the whole, a difficult writer to understand, and, at least on the surface, his *Meditations* and the *Discourse on the Method* – both masterpieces of clear philosophical style – are infinitely easier to grasp than Spinoza's exposition of the thinking in them. What we can read into his intentions might be a desire to see Descartes's world, as a philosopher, from within: to take it apart, to try its parts, to reassemble them and present them with his best advocacy. This is what his book does, and as such it remains one of the best philosophical studies by a great philosopher of another philosopher's thought, as a philosopher would understand it.[36]

The overt relationship between Descartes and Spinoza is not hard to see, and it will come up many times in these pages. To some extent,

---

[36] For a less positive view, see Edwin Curley, 'Spinoza as an Expositor of Descartes', in S. Hessing (ed.), *Speculum Spinozanum* (London: Routledge & Kegan Paul, 1977).

Descartes's questions were Spinoza's questions. The physics, the link between mind and body, the place of God in relation to the physical world, the priority of epistemology, the strength of the will: these were all on the Cartesian agenda. Much of Spinoza's technical language was common to his work and to the writing of Descartes; though traps lie in wait for the reader who believes that terms such as 'essence' or 'cause' necessarily shared common senses.

Spinoza saw the importance of Descartes and had to answer, or deal with, his questions. Some have believed that the Cartesian context is primary to an understanding of Spinoza's work.[37] However far that may be so, it cannot be overlooked that Spinoza placed a careful distance between himself and his great predecessor. His views on the relationship between the will and the intellect and between the mind and the body were argued explicitly against Descartes, and he does not hesitate to tell us where, and how foolishly, he believes that Descartes had erred. Far more significantly – in as much as it affects religion – he repudiated the order of thought with which Descartes mesmerised subsequent philosophers for several centuries. As early as 1663, in the *Principles*, Spinoza added a *Prolegomenon* explaining the Cartesian method of doubt. But in making its shortcomings, as he saw them, all too explicit, he distanced himself from it without direct criticism. And the *Ethics*, against all Cartesian thinking, arrives at epistemology – at what we can know, and how we know it – only towards the end of Part II. It was not to be the *first* issue, as it was for Descartes. This is of crucial importance in terms of the subject that came to be seen as the philosophy of religion: a subject tinged throughout with questions about the nature and validation of religious knowledge or faith in contrast – often not favourable – with other sorts of knowledge. Those questions were touched by Spinoza, but he never viewed them as prior to all others.

Descartes's attitude to religion has been a matter of debate.[38] The method of doubt may indeed have been intended as an aid to the defence of orthodoxy, as was declared piously in the dedicatory letter of the *Meditations* to the Fathers of the Sorbonne. But Descartes was far more interested in physics and mathematics than in religious polemics.

---

[37] The most persuasive case is given by Edwin Curley in *Behind the Geometrical Method: A Reading of Spinoza's Ethics* (Princeton University Press, 1988). Less clear, and with much reliance on Spinoza's early work, is Pierre Lachiéze-Rey, *Les origines cartésiennes du Dieu de Spinoza* (Paris: Vrin, 1950).
[38] See, for example, Stephen Gaukroger, *Descartes: An Intellectual Biography* (Oxford: Clarendon Press, 1995), pp. 354–61.

(And we who are not contemporary with the trial of Galileo may be in no position to comment on his cautiousness.)

What is of interest is the effect on religion of his work (a fact appreciated by those who anathematised it so promptly). Placing epistemology so persuasively at the beginning of first philosophy created an unavoidable pressure. Descartes's own positioning of God in relation to nature was unsatisfactory to the point of evident instability, whether or not we believe that he recognised that fact himself, or cared about it. His God was left as a cause, but as a supernatural cause, with infinite but self-limited will. Theological knowledge was left in limbo, surrounded by wary respect but unsupported by any reasoned context. Typically, Descartes welcomed the unintelligibility of the infinite as a helpful shroud over a delicate subject.[39]

It was in these areas of weakness that the effect on Spinoza took hold. Compromise and accommodation were alien to him (and he lived in safer times than Descartes). Whatever the reasons for the indirectness in the *Theological-Political Treatise*, there is no obliqueness in the theological assertions of Spinoza's *Ethics*. Without doubt, these would have taken him to the stake only a few years before, or in many other parts of Europe.

(i) The philosophical context for Spinoza was far wider than his knowledge of the work of Descartes, of course. The *Port-Royal Logic* of Arnauld and Nicole, published in 1662, was in his library; and much of his thought is not intelligible outside the framework of the *way of ideas* incorporated in it.[40] There was also a large inheritance (shared with Descartes) of terminology taken from late medieval thought. Much of seventeenth-century thinking can be understood in terms of trying to make sense of terms such as *substance, essence* and *cause* outside a context that had created a need for them, and inside a new context of natural science, where they had little use or value. It took a long time for it to be realised that those terms were more trouble than they were worth – philosophers today might conclude the same about *mind, meaning* and *concept*, for example – but in the meantime there were some wide and often unannounced shifts in their use. A good deal of the metaphysical terminology in Spinoza's *Ethics* looks the same as the apparatus employed in the *Summa Theologiæ* four centuries earlier, and we would be entirely right in assuming that

---

[39] *Principles of Philosophy*, I, 19 and 26, CSMK I 199, 201–2 = AT VIIIA 12, 14. Spinoza, as we shall see, regarded infinity as transparently intelligible.
[40] See Alan Donagan, *Spinoza* (New York: Harvester Wheatsheaf, 1988), Chapter 3.

Spinoza was well steeped in scholastic thought. But we might be entirely wrong in approaching his use of this terminology without the greatest of care.[41] To modern tastes, brought up on the rigours of formal logic, he was lamentably careless in his use and explanation of central terms which we might now categorise as 'logical', such as *essence* or *cause*. And it seems likely that he used some central terminology in his system – such as *attribute* or *mode* – in ways that deviated from Cartesian or from standard contemporary senses with only oblique explanations to alert his readers.[42] His *context of expression* was scholastic Latin: a context, by the end of the seventeenth century, near to breaking-point, and not only because of the spread of vernacular writing.

(j) We can see in Spinoza the influences of his predecessors in political philosophy, particularly Hobbes and Machiavelli. He shared many of Hobbes's problems and preoccupations, and the scale of intellectual debt to him is not in doubt. He shared with Machiavelli – 'that most acute Florentine'[43] – a clear-eyed view of the centrality of power and a desire to see political behaviour in terms of natural science.

These – less plainly than the influence of his Jewish upbringing or the underlying presence of a Cartesian agenda – are obvious strands in his work, consciously acknowledged and self-consciously appraised. Spinoza probably figured out for himself where he stood in relation to Hobbes, and in all likelihood had come to terms with it. This was not some deep, hidden undercurrent in his thought.

(k) The same must apply to the contexts brought to his work by more minor figures. Much study in recent years has been devoted, for example, to the work of Isaac La Peyrère[44] and to other, less eccentric, pioneers in textual interpretation of the Bible. We can see what Spinoza may have studied, where some of his thinking may have originated. Equally, we can see how a wayward figure such as Franciscus van den Enden, who, as a teacher, probably introduced Spinoza to Latin and to Cartesian philosophy in his early years, may have had some effect.[45]

---

[41] Spinoza 'uses terms and notions entrenched in the philosophical and exegetical tradition of the middle ages, seemingly accepting their validity, while inverting their meaning': Amos Funkenstein, 'Comment on R. Popkin's Paper', in J. E. Force and R. H. Popkin (eds.), *The Books of Nature and Scripture* (Dordrecht: Kluwer, 1994), p. 21.

[42] Edwin Curley was the first to make this evident, in *Spinoza's Metaphysics: An Essay in Interpretation* (Cambridge: Harvard University Press, 1969).   [43] *Political Treatise* x, §1 = G III 353/8.

[44] R. H. Popkin, *Isaac La Peyrère* (Leiden: Brill, 1987).

[45] Marc Bedjai summarises his pioneering research in 'Métaphysique, éthique et politique dans l'œuvre du Docteur Franciscus van den Enden', *Studia Spinozana*, 6, 1990.

This must be mentioned as part of the picture, but the need for a sense of proportion should be obvious. Philosophical quality is hard to pin down; but Spinoza is one of the greatest of thinkers. La Peyrère and van den Enden were not. If he had some debt to them, it was of the order of Beethoven's debt to Diabelli, not of Mozart's debt to Haydn.

(l) The work of Charles Schmitt and Richard Popkin has revealed the importance of a revival of interest in themes from ancient philosophy in the sixteenth and seventeenth centuries. Popkin's *History of Scepticism* has become a classic study of one line of thought.[46]

There was also a line of thinking from ancient stoicism, possibly filtered through the work of Lipsius, from the end of the sixteenth century. And Spinoza was part of that. His own temperament fitted well with the mentality of stoicism. Much of the *Ethics* rings with stoic nobility. Some of the underlying philosophy of nature, and of natural law, has parallels in stoic physics.[47]

Some of this, in a wide history-of-ideas sense, may have been an inexorable consequence of where Spinoza stood in relation to conventional religion and morality – there may indeed be only so many positions that can be occupied within an intellectual tradition.[48] Yet, for all that, he was not a stoic. He may not have appraised the full extent of whatever influence there was from stoicism, but he was aware of some of it. He took what he wanted and repudiated the rest. Stoicism is set aside overtly and crucially in the Preface to Part v of the *Ethics*, where he rejects the view that the will can restrain the emotions. And essential tenets in Part v, though rooted in premises shared with stoicism, lead to entirely anti-stoic conclusions: a man is bound to be a part of Nature and to follow its universal order . . . it is impossible for a man not to be part of Nature . . . man is necessarily always subject to passive emotions.[49] The power of reason is not only limited, but nature makes that so, and there can be no escape – the stoic project of control would be a complete mistake.

[46] R. H. Popkin, *The History of Scepticism from Erasmus to Spinoza* (revised from 1960) (Berkeley: University of California Press, 1979); C. B. Schmitt, 'The Rediscovery of Ancient Skepticism in Modern Times' (revised from 1972), in M. Burnyeat (ed.), *The Skeptical Tradition* (Berkeley: University of California Press, 1983).
[47] See Susan James, 'Spinoza the Stoic', in Tom Sorell (ed.), *The Rise of Modern Philosophy* (Oxford: Clarendon Press, 1993).
[48] The same might be said of his location in the history of ideas described in Arthur Lovejoy, *The Great Chain of Being* (Cambridge: Harvard University Press, 1936).
[49] *Ethics* IV, Appendix, 7; IV, 4; IV, 4, Corollary.

This multiplicity of contexts may give a confusing picture – too confusing, perhaps, to be helpful.[50] But even a short survey of Spinoza's contexts should be more valuable than the customary chapter of biography and *background* that often opens (or closes) philosophical studies. More than a few commentators interpret Spinoza almost exclusively under only one or another of the aspects that have been listed. And it can make some difference to describe philosophy in terms of a reaction to or a continuation of the thought of Descartes, as a piece of neoscholasticism, as Jewish mysticism or as an ideology for modern science. It is scarcely surprising that scholars who may have devoted years to one perspective or another may have come to see partial pictures. It would be more surprising if anyone were able to keep a fair balance between the many separate ways into his work.[51]

Spinoza himself, we can assume, could have had a view here. As we shall see in looking at his views on religion, *why* a belief is held could be seen indifferently as *causa, seu ratio* – as cause or as reason. He would have believed that the cause or reason for a philosopher's intellectual or religious position is created by family and community, education, study and experience, as well as by reflection brought about by, and in the context of, family and community, and so on. For him, an exhaustive and accurate historical account of origins and influences should fix a thinker precisely in our sights.

Yet we can see more than a little irony. If there is a common thread in the various contexts sketched for Spinoza in this Introduction, it lies in his capacity to absorb, reflect on and then measure his own distance from influences in his life. It is easy in some areas to see plain signs of influence from another thinker. It may be less easy to see – or more easy to miss, given understandably partisan scholarly enthusiasms – how carefully he could distance himself, openly taking what he needed and openly repudiating what he did not. This is not to say that he was able to achieve perfectly transparent self-awareness; but it is to suggest that he may have seen the value in such an enterprise, and may have travelled some way along such a path. His own view of autonomy, after all, was a

---

[50] More could be added, such as a considerable background in classical Latin literature, discussed e.g. in Fokke Akkerman, 'Spinoza's tekort aan woorden: Humanistische aspecten van zijn schrijverschap' and 'Pauvreté ou richesse du latin de Spinoza', *Studies in the Posthumous Works of Spinoza* (Meppel: Krips Repro, 1980).

[51] A point made well by Stuart Hampshire, 'Spinoza and the Idea of Freedom', *Proceedings of the British Academy* (1960), in M. Grene (ed.), *Spinoza: A Collection of Critical Essays* (Garden City: Anchor, 1973), p. 297.

freedom from external causes, and that applied as much to the intellect and to intellectual choices as it is more often applied to actions and to matters of morality. Intellectual originality for him would have to be seen in the same way as free will – impossible, if understood as uncaused, arbitrary, spontaneous creation; intelligible, if seen as clear awareness of the origins, value and balance of intellectual debts. Originality can be achieved in the same sense as freedom is achieved, by understanding as much as possible about one's contexts, influences and backgrounds.[52] One of the reasons for Spinoza's originality is exactly that he was able to absorb and appraise so many influences. The reading given here is as far as possible from the romanticised interpretation of Yovel, where Spinoza 'was a loner, the individual par excellence, who demands to be understood solely in terms of his private being and beliefs, not in terms of any social or historical framework supposed to provide him with the essential ingredients of his identity'.[53]

Difficulties in the location of Spinoza as a thinker, or even as a religious thinker, are not limited to finding a balance between the contexts for his work. Within his work there can be a balance of emphasis wider than for any other philosopher except perhaps Plato. The *Ethics* begins with cold logic and ends with the intellectual love of God. Few commentators have had the interests and expertise that could equip them to deal with both ends of the work even-handedly. Some have openly given up and have concentrated on what they can handle.[54] But a consideration of Spinoza's God could not leave that approach open: God appears at the beginning of the *Ethics*: Part I, *Of God*, is all about God's nature and God as cause. The end of the *Ethics* touches on eternity and the intellectual love of God. Nothing said by Spinoza in the *Ethics* – where we can see for ourselves the order of exposition – or in his other works, or in his correspondence, gives us a clue about the *direction* of his motivation. We may assume, in line with Bradley's cynical dictum, that metaphysics is the finding of bad reasons for what we believe upon instinct – that the logical machinery of Part I of the *Ethics* exists to support the quasi-religious

---

[52] This can be badly blurred by an apparently broad-minded generosity towards Spinoza: 'nobody is stupid enough to think that the greatest minds are explained by what nourishes them in their studies and their context; but the background allows for its own causality': E. Lévinas, 'Réponse au Professeur McKeon', in *Spinoza: His Thought and Work* (Jerusalem: Israel Academy of Sciences and Humanities, 1983), p. 49.   [53] *Spinoza and Other Heretics*, p. 173.

[54] Jonathan Bennett, for example, despairs of Part v of the *Ethics: A Study of Spinoza's Ethics* (Cambridge University Press, 1984), Chapter 15. Curiously, Russell seems to have derived a good deal from the later parts of the *Ethics* while regarding its logic as a mere mass of fallacies: Kenneth Blackwell, *The Spinozistic Ethics of Bertrand Russell* (London: George Allen & Unwin, 1985).

predilections unveiled in Part v – but we have no evidence for that, and might do well to reflect on why we might be inclined to believe it. The *Ethics*, as the title tells us, is supposed to be a practical book – a guide towards beatitude – but the practical is built on formidable theoretical foundations – as 'everyone knows' it must be 'based on metaphysics and physics'.[55] Here again there are questions of balance, between the practical and the theoretical. And once again, it is easy to assume that the practical must have taken priority; but that is to underestimate the power of *curiosity* – the search after truth – as a motive.

This study is overtly partial in its approach, taking only one among several angles on Spinoza's work. Other angles, therefore, may be under-emphasised or ignored. Not much will be said about his politics or his moral philosophy, and only what is necessary will be said about his philosophy of mind. No claim is made that looking at him from one angle is in accord with his intentions or his motivation; but then it would also be strange to deny that God and religion played a central part in his thinking.

A further question of balance needs to be noted, although no detailed defence will be elaborated. The assumption will be that Spinoza's *Ethics* represents his completed philosophical outlook, and that the *Theological-Political Treatise* – written during the composition (or before the completion) of the *Ethics* – tells us, together with his correspondence, most of what we need about his position on religion.

The development of Spinoza's work in a philosophical sense has been only poorly studied.[56] The ordering of his earlier writings has been established with reasonable certainty only in recent years,[57] and the alterations in the details of his views have received hardly any serious attention. Too many writers, unfortunately, quote indiscriminately from unpublished early work and from the *Ethics*, as if both can represent The Philosophy of Spinoza. We can assume uncontroversially – and this work assumes – that Spinoza must have laboured long and hard in saying what he wanted to say in the *Ethics*, striving to remove unclarities and inconsistencies in his earlier attempts at the same subject-matter. This is an important assumption at some crucial points – for example, in

---

[55] Letter 27; L 177 = G IV 160-1.
[56] This is not to say that there have not been the most excellent historical and bibliographical studies of his work, mostly originating from the Netherlands. The point is one about the development in his use of arguments.
[57] e.g. in the work of Filippo Mignini, 'Per la datazione e l'interpretazione del *Tractatus de Intellectus Emendatione* di B. Spinoza', *La Cultura*, 17, 1979.

the causal relationship between God and individuals, and on infinity – but it is one that is necessary to get through the subject at all. So this is not a work about the *development* of Spinoza's God – if such a book could be written. It is about the God of Spinoza's *Ethics* and the religion of the *Ethics* and of the *Theological-Political Treatise*.

Similarly, and finally, Spinoza raises for the commentator in a particularly forceful way the question of balance between historical and philosophical treatments.[58] It would be wholly pointless to detach his approaches to religious questions from the various contexts in which they could have been raised. We must see what those contexts were, if only to see what questions might *not* have been possible for him. We may never know in some areas what he *did* intend, but that by no means implies that we cannot rule out what he could *not* have intended.[59] Evidently, his main interest is as a philosopher, rather than as someone who held a historically curious amalgam of beliefs. Exactly how and why this is so is not easy to explain. There seems to be no satisfactory answer, other than the pragmatic compromise that historical location cannot just be driven into the background, but nor should it obstruct too much of the foreground. Sir Frederick Pollock's strength as a commentator – as an eminent lawyer – might well have come from his steady focus on the force of Spinoza's arguments and from his judicious appreciation of how those arguments add together to build a case. Pollock's introductory remarks on methodology sound quaintly naive in a more self-conscious age –

The only way to understand a great philosopher is to meet him face to face, whatever the apparent difficulties. A certain amount of historical preparation is indeed at least advisable; for to apprehend rightly the speech of a past time one must know something of its conditions. Apart from this, the author is his own best interpreter, and it has been my aim rather to make Spinoza explain himself than to discover explanations from the outside.[60]

– but they also remain entirely sensible.

---

[58] For an even-handed treatment: Michael Ayers, 'Analytical Philosophy and the History of Philosophy', in J. Rée, M. Ayers and A. Westoby (eds.), *Philosophy and its Past* (Brighton: Harvester, 1978).

[59] A policy commended by Quentin Skinner, 'Meaning and Understanding in the History of Ideas' (1969), in J. Tully (ed.), *Meaning and Context* (Cambridge: Polity Press, 1988), p. 48.

[60] *Spinoza, His Life and Philosophy* (London: Kegan Paul, 1880), p. xlii.

PART I

The God of the philosophers

Natural Philosophy teaches us the Causes and Effects of all Bodies simply and in them selvs. But if you extend it a little further, to that indeed which its Name imports, signifying the Lov of Nature, it leads us into a Diligent inquisition into all Natures, their Qualities, Affections, Relations, Causes and Ends, so far forth as by Nature and Reason they may be Known. And this Noble Science, as such is most Sublime and Perfect, it includes all Humanity and Divinity together GOD, Angels, Men, Affections, Habits, Actions, Virtues; Evry Thing as it is a Solid intire Object singly proposed, being a subject of it, as well as Material and visible Things But taking it as is usualy Bounded in its Terms, it treateth only of Corporeal Things, as Heaven, Earth Air Water, Fire, the Sun and Stars, Trees Herbs, flowers, Influences, Winds, Fowles Beasts Fishes Minerals, and Precious Stones; with all other Beings of that Kind. And as thus it is taken it is Nobly Subservient to the Highest Ends: for it Openeth the Riches of Gods Kingdom and the Natures of His Territories Works and Creatures in a Wonderfull Maner, Clearing and preparing the Ey of the Enjoyer.

Thomas Traherne: *Centuries*, III, 44 (*c.* 1670)

The God of the philosophers

CHAPTER I

How God exists

Does God exist, and if so, how?

Part I of the *Ethics* does offer answers to those questions, but that is not to say that Spinoza asked them in those ways, and still less to say *why* he might have asked them.

This may seem a disconcerting start – a faltering before we even begin – but the point to be grasped straightaway is an essential one. Part I of the *Ethics* contains demonstrations of God's existence. The first fifteen propositions constitute a characterisation of God's nature. We can translate this material out of the scholastic language and the geometrical form in which Spinoza composed it; but then we may still be no wiser about its aims and intention.[1]

This chapter will aim to specify the place of Spinoza's God – what God is for. But to start with the missing context is not just a piece of routine, academic prefatory caution. *Why God is needed* – in the sense that God's existence is supposed to be proved by Spinoza – as we shall see, is not obvious. Spinoza never tells us why he is doing what he is.

WHY GOD WAS NOT NEEDED

It can help to exclude two possibilities immediately. First, the existence of God was not intended as a rebuttal to anyone – maybe an atheist or a sceptic – who might want to deny it. The demonstrations of God's existence were not meant to be proofs that might be used to persuade or convince an atheist or agnostic. This, too, is a disconcerting thought to anyone thinking in the context of subsequent philosophising about religion, or of religious polemics conducted against a possibility of genuine atheism. Nevertheless, it does seem wholly conclusive. Whatever the

[1] 'The book contains . . . the answers to questions; it does not state the questions themselves', G. H. R. Parkinson, Introduction and Notes to Spinoza, *Ethics*, revised edn (London: Dent, 1993), pp. ix–x.

progress of atheism by the mid-seventeenth century,[2] Spinoza paid no attention to dealing with it. His first demonstration of God's existence surely illustrates that point for itself:

God . . . necessarily exists
Demonstration: If you deny this, conceive, if you can, that God does not exist. Therefore his essence does not involve existence. But this is absurd. Therefore God necessarily exists, q.e.d.[3]

This could not be seen as persuasive rhetoric in any sense. No atheist could be swayed by it.

Spinoza's intention in writing that way was not merely to strip every unnecessary word from the crucial propositions in his work. Nowhere else, within or outside the *Ethics*, do we find the existence of God argued as a case against someone who might not want to accept it, for whatever reason. We shall see later (in Chapter 3) that Spinoza was not concerned to argue against the possibility of Cartesian doubt – the possibility, for example, that his rationality might be radically at fault. Rather, he wanted to block the possibility that such doubt could ever arise: the context in which it might arise could not even be constructed. In analogy, this applied to the existence of his God. Nowhere do we find him addressing the possibility that God might not exist, and therefore seeking to deploy a case against someone who chose to adopt such a position. The reason is not obscure. It gives us our first instance of the blunt consistency that Spinoza found so easy and which his readers found so unsettling (and so similar to crude dogmatism): 'Conceive, *if you can*, that God does not exist . . . God necessarily exists.' But you *can't* conceive this. Perhaps the thought can be imagined or entertained, as a supposition in a *reductio ad absurdum*, but it cannot be conceived –

Note that, although many may say that they doubt the existence of God, they have in mind nothing but a word, or some fictitious idea they call God. This does not accord with the nature of God . . .[4]

The existence of God was not 'self-evident',[5] though the non-existence of God would be incoherent. Atheism would be a case that cannot be

[2] See Gaukroger, *Descartes*, pp. 196–7. The standard study is Michael Buckley, *At the Origins of Modern Atheism* (New Haven: Yale University Press, 1987).
[3] *Ethics* I, 11, Demonstration 1. (The demonstration contains references to a previous conclusion (Proposition 7) and an Axiom (7).)
[4] *Treatise on the Emendation of the Intellect* §54, p. 245, note t = G II 20. Later – *Theological–Political Treatise*, note 6 – 'We doubt the existence of God, and consequently everything else, as long as we do not have a clear and distinct idea of God, but only a confused idea.'
[5] *'per se nota'*, S 127 = G III 84/23–4.

formulated. So, like extreme sceptical doubt, it cannot be a target. So there need be no real argument against it.

Equally, Spinoza was not trying to demonstrate the existence of God as the object of conventional or historical religions, whether or not his results could be adopted for that end. The God whose existence is claimed, or assumed, in Part I of the *Ethics* may relate in some way to a God who can be an object of prayer or devotion, and may be brought into some relation with the God of historical religions discussed in the *Theological-Political Treatise*; but these relations are not at all evident.[6] God was said to be *unique* (though, as we shall see, there must be interesting reservations about the thought that *one God exists*) and to that extent at least, Spinoza's assertions would seem completely out of line with historical polytheisms (and perhaps, in his own mind, with Christian trinitarianism as well[7]); but beyond these minimal points, the lack of bearing – positively or negatively – on actual religions in Part I of the *Ethics* is absolute. As Heidegger put it more colourfully: 'man can neither fall to his knees in awe nor can he play music and dance before this god'.[8]

THE GOD OF THE PHILOSOPHERS

Spinoza is thought to have broken off the writing of the *Ethics* after Parts I and II (and when Part V may have existed as well) to write a different sort of work, the *Theological-Political Treatise*, devoted almost entirely to historical religions rather than to philosophy (as we now understand these). The God of the *Ethics* looks like the archetype of what Pascal thought he was disparaging not as the God of Abraham, but as the God of the Philosophers, considered apart from, and outside, the historical reality and practice of religion. So it might seem that we have a tidy separation between the natural theology of the *Ethics* and the study of historical religions in the *Theological-Political Treatise*.

That may be true to some extent. Spinoza may have believed – though he never said this – that he was able to isolate and discuss the *essential features* of God, or of a God, and that these could be discussed separately and independently from any discussion of practised religion.

---

[6] See E. M. Curley, 'Notes on a Neglected Masterpiece (II): The Theological–Political Treatise as a Prolegomenon to the Ethics', in J. A. Cover and M. Kulstad (eds.), *Central Themes in Early Modern Philosophy* (Indianapolis: Hackett, 1990), for a detailed examination. For a wider view, A. Matheron, *Le Christ et le salut des ignorants chez Spinoza* (Paris: Aubier-Montaigne, 1971).

[7] See Letter 73; L 333 = G IV 309: to be discussed in Chapter 9.

[8] *Identity and Difference* (1957), trans. J. Stambaugh (New York: Harper Torchbooks, 1974), p. 72.

That might accord with a Socratic principle that philosophers should seek to minimise their presuppositions, and it is an approach we can imagine that he could well have found sympathetic. Yet we should be careful in assuming that he followed it, and we would be wholly wrong to imagine that this is self-evident or uncontroversial. All the argument of the *Theological-Political Treatise* suggests that religions are inextricably historical. Spinoza's 'dogmas of the universal faith – the basic teachings which Scripture as a whole intends to convey'[9] – may be presented as minimalist or essentialist *religion*, but there is no suggestion of essential *theology*.

The God of Part I of the *Ethics* may be a God of the Philosophers, but we must be wary about what we may be taking for granted in that assumption. *Not*, for example – to put it negatively – that God can be separated, even for the purpose of discussion, from religion. Spinoza made that supposition in practice; but it was in practice, not in theory, and it was done with exquisite care. The creation of a subject with a label of 'philosophy of religion', in which God's existence can be debated in the absence of any possible God that might matter to anyone, cannot be attributed to him.

The God of the Philosophers, it may need to be said – since it was too obvious to Pascal to need saying – was almost entirely a God of Christian, and largely Catholic, philosophers. One preoccupation that Spinoza certainly did *not* share was any need to make his God consistent with, or even particularly palatable to, Christian, or specifically Catholic, thinking. And since a lot of effort has gone into showing that a God of Christian philosophers need not be seen as being in conflict with a Christian God,[10] this is relevant to what we can discern of Spinoza's aims: he did not share some of them with Christian philosophers.

Yet he did share some aims with them. The God of the Philosophers in the seventeenth century came into being because of the development of scientific – 'philosophical' – knowledge. New methods for understanding nature had to be fitted in with traditional forms of explanation, and with well-fortified theological claims. This induced a crisis in knowledge which manifested itself in various forms. One overt form was in the challenge of doubt articulated (for whatever intention) by Descartes. Others, less directly, came in the shape of arguments (pursued most famously by Leibniz) about limits on divine choice or free will, or in

---

[9] S 224 = G III 177–8.
[10] To some extent duplicating discussions in the Islamic world in its early centuries.

erosions of the senses of the conventional central terminology of *substance, essence* and *cause.*

The priorities for Spinoza, so far as we can judge them from the *Ethics*, were in these areas, and they make up the subject-matter of the first part of this book: the integration of theological with scientific explanation; the sense of divine causality and the scope for divine choice in the context of natural causality; and the places to be given to knowledge of God and to God in knowledge.

GOD, OR NATURE

A natural metaphor to help with an understanding of Part I of the *Ethics* is one of nuclear structure. In the rest of the work, and in the political and theological ramifications that follow from it, Spinoza unravelled the consequences of his views on how the world is made up and how it operates. The opening sections tell us about the fundamental components in the nucleus of the system, and about the forces – some might want to say the *logic* – that bound them together. A nuclear metaphor is apt because of a feature of his thought that one commentator has called his 'conceptual minimalism'.[11] We see an implosion or compression of terminology, where technical language seems to be crushed together in a way that can look in the end like a circular trick with mirrors. At times the effect can be claustrophobic in its concentration –

we have demonstrated . . . that Nature does not act with an end in view; that the eternal and infinite being, whom we call God, or Nature, acts by the same necessity whereby it exists. That the necessity of his nature whereby he acts is the same as that whereby he exists has been demonstrated . . . So the reason or cause why God, or Nature, acts, and the reason or cause why he exists, are one and the same . . .[12]

Spinoza takes orthodox scholastic terminology – the latinised vocabulary of Aristotle – and packs it together into a dense core. At the centre, God, substance and nature are brought into complete equivalence. We see 'God, or Nature' in the quotation above. In *Ethics* I, II we see a demonstration for the necessary existence of *God, or substance.* For most of

[11] Bennett, *A Study of Spinoza's Ethics*, pp. 38–41, but not on this subject. The density of style in the *Ethics* is discussed briefly but illuminatingly in Fokke Akkerman, 'Pauvreté ou richesse du latin de Spinoza', p. 25.
[12] *Ethics* IV, Preface, p. 153. The translator has tried hard here with one of the rare passages where Spinoza refers to 'God, or nature'. *Deus* is grammatically masculine and *natura* is feminine. It is very doubtful indeed whether we can read any significance into that, although it is absolutely certain that 'God' cannot be read without serious reservation as 'he'.

the *Ethics*, Spinoza chose to write about God, rather than to use the alternative titles of *substance* or *nature*, even where he was plainly concerned
with our natural knowledge of nature (as in the propositions at the end of
Ethics Part II that provide his grounding for the natural sciences). He
could have done otherwise. God, or Nature remains a surprising equivalence, and much of what is said about nature sounds far more surprising
when written as though it were about God. The extent to which this was
more than only a rhetorical preference is not clear. Though the question
seems interesting, there is no way to resolve it, because Spinoza left no
clues.

The formula *God, or Nature* appears only seldom and, it seems, rather
casually in the *Ethics*. The equivalence of God with nature is more
prominent, if obliquely, in the *Theological-Political Treatise*. There,
although Spinoza stressed that 'God's direction' is to be understood as
'the fixed and immutable order of Nature' – 'the universal laws of
Nature' are 'nothing but God's eternal decrees'[13] – it suited him to write
in terms of nature, not God. We read, for example, that man is part of
nature, acting in accordance with natural law,[14] whereas in the *Ethics* 'the
essence of man is constituted by definite modifications of the attributes
of God'.[15] The equivalence of natural law with divine law could scarcely
leave the equivalence of nature with God in any doubt, though that
implicit equivalence was never elaborated, for understandable rhetorical
reasons, in the *Theological-Political Treatise*.

More evident, perhaps, is the reason why *substance*, having been
brought painstakingly into equivalence with God and with nature in Part
I of the *Ethics*, was hardly mentioned afterwards. How substance came
into philosophy, the purposes it served and the reasons for its extinction,
is a massive subject, launched in all its complexity from the very outset,
in Aristotle's *Metaphysics*, Z. The whole subject became even more difficult with the translation of its terminology from the Greek Christian
fathers into Latin.[16] Christian philosophers felt a need for substance in at
least two crucial theological doctrines: of the eucharist and of the
Trinity. Consecrated bread was said to *become* the body of Christ, raising
questions about change, underlying nature and continuity. God was said
to be one being in three persons, raising questions about existence, unity

---

[13] S 89 = G III 46/3.   [14] S 101 = G III 58/9ff.   [15] II, 10, Corollary.
[16] Christopher Stead, *Philosophy in Christian Antiquity* (Cambridge University Press, 1994), Chapter 14,
     has a short but extremely useful discussion. A more discursive view of the same point is given by
     Emmanual Lévinas, e.g. in 'Ethics of the Infinite', interview (1981) in Richard Kearney (ed.), *States
     of Mind* (Manchester University Press, 1995), pp. 184–5.

and identity. These questions became trials for any philosophical claims about what exists. Attempts to advance an understanding of nature – of *what exists* – had to answer them, to steer a way around them or – by the time of Descartes – to ignore them with an air of pious unwillingness to tackle the mysteries of theology.[17]

But these were not, of course, Spinoza's questions. He had no interest in the theology of the eucharist and he saw the Christian Trinity as being as near to absurdity as tact would allow him to reveal.[18] The Christian theological agenda underlying thought about substance, and Spinoza's complete liberation from it, can be easy to miss. Substance had existed for a long time for particular reasons, but many of those reasons had no force for him. There were other questions that had created a philosophy of substance, and some of these are resolved in Part I of the *Ethics*: what exists? How was it created? From what? As we shall see, he thought he could deal with these questions in a short and conclusive way; but we should not underestimate how the directness of his treatment was eased by the avoidance of the traditional theological background. Some questions about substance needed to be faced, but substance was hardly needed, apart from nature, to solve questions within his thought. So, perhaps, we hear mostly about God, or sometimes nature, instead.

Spinoza takes us to his God not from a theological or moral direction – for example, in the manner of Descartes, from a quasi-moral notion of *perfection* – but by using a mathematical or physical notion: God is defined as 'an absolutely infinite being',[19] where to be finite, by a previous definition, is 'to be limited' (*terminari*). As a premise, this seems theologically innocuous: how could God *not* be said to be infinite by anyone in a monotheistic tradition? And it hardly seems innovative: Wolfson anatomises its antecedents in medieval Arabic writing.[20] Spinoza's subsequent arguments knit together an unlimited, infinite God with two characteristics of substance that might – taken alone, in their purified forms – be seen as commonplace at the time: it was 'that which is in itself and is conceived through itself' and 'that which is self-caused', 'whose nature can be conceived only as existing'.[21]

---

[17] An exception: his discussion about the eucharist, *Fourth Replies*, CSMK II 172–8 = AT VII 247–56.
[18] See note 7 above.
[19] 'the idea of a supremely perfect and infinite being': *Third Meditation*, CSMK II 31 = AT VII 46; *Ethics* I, Definition 6. On this difference of approach, see Jean-Marie Beyssade, 'The Idea of God and the Proofs of his Existence', in J. G. Cottingham (ed.), *The Cambridge Companion to Descartes* (Cambridge University Press, 1996), pp. 186–8.
[20] H. A. Wolfson, *The Philosophy of Spinoza* (reprint from 2 vols., 1934) (Cambridge: Harvard University Press, 1983), vol. I, pp. 133–41. [21] *Ethics* I, Definitions 3 and I.

Although we know nothing explicitly about the development of this essential core of Spinoza's thought, we must assume that the intricate web of his arguments has *some* forensic direction. Their logic has been much studied,[22] but in formal terms that takes us little further than the most cursory initial impression: that is to say, an impression that the axioms and definitions do not strike us as being self-evident, while the ensuing arguments seem to be interlocking to a point of circularity. That impression may be justified in a formal sense, but it is certainly not fair. No reader of the *Ethics* could possibly imagine that its arguments could have been meant to derive the less obvious propositions from the more obvious axioms or – as already mentioned – that its demonstrations were meant to persuade the wavering or the sceptical,[23] or even to remove the obstacles to faith in the traditional manner.[24] It is far more likely that his aim was to show how his machinery could be fitted together. Those who accepted his premises would need to show how they might not want his conclusions. And – more relevantly from our point of view, where we may not care about the premises – those who may have wanted some of the conclusions might need to show how they could get by without some of the others.

God, as self-caused substance, is allegedly shown to exist necessarily, to be 'unique' and to be indivisible. Some of this characterisation seems harmless, and would always have seemed harmless. But not all its consequences, in Spinoza's mind, were commonplace. Above all we see the equivalence between God as substance and the whole of nature: 'nothing can be or be conceived without God', we find, can be read in a literal way, though it is not until the beginning of Part II of the *Ethics* that the most puzzling corollary is drawn out explicitly: 'God is an extended thing' (*Deus est res extensa*). Yet Spinoza has told us that it is a gross error to regard God as 'corporeal'.[25]

GOD AND THE WORLD

This seems paradoxical. An extended God suggests physical pantheism (and it suggested this to many of Spinoza's most virulent critics). The denial of a corporeal God might suggest a denial of pantheism. The relationship between God and individual people or things in the world –

[22] e.g. Charles Jarrett, 'The Logical Structure of Spinoza's Ethics, Part I', *Synthèse*, 37, 1978.
[23] We shall see in Chapter 3 that Spinoza rejected a need to start from what is said to be *most certain*, in the manner of Descartes: to rebuild the structure of what is known after sceptical dismantling.
[24] As in *Summa Theologiæ* 2a2æ. 2, 10.   [25] *Ethics* I, 15, Demonstration; II, 2; I, 15, Scholium.

in nature – is one of the most difficult and contentious areas of Spinoza's thought – deeply technical, in the sense that it is encrusted in his most unhelpfully baroque terminology, but also centrally relevant, in the sense that it underlies almost all his other thinking.[26]

The challenge posed by that relationship has a long theological pedigree in Christian, Islamic and Jewish traditions. God may be said to be infinite. We, and the rest of creation, are finite. Yet there are supposed to be some connections: possibly in terms of ontology – where God exists – *outside, inside* or *as the totality of* the world; or in terms of causality – where God may be said to cause events *sometimes* (providentially), *rarely* (miraculously) or perhaps even *routinely*.

Spinoza's approach to this challenge in the *Ethics* was almost exclusively mathematical, ignoring entirely its historically theological dimensions. Yet one of his most direct explanations of the relationship between God and the world is given in language taken from medieval theology.[27] He makes use of the terms *Natura naturans* (nature naturing) to cover 'that which is in itself and conceived through itself' – God as substance; and *Natura naturata* ('nature natured') to mean 'all the modes of God's attributes in so far as they are considered as things which are in God and can neither be nor be conceived without God'.[28]

But this gives us only words, and not helpful words in that we still have a problem plus a load of dense terminology. What is the connection between *Natura naturans* – substance – and *Natura naturata*, which we see to be 'modes'? Are they separate, connected or, in some way, the same thing?

In Spinoza's early thought they may have been separate, and the connection between them was partially veiled in theological mist. In the *Short Treatise*, written before the *Ethics*, the 'whole of Nature' was divided into *Natura naturans* and *Natura naturata*. *Natura naturata* appeared at least in part in a theological guise as 'a Son, product or effect, created immediately by God' and 'an immediate creature of God, created by him from all eternity . . .'. This suggests that God may have been seen as divided from creation[29] with an indistinct causal relationship to it.

In the *Ethics* the mist dispersed, although the picture could hardly be

---

[26] It is also an area where the signs of development or change in his thought are apparent, but where they remain exasperatingly implicit, never spelled out as we might hope.

[27] For example, *Summa Theologiæ* 1a2æ. 85, 6.   [28] *Ethics* I, 29, Scholium.

[29] Though the Dutch word translated from the *Short Treatise* as 'divided' – *schiften* – could also mean 'separated' in the less distinct sense as seen in 'separated milk': *Short Treatise* I, 8 and 9; Curley, pp. 91–2 = G I 47/20–3 and 48/19–22.

said to be clear. The most important change was implicit: the connection between God and things became intelligible and non-metaphorical – talk of a 'Son' of God, with its obvious theological undertones, vanished. The context, instead, became not theology but geometry. Less obviously, the hint of division went too. *Natura naturans* is God as substance in so far as[30] God is considered a free cause. *Natura naturata* is God considered as modes – things – in so far as they are 'in God and can neither be nor be conceived without God'.[31]

We shall look at the causal relationships between God and 'modes' in the next chapter, in considering how God is meant to act. For now – so far as this can be taken separately – we can look at the ontological relationship.

At first that seems clear enough: 'Nothing exists but substance and its modes.'[32] The support summoned by Spinoza for this declaration was, to him, simple: 'All things that are, are either in themselves or in something else'; substance is in itself; a mode is in something else.[33] Modes are things. They may be individual things, such as people or thoughts, which are 'finite'; or they may be 'infinite'. Either way, they exist 'in' substance.

That looks like some form of dependence, in that free-standing existence is, seemingly, being denied. But the central relation of existing 'in', of course, remains unexplained.

That relation, between modes and substance, has been one of the most divisive areas of Spinoza scholarship. The ground was cleared decisively by Edwin Curley in 1969 with his *Spinoza's Metaphysics: An Essay in Interpretation*, the pioneering work for the modern study of Spinoza. Curley finally set aside a view of substance as a substratum in which modes 'inhere' as qualities – a view he ascribed to Descartes, Bayle, Joachim and (in more recent writing) to Jonathan Bennett.[34] Most importantly, Spinoza 'did not intend to say that the relation of particular things to God was in any way like the relation of a predicate to its subject' in a grammatical or logical sense. Equally, Curley buried a view, ascribed to Wolfson, where 'the relation of mode to substance is a relation of species to genus'. He rightly drew attention to remarks of Spinoza which stressed the individual, non-illusory existence of modes[35] – 'the very existence of particular things'; 'Each thing, in so far as it is in itself, endeavors to

[30] *quatenus* – a crucial term for Spinoza. Shirley offers an interesting note on its use in his translation, p. 26. *Ethics* I, 29 = G II 71/12.   [31] *Ethics* I, 29, Scholium.
[32] *Ethics* I, 28, Demonstration: *præter [enim] substantiam, & modos nil datur.*
[33] *Ethics* I, Axiom I, Definitions 3 and 5.
[34] See Curley, *Spinoza's Metaphysics*, Chapter I and 'On Bennett's Interpretation of Spinoza's Monism', in Yirmiyahu Yovel (ed.), *God and Nature: Spinoza's Metaphysics* (Leiden: Brill, 1991).
[35] Curley, *Spinoza's Metaphysics*, pp. 37, 28, 73.

persist in its own being.'[36] Individual things really exist. Curley's positive view was that substance for Spinoza 'is what is causally self-sufficient, that a mode is something which is not causally self-sufficient and that the relation of mode to substance is one of causal dependence, not one of inherence in a subject'.[37] That seems undeniable to the point of self-evidence in the light of Spinoza's insistence on causality in the early propositions of the *Ethics*, though (as we shall see in the next chapter) the mechanism of causation remains to be filled in: a task not without difficulty.

But an agreement that modes do not relate to substance – individuals and the world to God – as qualities to a substratum, as predicates to a subject or as species to a genus, and an agreement that such a relation is somehow 'causal', do not imply anything specific about the forms of existence of modes and substance. Curley adopted a radical view. He saw Spinoza's identification of God with nature not as 'the totality of things' but as 'the most general principles of order exemplified by things'.[38] God or nature became not nature in the sense of the world as we know it, but as more like 'those most general principles of order described by the fundamental laws of nature'.[39]

PANTHEISM?

Such an approach distances Spinoza from pantheism. As we have seen, though, he was clear enough that he did not want to identify nature or God with *corporeal* nature – a point stressed in a letter of 1675 to Oldenburg:

as to the view of certain people that the *Tractatus Theologico-Politicus* rests on the identification of God with Nature (by the latter of which they understand a kind of mass or corporeal matter) [*massam quandam, sive materiam corporem*], they are quite mistaken.[40]

If nature–God–substance *were* seen by Spinoza simply as the 'totality of things', then he might be described rightly as a pantheist;[41] and if we see

---

[36] *Ethics* II, 45, Scholium; III, 6.
[37] Curley, 'On Bennett's Interpretation of Spinoza's Monism', p. 37.
[38] Curley, *Behind the Geometrical Method*, p. 42.
[39] *A Spinoza Reader* (Princeton University Press, 1994), p. xxv.
[40] Letter 73; L 332 = G IV 307/11–14; another, less direct, repudiation of pantheism appears in Letter 43; L 239 = G IV 223/5–8.
[41] The fullest recent study of pantheism is surprisingly unhelpful on this. 'What makes Spinoza a pantheist, if anything, is what it means to say that for him everything is the self-expression of the Absolute', where this is not explained exclusively in terms of substance lineage'; but later, and scarcely less opaquely, we read in a footnote that, 'Although Spinoza is, by far, the most prominent "pantheist" – it may be that he is not really a pantheist at all', M. P. Levine, *Pantheism* (London: Routledge, 1994), pp. 137, 362–3, n. 7.

reasons to avert that conclusion we can understand how Curley might
have wanted to put God on to altogether a different plane from physical
nature.

But substance cannot be a totality of things. As Alan Donagan put it
perhaps rather too succinctly: 'Since finite modes are not self-caused,
their totality cannot be self-caused either. Spinoza is not a pantheist. Yet
if everything that is not God is in God,[42] there is no gulf between anything and God.'[43]

The motto on the title page of the *Theological-Political Treatise* was from
the First Epistle of John (4: 13): 'Hereby we dwell in God and He in us,
because He has given us of his Spirit . . .', though only the moral, not the
ontological relevance of that was drawn out in the book.[44]

INFINITY

The relationship between things and God can be spelled out more fully
by looking at Spinoza's thought on infinity, expressed (we must assume)
in its perfected form in the *Ethics*, largely in the Scholium to Proposition
15 of Part I – 'Whatever is, is in God, and nothing can be conceived
without God' – but also in his letters, including Letter 12 of 1663, given
the title *The Letter on the Infinite*.

On the most decisive point we see in a late letter, of 1676, that Spinoza
understood the complete difference between an infinity and a 'multitude
of parts'; in fact that 'multitude' and 'infinity' were not comparable.
Typically – but not perhaps most persuasively for theologically minded
readers – he used a geometrical example:

in the entire space between [the] two non-concentric circles we conceive there
to be twice the number of parts as in half that space, and yet the number of
parts both in the half as well as the whole of this space is greater than any
assignable number.[45]

Spinoza's resolution of the relationship between the finite and the infinite is simple, although cloaked in rebarbative language. What he calls
finite modes – for practical purposes, individuals – together make up what
he calls *infinite modes*. This we see, for example, where he tells us how we
can 'readily conceive the whole of Nature as one individual, whose parts
– that is, all the constituent bodies – vary in infinite ways without any

---

[42] In Letter 73, Spinoza agreed 'with Paul' that all things are 'in God and move in God'; L 332 = G IV
307/6–7.   [43] Donagan, *Spinoza*, p. 90.   [44] S 223 = G III 175–6.
[45] Letter 81; L 352 = G IV 332/11–15: *omni assignabili numero major est.*

change in the individual as a whole'; or where we learn that our mind, together with other minds 'all together constitute the eternal and infinite intellect of God' (and we know from a letter that 'infinite intellect' was an example of an infinite mode).[46]

At first sight, this looks unhelpfully wrong. How can finite individuals together *constitute* infinite modes? That looks to be exactly the error diagnosed by Spinoza, of thinking that infinities could be large totalities: that God or nature is *made up* of individual parts.[47]

He believed that things may be understood in different ways. If we 'imagine' quantity, for example, 'superficially', then

we find it to be finite, divisible and made up of parts. But if we consider it intellectually and conceive it in so far as [*quatenus*] it is substance – and this is very difficult – then it will be found to be infinite, one, and indivisible.[48]

This makes use of the distinction – familiar in outline to readers of Descartes[49] – between what we can imagine or picture to ourselves and what can be intellectually conceived. To Spinoza, God cannot be 'imagined' but can be understood.[50] But, whatever the details, we seem to get a purely verbal solution: a collection may be imagined as divisible and finite or conceived as indivisible and infinite: so *is it* infinite or not?

The answer lies in another distinction, drawn in the *Letter on the Infinite*, between 'that which must be infinite by its very nature' and 'that which is unlimited ... by virtue of its cause'.[51] Substance is said to be the 'cause of itself', modes are not, as we have seen, though the sense of this has not yet been explored.

The relationship between finite and infinite modes is constitutive not 'causal'. The relationship between the infinite modes and substance will be a matter of two ways by which the same reality may be considered: as *Natura naturans* and *Natura naturata*, or as cause and effect. In technical language, the machinery seems to be that finite modes together make up or constitute aggregations which may be imagined to be infinite. These 'infinite modes' are also infinite by virtue of being 'caused' in Nature.[52] Here, nature-as-effect – the infinite modes – will be *Natura naturata*. If this

---

[46] *Ethics* II, Lemma 7, Scholium = G II 102/11–13; *Ethics* V, 40, Corollary, Scholium: *omnes simul Dei æternum, & infinitum intellectum constituant*; Letter 64; L 299 = G IV 278/25.
[47] He did write at times as if individuals were 'parts' of nature – e.g., strikingly, Letter 32; L 194 = G IV 172–4 – but his clarity on the indivisibility of nature leaves no doubt of his more carefully considered view.   [48] *Ethics* I, 15, Scholium. He goes on to use a wholly inadequate example: water.
[49] *Sixth Meditation*, CSMK II 50–1 = AT VII 72–3.   [50] Letter 56; L 278 = G IV 261/10–11.
[51] Letter 12; L 101 = G IV 53/2–5.
[52] There is a complicating distinction between 'mediate' and 'immediate' infinite modes, deriving from *Ethics* I, 21–3, but this has no relevance here.

is seen in terms of nature-as-cause, it will be *Natura naturans*, or substance.

The point of this terminological compression is exactly to allow for infinities. Thinking in Spinoza's favourite terms, for example, if geometry[53] is to be able to make use of continuous or infinitely extended lines, or of areas containing infinite numbers of points, some scope must be allowed for these in nature. For the development of mathematical physics, infinite extension and infinitesimal points may be needed. So we get 'infinite modes'. We see this, but far from clearly, where possible infinite geometrical constructions do not exist 'except in so far as the infinite idea of God exists'.[54] This 'idea' is an infinite mode.

Where does all this get us – away from Spinoza's technical machinery – with his alleged pantheism? What sorts of things, after all, are supposed to exist? *Not* substance, infinite modes and finite modes as separate items on a list. All of these, in one sense, are the same thing, but understood in different ways. It would be wrong, though, to infer that Spinoza just identifies God or nature with, for example, physical objects individually (as parts) or together (as a whole) – as bad a mistake as to assert that 'a body is composed of surfaces, surfaces of lines, and lines of points'.[55]

His resolution of the infinity of God against the finitude of creation makes ingenious use of 'infinite modes' as a kind of hinge. We know that there are recognisable, unmysterious infinities in nature: as where there may be an infinite number of points on a line. Individuals 'make up' infinities in one loose, 'imaginative' sense. The infinity of nature is 'made up' of parts in that sense: nature understood[56] 'modally' is divisible. The same nature understood as substance or cause is not divisible. The corporeal (and mental) contents of nature do make it up. But they are not 'made of nature', in the sense that nature, substance or God is some sort of material that constitutes objects.

WHAT EXISTS?

If that seems unsatisfying, it might be less so in the light of Spinoza's wider thought about ontology: about what is supposed to exist.

It is easy and natural to assume that a philosopher might try to prove

---

[53] There are problems with arithmetic: see p. 40.
[54] *Ethics* II, 8, Corollary. The point here is one basis for the discussion of possibility, to be considered further in Chapters 2 and 3, and of eternity (in *Ethics* V, 23), to be considered in Chapter 10.
[55] *Ethics* I, 15, Scholium.
[56] More fully and correctly: understood 'through each attribute', a point to be considered later in this chapter, though it does not affect the discussion now.

the existence of God as part of an answer to the question: What exists? The answer would then indicate that God, among other entities, exists. And the notion of an *entity* would already suggest some categorisation of things as existing.

It is even easier to assume that a philosopher who goes on about substance might be thinking along such lines, because one of the ways in which substance came into philosophy in the first place was as part of an answer to the question, what sort of thing or things exist? And one answer would be, the sort of thing that exists is substance. A philosopher can then go on to ask, how many substances, or kinds of substance, are there? And so on. This is *ontology*.

It would be a great error to see Spinoza in that way. He did, of course, offer demonstrations for the necessary existence of God-as-substance, and he did claim that there is only one kind of substance which is also (carelessly expressed) numerically unique. But he was not an ontologist in the sense of offering any account of what kinds or numbers of things exist. In fact, the tendency of his thinking is to take ontology – questions about what exists – out of philosophy, as we might understand it, altogether, leaving them for physics.

His approach was grounded in an uncompromisingly consistent understanding of necessary existence. 'Ontological' proofs have had a bad reputation as, basically, a way of proving necessary existence from a definition (and that has been seen as patently unacceptable). But it is interesting that Spinoza seems to have welcomed such an interpretation in a letter of 1676 to Tschirnhaus:

Simply from the fact that I define God as an Entity to whose essence existence belongs, I infer several properties of him, such as that he necessarily exists, that he is one alone, immutable, infinite, etc.[57]

This has all the appearance of the self-supporting logic which (as in the opening propositions of the *Ethics*) could only persuade a reader already willing to accept its conclusions. But that assumes that we see here a 'proof' which is meant to convert an unbeliever; and that is entirely unlikely. And the function of 'proof' – *demonstratio* – is more like one of dismantling a clock to demonstrate how its parts work together.

It is worth noting, though, that Spinoza's comment to Tschirnhaus does not embody the kind of vicious circle that seems most obviously present. 'I define God as an Entity to whose essence existence belongs'

---

[57] Letter 83; L 355 = G IV 335/4–7.

might be understood by an unwary modern reader to mean that it is necessary (or necessarily true) that God possesses the property of existence;
from which it looks as if we may deduce – 'prove' – that God has the
property of existing necessarily; and that would surely be flagrantly
question-begging. Jonathan Bennett, for example, reads Spinoza like
that:

the argument takes it to be a necessary truth – a matter of the definition or
concept of God – that God has every property in some domain of properties of
which existence is one of the members: the domain may be perfections, or kinds
of reality, or whatever. From this it is inferred that necessarily God has existence,
i.e., that necessarily God exists.[58]

But in an earlier letter, and in other writing, Spinoza emphasised that a
definition should express the 'efficient cause' of something (or, what
seems to be the same, its 'nature'[59]) from which its properties could then
be deduced. He disagreed explicitly with the allegedly Aristotelian idea
that a definition should be a list of necessary or essential properties.[60]

The cause for the existence of a thing must either be contained in the very
nature and definition of the existent thing (in effect, existence belongs to its
nature) or it must have its being independently of the thing itself.[61]

Spinoza compressed together the notions of *cause*, *definition* and *nature*.
Substance-or-God acts as its own cause, and that cause is its definition:
being self-caused.

But this, in so far as it seems to make sense at all, looks even more
unhelpfully circular than the plainer assertion, in Bennett's reading, that
God's necessary existence follows from an assumption that God necessarily possesses the property of existence.

Yet Spinoza did not express his arguments in terms of a 'domain of
properties', and he did not say that it is a 'necessary truth' that God has
properties. To read him like that is to translate his arguments into the
terms of a logic where it heads inexorably for the trap sprung by Kant:
existence is not a property like other properties; and absurdities arise

---

[58] Bennett, *A Study of Spinoza's Ethics*, p. 70: he is writing about the demonstrations in *Ethics* I, 7 and 11,
not directly about Letter 83. Also H. A. Davidson, *Proofs for Eternity, Creation and the Existence of God
in Medieval Islamic and Jewish Philosophy* (Oxford University Press, 1987), p. 395.

[59] Letter 60; L 290 = G IV 270–1; G II 50/20ff.

[60] See *Ethics* II, 40, Scholium 1 = G II 121/30–2, where definitions of 'man' as a featherless biped or as
a rational animal are mocked; or *Treatise on the Emendation of the Intellect*, p. 257, §95 = G II 34/29ff,
where it is said that a definition should not use properties instead of causes to explain. Spinoza
would think in terms of real, rather than nominal, definition, though the existence of that contrast would beg the question here.   [61] *Ethics* I, 8, Scholium 2 = G II 50/31–3.

from attributing or predicating existence to anything in the same way as other properties such as shape or colour.[62]

Spinoza's argument was simpler, and the core of it can be stated in terms of reasons or (as he would say) causes. The first premise would be that everything has a cause; the second that everything is caused either by itself or by something else. The existence of substance is not caused by anything else. So it must be caused by itself; and that constitutes its definition.

The first premise was a cardinal thesis for Spinoza – 'For every thing a cause or reason must be assigned either for its existence or for its non-existence'[63] – much more on this in the following chapters. The second premise comes from Spinoza's axioms. Substance is seen from the outset as being its own cause.[64]

But even if the logic of the connections in this argument does not break down in fallacies, we remain with conclusions and premises which – to say the least – look disconcertingly close together.

Spinoza was taking assumptions that might have been widely accepted in his time and was, at the same time, pushing these to their logical extremes and fitting them together into a set of working machinery. The idea of a God without limits, or infinite, would not be surprising. God as a substance was a commonplace. Descartes made use of the notion of 'cause of itself' and had a good deal of theological trouble with it.[65] He also wanted God to be a substance, but was unable to deny that other substances – souls, for example, to give the most tricky case – existed as well. Spinoza's resolution of these terms might not have been harmfully circular if it could have fitted them together without inconsistencies.

More important, though, is the sense of what he was trying to show. Iris Murdoch, in an extended discussion of 'ontological proofs' for the existence of God, puts the essential point well:

The definition of God as having *necessary* not contingent existence is an important clarification for any interested party. God cannot be a particular, a contingent thing, one thing among others; a contingent god might be a great demonic or angelic spirit, but not the Being in question. Anything that happens to exist,

---

[62] Bennett also assumes a modal inference that could not apply for Spinoza: 'It is necessarily true that A has x' (*de dicto*) entails 'A necessarily has x' (*de re*). This will come up in a different context in the next chapter.   [63] *Ethics* I, II, Demonstration 2.

[64] *Ethics* I, Axioms 1 and 2; Definitions 1 and 3.

[65] e.g. *First Replies*, CSMK II 79–80 = AT VII 108–12; Letter to Mersenne, 18 March 1641, CSMK III 175–7 = AT III 334–8.

and could perhaps not exist, or about whose existence one could speculate as about empirical discoveries, or about which one could state 'what would it be like' *if* it existed, is not what is thought of here. God's necessary existence is connected with his not being an object. God is not to be worshipped as an idol or identified with any empirical thing; as is indeed enjoined by the Second Commandment.[66]

This applied to Anselm's original ontological 'proof', but the sense applies as well to Spinoza. His God was not 'an object' for whose existence proofs might be convincing or not. The conclusion that God necessarily exists does not mean, as Bennett assumes, that a proposition that God has the property of existence is necessarily true.[67] God is the same as nature in the sense that there is nothing that is not nature, and in that there is no point in arguing that nature does not exist. If we were thinking in terms of God as 'an object', we could ask why, or if, that object exists, and maybe search for a convincing proof. But there will be no external explanation for the existence of nature if we understand it as being without limits.

And maybe that is one reason why Spinoza took infinity as the main thread leading into his web of terminology: in the plainest terms – if you take seriously the claim that God is infinite, how can you then say that anything in nature can be excluded from God?

ETERNITY

The same thinking applies to eternity. The ascription of eternity to God would not seem too controversial to any modern European thinker who accepted a God at all; but Spinoza's notion of eternity could only be called provocatively unhelpful as it appeared first in the *Ethics* – 'By eternity I mean existence itself in so far as it is conceived as necessarily following solely from the definition of an eternal thing.' Such eternity 'cannot be explicated through duration or time, even if the duration be conceived as without beginning and end'.[68] With the aid of a few other central assumptions, it was said to follow that God is eternal.[69] In addition, unusually, Spinoza refers us back to an earlier work, his *Descartes' Principles of Philosophy Demonstrated in the Geometrical Manner*. There, the nub of the point had been simple enough: 'God has not a limited, but an infi-

---

[66] *Metaphysics as a Guide to Morals* (London: Chatto & Windus, 1992), p. 395.
[67] Whatever Spinoza meant by 'eternal truth', it was not this: *Ethics* I, 20 Corollary; 19, Scholium.
[68] *Ethics* I, Definition 8 and explication.   [69] *Ethics* I, 19.

nite existence, which we call eternity.'[70] This relied, again, we see, on the fundamental notion of being limited or unlimited – finite or infinite. We shall return in more detail (in Chapter 10) to the use of eternity in Part v of the *Ethics*.

The unity of God is of more immediate interest.

It does not seem too rash to speculate that one legacy of Spinoza's Jewish upbringing that never left him was a repudiation of any thought of many gods, or of some kind of multiple God.

So much is clear. His understanding of the unity of God is far less straightforward. In his *Descartes' Principles of Philosophy*, he distanced himself from a Cartesian route to divine unity from an angle of divine perfection, preferring what he saw as a more direct argument: 'it follows necessarily from the mere fact that some thing involves necessary existence from itself (as God does) that it is unique'.[71]

The most explicit demonstration in the *Ethics* goes along similar lines. 'God is one, that is . . . in the universe [*in rerum natura*] there is only one substance, and this is absolutely infinite' appears as a corollary of Part i, Proposition 14: 'There can be, or be conceived, no other substance but God.' The support for these conclusions is assembled by welding together conceptions of infinity, substance, nature and God. Spinoza's wish is to show that more than one substance, as he understands it, makes no sense. He tries to achieve this by *reductio ad absurdum*: suppose there could be two substances – but then these could be neither dependent on each other nor independent of each other, finite or infinite, and so on.

The aim has to be to show that there cannot be more than one sub-stance because, as he says in a letter, he does not try to show that there is *one* substance, strictly speaking; and in this sense he is inaccurately described as a monist,[72] if that is taken to mean that he counted only one existing substance: 'it is certain that he who calls God one or single [*Deum unum, vel unicum* . . .] has no true idea of God, or is speaking of him very improperly'.[73]

---

[70] Curley, p. 261 = G i 178/18–19. This seems to sail very close to the wind in making eternity sound like an unlimited duration, or a very long time, or sempiternity; but Spinoza strove to dispel that impression in Appendix ii, 1 to the *Principles*.

[71] Curley, p. 255 = G i 169/18–23, also G i 253/16–21.

[72] Like, perhaps, even Parmenides nowadays, according to one commentator: Jonathan Barnes, 'Parmenides and the Eleatic One', *Archiv für Geschichte der Philosophie*, 61, 1979.

[73] Letter 50; L 260 = G iv 240/3–5 = 23–5.

His reason for saying this is far more revealing than his explicit demonstration of God's unity. Frege, in *The Foundations of Arithmetic*, noted with approval Spinoza's observation that 'we do not conceive things under the category of numbers, unless they are included in a common class'.[74] There could not be *one sort of thing* that God or nature is, because it could not form a category of things that could be counted at all. Frege went on, though, to attribute to Spinoza the

> mistake of supposing that a concept can only be acquired by direct abstraction from a number of objects. We can, on the contrary, arrive at a concept equally well by starting from defining characteristics; and in such a case it is possible for nothing to fall under it. If this did not happen, we should never be able to deny existence, and so the assertion of existence too would lose all content.[75]

As we might expect from Frege, this was a penetrating observation. It is revealing, but not as he intended. Spinoza's own thinking about arithmetic, such as it was, was grounded in his belief that number derived from imagination rather than pure intellection (in contrast with geometry). And that belief, despite the great efforts of commentators to present its positive aspects,[76] is surely irredeemable. Here, though, this does not matter. Spinoza's thought was not that we cannot acquire a concept such as 'two substances' because such a number of substances cannot exist. (That could not be right because we see him arguing by *reductio ad absurdum*: suppose there was more than one substance . . .) His thought actually was very much more like what Frege says: we may 'arrive at a concept . . . from defining characteristics'. But the defining characteristics of substance imply that not more than one substance can exist.

Yet in a way it is correct to say – and important to see – that the assertion of the existence of only one object in nature would be without 'content' [*Inhalt*].[77] As we have seen, the existence of God is not proved like the existence of an 'object'. The direction of the apparent logical problem is indicated by Richard Rorty:

> Spinoza would like to say that he knows all about finite modes and can describe what they are in a vocabulary which gets them right. But . . . getting something

---

[74] Letter 50; L 259 = G IV 239/9–10/30–32.

[75] *The Foundations of Arithmetic* (1884), trans. J. L. Austin (Oxford: Blackwell, 1968), p. 62.

[76] For example Martial Gueroult, *Spinoza I: Dieu* (Paris: Aubier-Montaigne, 1968), Appendix 17, pp. 578–84.

[77] This means that Spinoza wholly escapes the argument produced by Hampshire against a metaphysician who tries to claim that 'it makes sense to talk of Nature as a single system' (*Spinoza* (Harmondsworth: Penguin, 1951), pp. 221–2); whoever this is, it is not Spinoza.

right, representing it accurately, seems to be a relation between two things. Yet the whole point of monism is that there is only one thing.[78]

But Spinoza's God, as we have seen, is hardly a 'thing', even in a wide logical sense; and his very point here, as Frege sees, is to say that you cannot start counting at all where you can only count to one. (Lévinas: 'Le monothéisme n'est pas une arithmétique du divin.'[79])

This is why Spinoza can only be seen in a very weak sense as engaging in 'ontology'. It would be more accurate to say that his approach deprives philosophical ontology of any point. The answer to the question, what, basically, exists? is that substance and its modes exist. But that, as Spinoza understands it, tells us nothing at all – nothing physical, for example – about what specific things might or might not exist, or why. Pollock put it well: 'to say of the universe . . . that its essence involves existence, does not really import any greater assumption than that something does exist'.[80] The view that nature exists – that there is nature – leaves open any question of *what* exists in nature – of what exists: open for scientific inquiry, perhaps.

HOW GOD EXISTS

The unity of God leads us on to the question of *how* God exists for Spinoza. Substance is not only 'unique' in a numerical sense (though not wholly accurately, as we have just seen), but in the sense of being simple: there are not, as it were, different sorts of substance.

This is the territory of Spinoza's writing on what he called 'attributes' – surely, as we will see, one of his most damagingly misleading choices of terminology. What he says can be read as an answer to several, apparently quite different, theological and philosophical questions. 'Read' *as* an answer, we must say, because we do not know – and we are not told – the order of priority in his thinking. It can be tempting to assume that theological or personal motivations must have taken precedence over philosophical needs; but Spinoza's writings can be quoted in both directions. What we can assert with reasonable confidence is that a highly

---

[78] *Essays on Heidegger and Others* (Cambridge University Press, 1991), p. 90. Rorty also thinks that Spinoza makes individuals – finite modes – 'unreal'.

[79] 'Monothéisme et langage' (1959), in *Difficile liberté* (Paris: Albin Michel, 1963), p. 178. A similar point was made by Aquinas: *Summa Theologiæ* 1a. 11, 3. Hermann Cohen opened his *Religion of Reason* by saying that 'It is God's uniqueness, rather than his oneness, that we posit as the essential content of monotheism'; but from that he drew conclusions very different from Spinoza's (*Religion of Reason, out of the Sources of Judaism* (1919), trans. S. Kaplan (trs.) (New York: Ungar, 1972), p. 35).

[80] *Spinoza, His Life and Philosophy*, p. 162.

compressed theory – or rather, a theory compressed down to just an item of terminology – goes to work on several fronts at the same time.

First there is an ancient theological problem about the simplicity of God. Is God, basically, of a simple, united nature? Or is the nature of God better expressed by the infinite multiplicity of creation? Or, indeed, both equally (if paradoxically)?[81]

Although abstract, this was an issue where religious intuitions – or perhaps temperaments – had been divided: in contrast with the less schismatic issues of the numerical unity, the infinity or the eternity of God. Even mystical insights could point with equal force in opposite directions – towards simplicity and towards multiplicity – maybe creating the temptation to smother the issue in a blanket of ineffability or divine unintelligibility.

The simplicity of God was by no means only a Christian problem, but it did generate a specifically Christian sub-problem, in thought about the unity of the Trinity. A delicate balance had to be found, or defined, between the simple nature of one God, and the non-simplicity of God's three persons. *That* sub-problem, at least, we can be certain was not in the front of Spinoza's mind.

Another sub-problem, not specifically Christian, can be expressed in terms of the objectivity or subjectivity of God's simplicity. Was God really simple in nature – only appearing complex to mortal eyes – although maybe united to those with higher forms of mystical vision? Or could the evident multiplicity of nature be seen as itself intrinsic? Is human perception or judgment that things are not simple in fact a correct view of how things are?

Then, too, there was a theological–philosophical question about degrees of reality. It had seemed natural to claim that God was 'most real' in the sense that *if* 'reality' contained some sort of graduated scale, God could hardly be denied a place on the top rung of the ladder. The traditional subject-matter of ontology could contain not only the question, what exists? but also, what sort of things exist? leading on to questions about whether some things exist *more*, or more *really*, than others. What exists can be called *substance*, and one can then ask whether substance exists in more than one way or form and, if so, whether such forms contain, or express, varying degrees of reality.

Descartes had left this corner of the subject in a state of acknowl-

---

[81] Gerard Hughes, *The Nature of God* (London: Routledge, 1995): Chapter II has a clear account. Spinoza's exposition of Descartes's view was contained in Appendix II, 5 to the *Principles of Philosophy*, Curley, pp. 323–5 = G I 257–9.

edged confusion. God was a substance, and certainly the most real substance or sort of substance. But there was mental or spiritual substance, constituting the fabric for human self-consciousness and (perhaps – Descartes was innovatory on this) the fabric of the immortal soul. There was also corporeal substance: bodies in the physical world. There was a 'real distinction' between mental and corporeal substances – crudely, between the human mind and the human body – which Descartes expressed himself anxious to establish. There seemed to be a wholly insoluble deadlock on causal relations – both from the mental to the corporeal, in terms of willed bodily actions, and from the corporeal to the mental, in terms of perception, as well as from the divine to the mental and the corporeal in terms of determinism or freedom. Since substance, or substances, were supposed to be causally independent, such relations could be puzzling.[82]

This is not a book about Descartes – and it is worth stressing that every word written here about his work will have been the subject of scholarly dispute – but we should notice how the theological framework restricted the solutions available to him. *If* we need to bring in substance at all, then there is an unavoidable legacy of God as the 'most real' of substances. If souls or spirits are to have some lasting reality, then maybe some degree of substantiality cannot be denied to them. But then substance had become tied up with the idea of causally independent existence. Sorts-of-things that are supposed to be causally independent cannot interact, by definition. So how can the mind and the body affect each other?

Spinoza's solutions can be stated clearly enough, though interpretations of their sense have varied at least as much as on any area in his philosophy.

One initial point is so obvious that it can be easy to overlook; yet in a way it is the key that unlocks everything else: he treated this whole tangle of issues as *solvable*. He could not see the form of existence of God or nature as unintelligible. The thought that there could be something impenetrable, ineffable or in any way mysterious in any tension between the unity of God and the diversity of nature was impossible for him; as impossible as the thought that the connection between body and mind might be, in some way, unsolvable. His respect for Descartes was

<hr>

[82] A neat summary of the tensions within Cartesianism is given in R. A. Watson, *The Downfall of Cartesianism, 1673–1712* (The Hague: Nijhoff, 1966), Appendix I, p. 147; a longer and more trenchant diagnosis is in Jean-Luc Marion, 'The Essential Incoherence of Descartes' Definition of Divinity', trans. F. P. Van de Pitte in A. Oksenberg Rorty (ed.), *Essays on Descartes' Meditations* (University of California Press, 1986).

undeniable, but he used the strongest terms for a resolution to the relation between mind and body which, he thought, had produced 'a theory more occult than any occult quality' – a view, he said, 'which I could scarcely have believed to have been put forward by such a great man, had it been less ingenious. Indeed, I am lost in wonder'.[83]

For Spinoza, there is only one sort of substance: God or nature. But then 'The more reality or being a thing has, the more attributes it has.' And God has been defined as 'an absolutely infinite being; that is, substance consisting of infinite attributes, each of which expresses eternal and infinite essence'.[84] And here is a response to theological concerns about degrees of reality. It looks orthodox enough:

since the ability to exist is power, it follows that the greater the degree of reality that belongs to a thing, the greater the amount of energy [*plus vivium a se*] it has for existence. So an absolutely infinite Entity, or God, will have from himself absolutely infinite power to exist, and therefore exists absolutely.[85]

God consists of an infinite number of attributes, each in some infinite way. Only two attributes are – can be – accessible to us: thought and extension. 'Man consists of mind and body', where 'mind and body are one and the same thing [*una, eademque res*], conceived now under the attribute of Thought, now under the attribute of Extension'.[86]

The apparatus which was to resolve the Cartesian deadlock seems mechanically polished: God will be simple *as* one substance, but complex *as* infinite attributes. Things or events 'conceived under the attribute' of thought may cause or explain one another, a special case of causality among individuals in general.[87] Thought may cause thought, and bodies may be the cause of bodies, but these two causal orders are completely independent of each other. The relationship between thought and extension – in people, mind and body – cannot be causal. It is a *sui generis* relation of an 'idea' to what Spinoza calls its 'ideatum': 'The object of the idea constituting the human mind is the body.'[88]

This is appealingly neat. It has immediately alarming corollaries. If everything is constituted somehow of thought and extension then what applies nicely to people is also 'of quite general application, and applies to men no more than to other individuals, which are all animate, though to different degrees',[89] raising the apparent prospect of thinking rocks. And the exact parallel between idea and object, mind and body, seems to

[83] *Ethics* v, Preface. [84] *Ethics* I, 9; *substantiam constatem infinitis attributis*, I, Definition 6.
[85] *Ethics* I, 11, Scholium. [86] *Ethics* II, 13, Corollary; *Ethics* III, 2, Scholium = G II 141/24–5.
[87] *Ethics* II, 9; I, 28. [88] *Ethics* II, 3.
[89] *omnia, quamvis diversis gradibus, animata tamen sunt; Ethics* II, 13 = G II 96/28.

create great difficulty for a philosopher who might want to argue that any part of the mind might exist eternally.

We shall have to come back to these questions seriously in Chapter 10, in looking at Spinoza's conclusions about eternity. For now, we must consider his use of the attributes of God or nature in general.

One impression might be that any success of his account is purely terminological. *Cause* and *substance* are brought into a tight definitional relation so that two sorts of substance – even if they could exist – could not interact. Mental and corporeal causal orders are established which are, if anything, even more distinct than the mental and corporeal substances of Descartes. The relationship between them, instead of being opaque, is defined as that of idea to object. Yet that looks to be *only* a definition: to advance discussion only by applying a defined term to the problem. Can we say more?

THE ATTRIBUTES

Attribute, as a technical term, was used at the heart of Spinoza's metaphysical system, in the *Ethics*; but his specialised use of it is hardly seen elsewhere in his major work: it scarcely appears in the *Theological-Political Treatise*, for example,[90] and no clue is given that the usage might be unconventional. Sometimes, confusingly, he used the term in a quite untechnical way.[91]

And as a technical term, *attribute* has no self-evident sense. What Spinoza did *not* mean by his use of it is far more clear than what he *did* mean. He had little sympathy or patience for explaining himself to his puzzled correspondents. Even more than elsewhere, inquiries about what he had in mind were met by repetitions of what he had said already, sometimes with minor variations that have maddened subsequent commentators.

It is evident that the attributes of God were in no way comparable to attributes of people, as normally understood, though the exact point of difference was not spelled out:

in philosophy . . . we clearly understand that to ascribe to God those attributes which make a man perfect, would be as wrong as to ascribe to a man the attributes that make perfect an elephant or an ass.[92]

Maybe the most natural understanding of an attribute would be as a quality or property, and that would hardly be surprising, because that

---

[90] S 80 = G III 37/12–13; S 216 = 169/12–13.   [91] As in his *Hebrew Grammar*, see G I 303/18.
[92] Letter 23; L 166 = G IV 148/5–8.

was its standard use in scholastic terminology. Bennett understands attributes to be 'basic and irreducible properties' or 'most general' properties, though also as something like a 'basic and irreducible way of being'.[93] We owe the comprehensive rebuttal of that reading, again, to Edwin Curley's *Spinoza's Metaphysics*, which draws attention to the fact that 'Spinoza, unlike Descartes, does identify substance with its attribute, or rather, with the totality of its attributes', a point difficult to dispute in that Spinoza wrote explicitly of 'substance consisting of infinite attributes'.[94]

Whatever an attribute is meant to be, it cannot be a property or quality inhering in substance in a predicative or adjectival sense. Nowhere does Spinoza say or imply that thought and extension 'belong to' substance, in that substance 'underlies' them, or that they may be ascribed to it. Attributes máy be perceived as constituting the essence of substance, but, as we have seen, it is incorrect to see Spinoza's use of 'essence' in a predicative sense (that is, as the ascription of a set of necessary properties). Even in his early work, he was keen to differentiate 'things commonly ascribed to God', or '*Propria*', from God's attributes. Ferdinand Alquié puts it tersely: 'Les attributs ne sont pas des qualités de Dieu, ils sont Dieu même.'[95]

Equally, we can be safe in putting aside any understanding of Spinoza's attributes in a subjective sense – as if nature-as-extension, for instance, were in some way a result of how things are seen, in the sense of depending causally on human perception. Such a reading might seem attractive in the light of Spinoza's cryptic definition – 'By attribute I mean that which the intellect perceives of substance as constituting its essence'[96] – but F. S. Haserot, in a conclusive article in 1953, assembled an overwhelming body of commentary and argument which laid that reading to rest. As he put it, 'God's nature, though indivisible, contains

---

[93] *A Study of Spinoza's Ethics*, p. 61. How a 'way of being' can be a 'property' is not explained, however.

[94] *Ethics* I, Definition 6, and Letter 2; L 61 = G IV 7/24ff; Curley, *Spinoza's Metaphysics*, p. 16. But Bennett does dispute it, or rather he seems to simply dislike it, first interpreting it as a treatment of substance 'as an aggregate or collection with members or parts' and then suggesting that a language of identity between substance and attribute, or talk of 'constitution', are 'exaggerated expressions' by Spinoza (*A Study of Spinoza's Ethics*, pp. 61–4). His later thoughts appear in 'Spinoza's Metaphysics', in Don Garrett (ed.), *The Cambridge Companion to Spinoza* (Cambridge University Press, 1996), pp. 85–8.

[95] *Short Treatise*, Curley, p. 88, note a = G I 44/27–31, 45/12–14. F. Alquié, *Le rationalisme de Spinoza*, 2nd edn. (Paris: Presses Universitaires de France, 1991), p. 114.

[96] *Ethics* I, Definition 4 – '*tanquam ejusdem essentiam constituens*': four words that have generated more debate than anything else that Spinoza wrote.

the ground for all possible differentiation in the world':[97] this is not a subjective matter.

Curley, in 1969, took the view that the relation between the attributes
of thought and extension could be seen reasonably as 'an identity of true
proposition and fact' – 'my body is a set of facts, my mind a set of
propositions describing those facts'.[98] Later in his work, attributes are
seen in wider terms, as 'permanent and pervasive features of the
world';[99] although that must have been meant as an illuminating para-
phrase rather than as an explanation. Yet to be told that substance *consists*
of attributes is to be told very little, given the explanatory load that has to
be carried.[100]

It may be useful to recall that what Spinoza said about attributes was
not used only, or primarily, to address the legacy of Cartesian problems
about mind and body, even though that is where almost all commentary
and discussion has been concentrated. Attributes were used first in
connection with the (apparently) more arcane matter of the reality of
God. Again, 'The more reality or being a thing has, the more attributes it
has.'[101]

In response to the question, *how* does God exist? Spinoza's thought
was that God exists in infinite ways as one substance. That was not an
answer or a solution – just as the 'question' was never put so directly. It
was not an answer because the basic thought that God exists in infinite
ways as one substance advances a discussion hardly at all in itself. It helps
only in so far as we understand that Spinoza meant to take his assumptions as literally as he stated them, and in that he intended to pursue
them consistently.

There were, he believed, different ways in which nature – things in
nature – can be conceived. In the most general terms he was able to
frame, nature could be conceived as thought or as extension. Nature
cannot be conceived *except* in those ways, in that we do not know what
could be made of something that was not thinking or not extended ('it is
clear beyond all doubt that every entity is conceived by us under some
attribute'[102]). Hence, the ways in which nature can be conceived must be
fundamental to it; as fundamental as its existence.[103]

---

[97] F. S. Haserot, 'Spinoza's Definition of Attribute' (1953), in S. P. Kashap (ed.), *Studies in Spinoza*
(Berkeley: University of California Press, 1972), p. 42.   [98] *Spinoza's Metaphysics*, pp. 123, 127.
[99] *A Spinoza Reader*, p. xxiii.   [100] Bennett, *A Study of Spinoza's Ethics*, p. 64.   [101] *Ethics* I, 9.
[102] Letter 9; L 92 = G IV 45/18–20 and *Ethics* I, 10, Scholium; G II 52/10–11.
[103] There is a significant problem over the apparent priority of the attribute of thought, raised by
Tschirnhaus in Letter 65, but that need not be pursued here.

Spinoza was as explicit as he could be about the identity of substance and attribute, although his explanation of it was not useful, almost to the point of being misleading. Writing in 1663, he cited a definition in an early version of his *Ethics* –

By substance I understand that which is in itself and is conceived through itself; that is, that whose conception does not involve the conception of another thing. I understand the same by attribute, except that attribute is so called in respect to the intellect, which attributes to substance a certain specific kind of nature.[104]

As we have seen, it is an error to regard 'in respect to the intellect' in a subjective sense. The two illustrations given by Spinoza in this letter are puzzling. First, 'Israel' and 'Jacob' were two names for the same person, but under different descriptions: Israel as the third patriarch, and Jacob under the name given because he had seized his brother's heel. Second, 'by "plane surface" I mean one that reflects all rays of light without any change. I mean the same by "white surface", except that it is called white in relation of a man looking at it.' What is odd here is that Spinoza is not illustrating how the same thing could be conceived in two ways, as thought and extension, for which his examples might well be apt; but how the same thing might be conceived as substance and as attributes. If that reading is right, his illustrations are out of focus. Substance and attributes may indeed be like the same thing which can be designated by two names[105] but substance is conceived as something as it exists, whereas an attribute is more like *how* it is conceived to exist.

The infinite unknown attributes of God or nature cannot just be an embarrassing appendage to Spinoza's account, of some mystical origin or significance.[106] Just as the infinite modes allow scope for infinity in geometry, and so in the development of physics, so the infinite attributes may allow scope for infinite ways in which nature can be understood. These ways were not known to Spinoza; and in fact he produced an unwise argument that they could not be known in principle along the lines (regrettably) that we cannot conceive other ways of conceiving nature because we cannot conceive them.[107]

We might speculate, though, on other ways in which nature might be conceived in a fundamental and comprehensive manner – the plainest example being, perhaps, electromagnetically. Here, an entire form of description would be, as it were, conceived through itself without being

---

[104] Letter 9; L 93 = G IV 45–6.   [105] *eadem res duobus nominibus insigniri possit*; L 93 = G IV 46/26 = 8.
[106] Bennett, for example, tries to demystify: *A Study of Spinoza's Ethics*, pp. 65–6.
[107] Letter 64; L 298–9 = G IV 277–88.

reducible to, or commensurate with, another form of description. In fact, it is possible that the present state of physics shows us several ways – indeed, even rather too many for theoretical elegance – in which fundamental particles can be characterised and which, as yet, seem to be independent of each other. (And in fact it is quantum mechanics which can provide the most obvious analogy for the non-subjectivity of the attributes: the same phenomena may be conceived by the intellect as waves or as particles.[108])

What Spinoza needed was a framework to capture the notion that God or nature could be characterised in the most basic sense, in an unlimited number of ways. And he could not have wanted to interpret that notion so that it might impute to God any kind of unintelligibility. So he indicated two fundamental ways in which God or nature is understood, and indicated that there must be others, unknown.

As we shall see in the next chapter, he wanted nature to be intelligible. His attributes deal with two threats to intelligibility at the same time. First, nature has infinite faces: there is a lot of science not yet discovered. Second, there is the non-causal relationship between mind and body. He feels he can deal with infinity well enough without appeal to mystery.[109] The infinity of God is, prosaically, discussed using analogies from plane geometry. To say that there are infinite ways in which God can be expressed, or nature understood, becomes no more opaque than saying that there are infinite points between any two points on any line. The relationship between mind and body is handled in a similar way. By making it non-causal, Spinoza makes it, by definition, non-intelligible, in that mind cannot be 'understood through' – reduced to – body, or body through mind.

In a sense, this is an arbitrary account. To sharpen his point, for example, Spinoza had to create a far *more* distinct division between mind and body than did Descartes.[110] Because thought and extension have to be only conceived through themselves, the mental and the corporeal causal orders have to be wholly distinct, though reflecting each other.

---

[108] Any unease created by this analogy mirrors the remaining unease we are bound to feel about Spinoza's meaning.

[109] Unlike Descartes, as mentioned above: 'since we are finite, it would be absurd for us to determine anything concerning the infinite; for this would be to attempt to limit it and to grasp it', CSMK 1 201–2 = AT viiiA 14. Meyer, in his Preface to Spinoza's book on Descartes, pointed out that intelligibility was an important point of difference between the two philosophers: Curley, p. 230 = G 1 132/25ff.

[110] A point often missed by philosophy students enthused by the apparent simplicity of his approach. See Alan Donagan, 'Spinoza's Dualism', in R. Kennington (ed.), *The Philosophy of Baruch Spinoza* (Washington: Catholic University Press, 1980).

And, in its way, this is as unfortunate as were Descartes's less consistent compromises. Spinoza is arbitrary, too, in the sense that we are asked to go along with some arbitrary assumptions: that nature is conceivable in an unlimited number of irreducibly different ways, for example. Although we might ask what, scientifically, would be implied by denying such an assumption: that only a limited number of forms of understanding could be available?

Just as Spinoza's view of God's existence is not a theory about what exists – it removes questions about what exists from philosophical or theological debate – so his theory of attributes is not really a *theory* about mind and body. In a way it is a non-theory, or a refusal to formulate a theory: simply a claim that no story could be constructed that could explain mental or corporeal events in terms of each other. This could be said to create or define a framework for the understanding of nature. Everything in nature is to be understood. There can be no areas of mystery, ineffability or unintelligibility. Yet there will be distinct forms of understanding, or explanation, that cannot be translated into each other. Because nature is unlimited, these forms of understanding will be unlimited. The connection between them will be clear, to the point of perfect transparency.

CHAPTER 2

How God acts

At the beginning of the Appendix to Part 1 of the *Ethics*, Spinoza summarised his conclusions up to that point in one long sentence:

I have now explained the nature and properties of God: that he necessarily exists, that he is one alone, that he is and acts solely from the necessity of his own nature, that he is the free cause of all of things and how so, that all things are in God and are so dependent on him that they can neither be nor be conceived without him, and lastly, that all things have been predetermined by God, not from his free will or absolute pleasure, but from the absolute nature of God, his infinite power.

The first part of this summary – on the 'nature and properties of God' – has been discussed in the previous chapter. We must now turn to the second part: how God 'acts solely from the necessity of his own nature'.[1]

Once again, it is worth stressing at the start that we do not know the roots of Spinoza's motivation. If a question could be characterised in the abstract – without any reference to who asked it, when or why – it would be, how does God relate to the world in terms of action? This is a question which has appeared in innumerable forms in different religious traditions, for differing reasons; to the extent that there is an obvious risk of misrepresentation in thinking of a single, continuing question. We can see some of the contexts in which Spinoza was working in the 1660s and 1670s. There were religious questions about providence, miracles and creation: God's place inside, alongside or outside history. There were questions arising from growth of the physical sciences: about how things happen, and how God's influence on things and events is law-like. There were questions that cut across both religion and physical science, that could be framed in terms of limitations on God's freedom: if geometry is inexorable, what is implied for God's place in nature? Is this

---

[1] *Ethics*, p. 57: '*ex solâ suæ naturæ necessitate*' = G II 77/22–3.

inexorability a result of God's will, or is God also subject to it? In general, if God acts, *how?*

We can see that Spinoza immersed himself in these questions and we can see without difficulty that they had long and intricate histories, much of which he knew. What we cannot say is how he balanced the priority between them, or where his thinking really started. We do not know this because he did not tell us, and his writing can point in different directions. It is tempting, for example, to represent his thinking as an attempt to get God out of history and physics; except that we may also see parallel arguments that bring God into the centre of history and physics. Much of his work seems to be an onslaught on what he viewed as delusions or superstitions about the interventions of God in history through miracles or providential action, and it is not unnatural to imagine that this might be what drove his thinking. Except that, it seems, he was driven with apparently matching force by a passion less common (and therefore less intelligible) than a taste for religious polemics, and one which is more difficult to imagine by those who may not share it: a passion for knowledge which, in his case, showed itself in a love for geometry and physical science. Near the beginning of his early work, the *Treatise on the Emendation of the Intellect,* he wrote of the 'supreme good' connected with 'the knowledge of the union which the mind has with the whole of Nature'.[2]

CAUSALITY

Anyway, whatever our uncertainty about Spinoza's intentions, what we do know is that the notion of a cause, or, as he put it, *causa, seu ratio* – cause or reason – was at the focus of his thought about the relations between God and the world. And we can see how readily we can frame questions about divine action in causal terms: does God *cause* events in history *all the time,* according to some providential plan, only *some times,* by way of miraculous intervention or revelation, or perhaps only *at the beginning* of history, in a moment of initial creation? These questions can be considered both in spiritual or mental and in corporeal versions: God's causal intervention might be deemed to be spiritual, for example, in a sense of prophecy, conversion or revelation, rather than in terms of merely physical manifestations. Some questions can also be raised by thinking about God's laws for the world, both moral and physical. Do

[2] §13, p. 235 = G II 8/26-7.

such laws *make things happen*, causally? And if so, how? And what scope is left for choice or freedom, including God's own causal freedom? As we shall see, these questions can be understood as an exploration of the territories of theological and scientific explanation, and their relationships. In general: if God is a causal agent, how does that causal agency operate?

The notion of causality may also be seen as central because – as with questions about substance – much of Spinoza's approach can be read in terms of a crisis in fundamental terminology. *Substance* had been doing too much, theologically and philosophically, and had been doing it in conflicting ways. Spinoza's treatment can be understood – more aptly than in some other ways – as an attempted resolution of those conflicts. Similarly, what constitutes or characterises a *cause* can be understood in apparently inconsistent senses. God, in Spinoza's time, had to be regarded as a – the – supreme causal agent. Things, or minds, if they were substances, possessed both some degree of causal independence and some degree of causal importance secondary to God's. The causal powers of nature, revealed by experiment, appeared to be inexorable, raising issues expressed in terms of *necessity* which hitherto had been reserved for God's causal activity.

As with substance, so with causality: Spinoza lacked a heritage of Christian theological concerns. The capacity of human freedom to attain salvation in the context of God's providence was at the heart of post-Reformation polemics, not infrequently acted out in terms of personal and international violence. His own Jewish background was not without its own problems on God's place in history and the meaning of divine law. But he cared not at all about the requirements of Christian theology. His lack of concern came out not just in the solutions he produced but, perhaps more importantly, in the presuppositions behind his approach. It never mattered for him whether or not a doctrine of divine predestination would sit badly with the saving power of voluntary faith,[3] and it mattered still less whether he would reach conclusions that suited the views of one religious faction or another. Here he differed markedly from Leibniz, whose published writings on freedom and divine causality, whatever their merits, were constrained by a desire to avoid an appearance of heterodoxy.

There has never been any real uncertainty over the general outline of

---

[3] A live issue then: Innocent X (in *Cum occasione*, 1653) had condemned the Jansenists' 'semi-pelagian' belief in 'the necessity of prevenient grace for single acts, even for the beginning of faith'.

Spinoza's approach to God's causality, and there is no excuse to make heavy weather of it. Propositions 17 and 18 of Part I of the *Ethics* are clear, short and decisive:

God acts solely from the laws of his own nature, constrained by none.

God is the immanent, not the transitive,[4] cause of all things.

From what was said in the previous chapter, we could not expect otherwise. God cannot be seen in any way as outside the created world. What happens within the world happens within, not outside, God. The rules or laws by which nature acts are the laws of God. Since God is supposed to act not by chance or whim but by necessity, what happens in nature happens necessarily:

By God's direction I mean the fixed and immutable order of Nature, or chain of natural events; for . . . the universal laws of Nature according to which all things happen and are determined are nothing but God's eternal decrees, which always involve truth and necessity. So it is the same thing whether we say that all things happen according to Nature's laws or that they are regulated by God's decree and direction.[5]

All of this has to apply as much to the human world, in the personal life of individuals and in history or politics, as it does in the rest of the natural order:

I shall . . . treat of the nature and strength of the emotions, and the mind's power over them, by the same method as I have used in treating of God and the mind, and I shall consider human actions and appetites just as if it were an investigation into lines, planes or bodies.[6]

Even human passions such as love, hatred and envy are seen as phenomena which are necessary, having 'causes by means of which we endeavour to understand their nature'.[7]

As we might expect, how God acts is related to how God exists. An anthropomorphic god, dwelling on Olympus, might be expected to have limited or arbitrary powers of intervention in human or worldly affairs. A God identified with nature might not be expected to act outside the powers of nature, though the assumption that nature acts non-arbitrarily is an extremely large one, perhaps not immediately plausible to anyone living in a world of plagues, floods, hurricanes, volcanoes or earthquakes.

---

[4] *transiens*: Shirley, in his Translator's Preface (p. 25), explains: 'A transient cause is one in which causation "passes over" from the cause to the effect, while cause and effect remain really distinct.'
[5] S 89 = G III 45–6.   [6] *Ethics* III, Preface; G II 138/23–7.
[7] *causas, per quas eorum naturam intelligere conamur: Political Treatise* I, §4; G III 274/35.

Spinoza's picture of God's action has often seemed repellent or just mistaken. It has seemed repellent because God seems to be deprived of any particular capacity to be interested in individual people or events. In so far as it remains appropriate to think of God's interest or attention at all, to think of a universal, impartial interest seems to be the same as thinking of *no* interest. Also repellent has been the apparently inexorable determinism, all too difficult to differentiate from fatalism in the minds of some of Spinoza's correspondents and critics.

'LOGIC?'

The consequences for a God of historical religions will be explored in Part II of this study. For now, we should examine the groundings of Spinoza's approach, rather than its seemingly irreligious consequences. The general picture, we have seen, looks simple and reasonably intelligible, but possibly not too convincing. If we go into the detail, we will find it far subtler, but also less easy to grasp than it seems as first sight. And the 'detail' is of crucial importance, to the extent that that may be a misleading way to describe it. We are thinking of the basic articulation of the system. If the machinery never worked properly it hardly even deserves a place in a museum of disused philosophical apparatus.

What has seemed badly wrong, in brief, and in fundamental terms, has been an apparent assimilation of causality into logical consequence, so that 'a causes b' ends up looking like a statement that one proposition or statement follows from another, so that what is said in 'a causes b' is subsumed in, or equivalent to, ' "b" follows from "a" '. A corollary could be that all such causal propositions might end up as necessarily true, thereby removing any contrast between necessity and contingency which we might feel to be valuable. Natural laws (in physics, for example) might become indistinguishable from propositions in mathematics, possessing their force by some sort of *logical* necessity.

Such a reading is found in Jonathan Bennett's *Study of Spinoza's Ethics*. And, not surprisingly, Bennett went on to conclude that 'Spinoza was no logician; his modal thinking seems to have been neither skillful nor knowledgeable'.[8]

This leads us to a more fundamental question, about the metaphysical apparatus of the *Ethics*: *what is it?* God as logician or as natural lawgiver,

---

[8] Bennett, *A Study of Spinoza's Ethics*, p. 124.

dealing with necessary propositions, may not be the same as God as physical agent, dealing with objects.

Bennett translates Spinoza effortlessly into propositional terms – into what is *said* – from which an interpretation of metaphysics in terms of *logic* is in effect an unavoidable step. Here he is, putting Spinoza into a logical checkmate:

> Now, there is a certain class of propositions all of whose members are absolutely necessary; they predicate attributes and infinite modes on God. Spinoza says that no particular proposition follows from any of them. Does that entail that every particular proposition is contingent?[9]

And earlier, Edwin Curley had gone some of the way down the same path. He noted that Spinoza had written in the *Ethics* about 'the necessity or impossibility of things, rather than of truths':

> and he speaks only of the existence of things, and not of the necessity or impossibility of their possessing certain properties or entering into certain relations. But this need not prevent us from translating what he says about things into talk about truths and developing a general account of necessary truth that will accord with Spinoza's intentions.[10]

This line of thinking – that we can safely translate 'talk about things' into 'talk about truths' – goes back a long way. Leibniz wrote a revealing paper *On Freedom* in 1679, three years after he had met Spinoza. Setting his question into a characteristic context he began:

> One of the oldest doubts of mankind concerns the question of how freedom and contingency are compatible with the chain of causes and with providence. And Christian investigations of the justice of God in accomplishing man's salvation have merely increased the difficulty of the matter.

He remarked how he had found himself 'very close to the opinions of those who hold everything to be absolutely necessary', but he was 'pulled back from the precipice by considering those possible things which neither are nor will be nor have been'. His route back from his precipice went through an assumption – never discussed – that questions about necessity can or should be discussed in terms of necessary truths. Here is the exact point where the step is taken:

> Having thus recognized the contingency of things, I raised the further question of a clear concept of truth, for I had a reasonable hope of throwing some light from this upon the problem of distinguishing necessary from contingent truths.[11]

[9] Ibid., p. 114.   [10] Curley, *Spinoza's Metaphysics*, p. 88.   [11] *c.*1679, Leibniz, p. 263.

In the previous chapter it was noted that Bennett understands the necessary existence of God in a sense where a proposition that God exists is
held to be necessarily true. This is a natural enough understanding in
twentieth-century terms,[12] but it embodies two important misunderstandings about Spinoza which need to be unravelled at length before it
is possible to give a coherent picture of what he says about God's action.

First, there is the idea that Spinoza should be translated into propositional terms – as seen quite openly stated in the passage just quoted from
Curley, and less openly in Leibniz.

Then, following that, there is the connected assumption that necessity
– the necessity of causality or of natural laws, for example – should be
seen solely or primarily in terms of the necessary truth of propositions.

Together, those two assumptions would suggest that Spinoza was
working in the field of *logic*, because that is where we now tend to locate
relationships claimed or established between necessary propositions.
Hence, natural laws may be read as having *logical* force, causal relations
may be seen as *logical* and so the existence of God may be seen as *logically
necessary*. And since all these corollaries have been widely viewed as
refuted since the time of Hume and Kant, the whole context from which
they seem to have emerged may also seem to have been vitiated.

To start on this tangle from the end – from the likelihood of the
conclusions, as it were – we can ask how plausible it is that Spinoza might
have wanted to think in terms of logic, logical relations or logical truth.

And the answer here is, surely, clear. He had no interest in logic and no
regard for it, seeing it as a branch of something like mental hygiene. It
was only mentioned once in the *Ethics*, and very rarely elsewhere in his
work.[13] This would seem a strange lapse in someone so keen to reduce so
much to logic, and it is a fact that, alone, ought to worry anyone wanting
to interpret his thinking in *logical* terms.

But perhaps he thought *logically* without using the term? Maybe by
reading him in a logical sense we are dispelling a confusion that he could
not have been expected to notice himself? Or clarifying his thought on
his behalf?

A notably strong logical reading of Spinoza is given by Yirmiyahu
Yovel; and this illustrates some of the problems. For Spinoza, we learn
'All necessity is inherently logical.' The laws of nature 'not only describe
how particulars behave but *make* them behave in these ways, though the

[12] Especially in view of the talk of the 'eternal truth' of God's existence; *Ethics* I, 20, Corollary 2; 19,
Scholium.   [13] *Ethics* V, Preface; G II 277/15.

causality they exercise is logical rather than mechanical'. A law is 'generated in nature by immanent logical derivation'.[14]

Although Yovel is anxious to argue for Spinoza's thoroughgoing immanentism, his idea of laws *making* things happen gives us a hint of another way of thinking. Natural laws may not be the decrees of an external lawmaker, but they may still be seen as a set of rules, with 'logical' force, *governing* how things exist and act.[15]

How likely is that ontologically? Where could 'logical' rules fit into Spinoza's world? Well, *inside* it, we might reply, since everything has to fit inside it; but then where inside it? Not as part of the corporeal world and not in the matching world of ideas. Spinoza gave us no hint that he wanted to ground logic (or modal logic: necessity and possibility) in the workings of language or in the mental operations of human beings. And there was no room anywhere in his world for a special, *sui generis* realm of propositions, logical or otherwise. If the necessity of nature stemmed from logic, or primarily from logic, even unconsciously, what did logic stem from – where did it get its force? That would seem a rather important loose end to leave hanging. (Hardly a trivial matter because the whole theological difficulty in the subject derives from worries about God's freedom. If nature is subject to logic, or to logically binding laws, where does God fit in? As the creator of logical truths and laws? As their subject or as their master?)

So far we have only looked at persuasive, rather than conclusive, points. After all, it may not seem quite so strange to resort to logic to make sense of Spinoza. The terminology he employed to interconnect the items in his metaphysical system looks – to cautiously formal, modern eyes – casually varied: *involve, express, conceive through, exist in, produce* and, most strikingly, *follow from*. Some things are said to *follow* in a way that sounds unremarkably logical: 'No attribute of substance can be truly conceived from which it would follow that substance can be divided.'[16]

In this, *what follows* sounds like a proposition – the proposition *that* substance can be divided; though what it follows from sounds more like an object or state of affairs than something that could be said, of propositional status: an attribute of substance.

[14] Y. Yovel, 'The Infinite Mode and Natural Laws in Spinoza', in Yovel (ed.), *God and Nature*, pp. 87, 93.

[15] A tendency that can be seen even in a good translator: Shirley, for example, translates *lex . . . universalis omnium corporum* as 'a universal law *governing* all bodies', S 101 = G III 57/33.

[16] *ex quo sequatur, substantium posse dividi, Ethics* I, 12.

The relationship between the propositions in Spinoza's system is also said to be one of *following*, as for example in *Ethics* I, 25, Scholium, full of logical language:

This proposition [i.e. 25] follows more clearly [*clarius sequitur*] from Proposition 16; for from that Proposition it follows [*ea enim sequitur*] that from the given divine nature both the essence and the existence of things must be inferred [*debet necessario concludi*].

Yet we also find *following from* in a more puzzling form:

A thing is termed 'necessary' either by reason of its essence or by reason of its cause. For a thing's existence necessarily follows [*rei enim alicujus existentia . . . sequitur*] either from its essence and definition or from a given efficient cause.[17]

Here, the *existence of a thing* follows. Then there are some assertions crucial to the edifice of arguments, such as:

All things . . . are in God, and all things that come to pass do so only through the laws of God's infinite nature and follow from the necessity of his essence . . .

From the necessity of [the] divine nature there must follow infinite things in infinite ways.[18]

In even more concrete terms, *natura naturata* ('all the modes of God's attributes in so far as they are considered as things which are in God and can neither be nor be conceived without God') is said to *follow from* the necessity of God's nature – 'that is, from the necessity of each one of God's attributes'.[19] We are deep in the thickets of Spinoza's densest terminology, but the sense is unavoidable: modes – including individuals – *follow from* the necessity of God's nature. Modes also *follow from* each other. And, most bluntly of all, right at the beginning of the *Ethics*: 'From a given determinate cause there necessarily follows an effect.'[20]

So, undeniably, Spinoza used the same language for the relations between, for example, the propositions in his system as he did between causes and effects or between God and modes. So are we justified in absorbing other 'causal' relations into a relation of consequence, whether or not we call that a 'logical' relation?

Almost all commentators who have focused seriously on this issue have tended to think so. 'One thing every interpreter of Spinoza agrees

[17] *Ethics* I, 33, Scholium I = G II 74/5–8.
[18] *Ex necessitate divinæ naturæ, infinita infinitis modis . . . sequi debent, Ethics* I, 15, Scholium, and 16.
[19] *Ethics* I, 29, Scholium.
[20] And the corollary, in an interestingly indirect form: 'on the other hand, if there be no determinate cause, it is impossible that an effect should follow', *Ethics* I, 29, Scholium; I, 28; I, Axiom 3.

on is that Spinoza connects the causal relation with the relation of logical consequence', writes Curley.[21] Many have thought that, in this, they have diagnosed a central problem for Spinoza. Because causal relations – has not Hume shown us? – are *not* like logical relations.

But we should also think about the alleged *direction* of any connection (or reduction) between causality and logical consequence. The suggestion seems to be that we know what logic is, and we are able to handle 'logical' connections, whereas causality may be more open to reduction.[22] An alternative perspective might be that we can achieve some understanding of causality,[23] whereas entailment and logical consequence have, so far, proved resistant to uncontroversial analysis, or even description. We might consider whether it helps us more to say that logic is like causality or that causality is like logic. A further possibility could be that Spinoza did not care about logic too much, but cared a good deal about causality, and therefore tended to think in causal terms.

THINGS

We can attempt a different reading of Spinoza, trying to see how his system fits together, and looking at how it may relate, or not, to logic.

We might start with his clear insistence that things cause things, that things follow from God's nature or that the world is a necessary effect of divine nature.[24] Then there are his declarations of the universality of causality:

For every thing a cause or reason must be assigned either for its existence or for its non-existence. For example, if a triangle exists, there must be a reason, or cause, for its existence . . .[25]

There must necessarily be a positive cause of each thing, through which it exists.[26]

---

[21] Curley, 'On Bennett's Interpretation of Spinoza's Monism', p. 48.

[22] This seems to be the case even for commentators who ask what kind of 'logic' Spinoza is presupposing. Don Garrett, for example, sets off by assuming that logical and metaphysical necessity are the same and then concludes that the only type of logic to fit the bill must be a relevance logic: 'Spinoza's Necessitarianism', in Yovel (ed.), *God and Nature*, pp. 192, 194.

[23] Or that causation is 'itself a basic feature of our world', even though we find it hard to understand: D. H. Mellor, *The Facts of Causation* (London: Routledge, 1995), p. 30, though this is not to imply that Mellor accepts a priority of causality over logic.

[24] Letter 54; L 268 = G IV 251/21–2.

[25] . . . *causa, seu ratio, tam cur existit, quàm cur non existit. Ex. gr. si triangulus existit, ratio, seu causa, dari debet, cur existit . . . Ethics* I, 11, Demonstration 2.

[26] Letter 34; L 201 = G IV 179/29–30; also *Ethics* I, 8, Scholium 2.

These strong assertions are framed entirely in terms of the existence of things, not the truth of propositions. There must be a cause or reason why every thing exists. No claim is made that there must be a ground for every true proposition.

Spinoza's elucidation of *necessity*, already quoted above, is only oblique and is given, like his full explanation of *essence*, long after he has started to make use of the term. Again, it relates explicitly to things:

A thing is termed 'necessary' [*Res aliqua necessaria dicitur*] either by reason of its essence or by reason of its cause. For a thing's existence necessarily follows either from its essence and definition or from a given efficient cause . . .[27]

Earlier, and more briefly, a thing is said to be necessary or constrained 'if it is determined by another thing to exist and act in a definite and determinate way'.[28] Being necessary and being caused are brought into equivalence.

The central items in the system are *things* and the central relationship is to be 'causality'. We saw in the previous chapter that the *essence* ('or nature'[29]) of something is what makes it what it is in Spinoza's causal sense, not a set of properties said to belong to it, 'necessarily' or otherwise.[30] Laws are not rules governing how things act but *are* how things exist and act as they do, in the same causal sense: Spinoza wrote, puzzlingly, of 'laws or nature'. 'A law which depends on Nature's necessity is one which necessarily follows from the very nature of the thing, that is, its definition.'[31]

For a thing to be necessary 'by reason of its essence', as he explained himself, is for its existence to follow from its essence: then, in such a case, it is 'a thing to whose nature it pertains to exist, or – and this is the same – a thing from whose definition existence follows'. But its 'essence, or definition' is also its 'cause' since 'we ought to define and explain things through their proximate causes'.[32] So it is its own cause: *causa sui*. Necessary existence, then, means existence by definition. The necessity resides entirely in the existence of a cause.

In addition to the causality of God-or-substance there is another type of causality: of the existence and action of individuals.

An individual man, man generally or any specific number of men, do

<hr>

[27] *Ethics* I, 33, Scholium I = G II 74/5–8. [28] *Ethics* I, Definition 7.
[29] *essentia, seu natura; Ethics* III, 56, Demonstration = G II 185/9.
[30] For example, as 'logically essential' 'characteristics': Garrett, 'Spinoza's Necessitarianism', p. 203: the force of 'logically' here is surely little more than rhetorical.
[31] *leges, sive natura*; Letter 32; L 192 = G IV 170/13 and *natura, sive definitione*; S 101 = G III 57/27–8.
[32] *Ethics* I, 19, Demonstration; G II 74/10; S 101 = G III 58/19–20.

not exist by necessity. That is because their reason for existence 'cannot be contained in the nature of man'.[33] To know why a particular man exists, we need to look not at his 'nature, or definition' but at an endless series of causes why he came to be where and how he is, and so on. 'Each particular thing is determined by another particular thing to exist in a particular manner.'[34] The causality for the existence and action of individuals will always be endless because it would include an endless series, spreading out through 'the whole of Nature and all its parts'; and we cannot know 'the actual manner of this coherence and the agreement of each part with the whole'.[35]

CONTINGENCY

It is this idea of endless causality that provided the basis for Spinoza's view of contingency. 'Individual things' are contingent in as much as their essence does not posit their existence. That only means that individuals viewed 'modally', not as substance, have causes, and 'we can conceive them as not existing'.[36] Because these causes spread right through nature they are endless and because they are endless we cannot know them thoroughly: 'because the chain of causes [*ordo causarum*] is hidden from us, then the thing cannot appear to us as either necessary or as impossible. So we term it either "contingent" or "possible".'[37] So contingency is related to a 'deficiency in our knowledge'. In reality, 'nothing in nature is contingent'.[38]

What Spinoza says about contingency is easy to consider as similar to the better-known views of Leibniz, but in fact it is different and more straightforward. Leibniz would assign contingency primarily to propositions, not things. For him, the predicate of a necessary proposition is 'contained' finitely in the subject. In a contingent proposition, the predicate is also contained in the subject (in reflection of his views about substances which contain all their properties) but its inclusion could be fully visible only to a being capable of performing an infinite analysis: God. God will see the infinite analysis and will therefore see such propositions as really necessary:

In contingent truths . . . though the predicate inheres in the subject, we can never demonstrate this, nor can the proposition ever be reduced to an equation

---

[33] *Ethics* II, Axiom 1; II, 10 Demonstration; I, 8, Scholium 2.   [34] *Ethics* II, 45, Scholium.
[35] Letter 32, of 1665; L 192 = G IV 170/3–6. As noted, the 'parts' of nature here is not in line with Spinoza's stricter expression, for example in *Ethics* I, 15, Scholium.
[36] *Res singulares* . . . *Ethics* IV, Definition 3; Letter 12, L 102 = G IV 54/11.
[37] *Ethics* I, 33, Scholium 1.   [38] *defectus nostræ cognitionis – in rerum natura: Ethics* I, 29.

or an identity, but the analysis proceeds to infinity, only God being able to see, not the end of the analysis indeed, since there is no end, but the nexus of terms or the inclusion of the predicate in the subject, since he sees everything which is in the series.[39]

Most obviously, Spinoza, could not make use of God as an external viewer or analyser of things or propositions. Endless chains of causes (mental or corporeal) exist 'in' God, but this cannot possibly be read as meaning that a God is thinking about them, or could be thinking about them in any remotely anthropomorphic sense. It should also be evident that an endless net or chain of causes is a good deal more transparent as an idea than the infinite analysis of a logical subject (or of the concept of a substance, as Leibniz sometimes puts it). That, in turn, reflects the fact that Spinoza ascribes his type of necessity first to things, not to propositions.

It is worth pausing, too, to consider what Spinoza's view of contingency suggests in terms of determinism. He is clear that we cannot attain the knowledge that would enable us to understand all causes, or perhaps even *any* causes for individuals, comprehensively. Again, the reason for this is simpler than Leibniz's. It *is* because we are not divine, but that cannot be understood, as it can for Leibniz, in contrast with the understanding of another being who *is* divine. To say that 'in God' everything is necessary is only another way of saying that everything in nature has a cause or reason. The endlessness of chains of individual causes is not used to suggest anything about mystery or unintelligibility; only the plain fact that we can never get to the end of them because no end is there.[40] This means that Spinoza's understanding of causal prediction in practice sounds even more reserved than Hume's: 'when we have regard only to the essence of Modes and not to the order of Nature as a whole, we cannot deduce from their present existence that they will or will not exist in the future or that they did or did not exist in the past'.[41]

That hardly sounds like a licence for a priori science, and could scarcely be an endorsement for a crude fatalism sometimes linked to determinism. I am here now for a series of reasons too long and too complicated to unravel. Where I am next may 'follow' from where I am now – my capacity to predict and affect that future may be improved by the

[39] Leibniz, p. 264; see pp. 203–4 for views directly on Spinoza.
[40] And note Leibniz's equivocation on that point: analysis is endless, so even God can't do it, but nevertheless God can 'see everything' in an infinite series – so can Leibniz's God comprehend infinity or not?
[41] Letter 12; L 102 = G IV 54/11–15; see also Letter 40; L 218 = G IV 198/8–11 = /26–30.

exercise of my understanding, but it remains limited. For practical purposes, the necessity of nature acts as a regulative or methodological principle: what determines the existence and acting of individuals should be
discoverable, but such discoveries could go on for ever. (Science can be
possible but it may be endless.) In the *Theological-Political Treatise* Spinoza
concluded that 'for practical purposes it is better, indeed, it is essential, to
consider things as contingent' because 'we plainly have no knowledge as
to the actual co-ordination and interconnection of things – that is, the
way in which things are in actual fact ordered and connected'.[42]

And it can be noted here that his infinite modes – discussed in the previous chapter – play no part in the causality of the existence and action of
individuals. As we saw, individuals – 'finite modes' – in a sense make up
nature-conceived-as-effect: *Natura naturata*. In as much as we need to take
account of infinite extension, infinite divisibility or (Spinoza should have
said) infinite mathematical series, the 'infinite modes' constitute nature
considered in that way – they could be the subject-matter of mathematics.
What they are *not* are causal intermediaries between God and finite individuals. Finite modes quite straightforwardly and unambiguously determine each other. In causal networks they determine each other mutually.[43]
The existence of an endless network of existing things can be conceived as
effects – infinite modes – or as cause – substance. But finite modes cannot
be said to have infinite modes as their causes, in whole or in part.[44]

This is more than a point of scholarly interest about the articulation of
Spinoza's machinery. How things are, how they have been and how they
will be is not deducible in practice by logic from the general principles of
nature. (And a crucial consequence of Spinoza's thinking is that the
notion that they might follow 'in principle' is without content. There is
no external, divine perspective from which that could apply: the 'principle' would be vacuous.) The infinite order of nature is there, is causally
ordered and that constitutes its necessity. All these assertions come down
to the same thing – not that I can ever deduce from known causes what I
shall be doing tomorrow; only that causes exist for what will happen and
that I can go on finding them.

---

[42] S 102 = G III 58/23–5.

[43] *quatenus earum natura invicem se accommodat*; Letter 32; L 194 = G IV 170/16.

[44] This is controversial, but there is no need to pursue the details here; for further argument, see my
'Spinoza on the Causality of Individuals', *Journal of the History of Philosophy*, 24, 1986, and 'How
Things Happen: Divine-natural Law in Spinoza', *Studia Leibnitiana*, XXVIII/I, 1996; for a different
view, see, for example, Joel Friedman, 'How the Finite Follows from the Infinite in Spinoza's
Metaphysical System', *Synthèse*, 69, 1986, or Errol Harris, 'Finite and Infinite in Spinoza's
System', in Hessing (ed.), *Speculum Spinozanum*.

NECESSITY

The compactness of Spinoza's treatment of necessity and contingency closely resembles the 'conceptual minimalism' mentioned in the previous chapter. One way into his thinking is to realise that several terms are doing the same work. *Being caused* – having a *reason*[45] – *the existence of* a cause or reason – being bound by a *law* – having a certain *nature, essence* or *definition* – and *being necessary* – all, it seems, crowd into the same territory. For something to be necessary is no more and no less than for it to have a cause or reason. The caused-ness of individuals is their nature, which is their acting and existing by law. There are no external rules of nature or logic above, behind, alongside *or within* the existing and acting of individuals which can explain them, or whose workings can explain or justify their necessity. There are only individuals and their actions.

In the same way that Spinoza's views about substance and attributes could be seen as a non-theory about what exists and how it exists, his view about necessity and contingency – which looks extraordinary – can be seen as a non-theory about modality. This is not at all to say that it was negligible or unhelpful; rather the reverse – it can be seen as an elaborate demonstration of why a theory of necessity is not needed.

His 'theory', so far as it is one, is that things have causes or reasons. That is how they are. Nature is like that. The fact that things have causes or reasons is their necessity. Necessity is not itself 'explained' by anything: it is simply the state or condition of having a cause or reason.

If this reading is correct it constitutes an extremely radical view, and is radically different from most other thought on the subject – maybe to the extent that there must be a temptation to reject it out of hand. We should look at some of its framework in Spinoza's thinking and at some of the consequences within his system.

First, the primacy of necessity within his system needs to be appreciated. As with Leibniz,[46] the status of contingency presented the problem, rather than the status or nature of necessity. In Spinoza, that approach reached its consistent extreme. For him, the necessity – the caused-ness – of nature was basic, self-evident and in need of no defence.[47] He believed that the cardinal error of empiricist philosophers was to have

[45] The equivalence of *causa* and *ratio* – apparently, of causality and explanation – will be discussed in Chapter 3.

[46] See H. Ishiguro, 'Contingent Truths and Possible Worlds' (1979), in R. S. Woolhouse (ed.), *Leibniz: Metaphysics and Philosophy of Science* (Oxford University Press, 1981), p. 64.

[47] Although some systematic support for it can be found, to be examined at the end of Chapter 3.

overlooked this and to have taken 'the objects of sense' as fundamental.
They had failed 'to observe the proper order of philosophical enquiry' –

Hence it has come about that in considering natural phenomena [*res naturales*],
they have completely disregarded [the] divine nature. And when thereafter
they turned to the contemplation of [the] divine nature, they could find no
place in their thinking for those fictions on which they had built their natural
science, since these fictions were of no avail in attaining knowledge of [the]
divine nature. So it is little wonder that they have contradicted themselves on
all sides.[48]

In bare summary this presents the most commonplace caricature of a
contrast between what used to be polarised as 'rationalism' and 'empiricism'. We need to see the extremity of Spinoza's attitude to bring it into
focus (though there are good reasons not to characterise it as 'rationalism', as we shall see). The philosopher who takes 'the objects of sense' as
basic will take brute contingent facts for granted: they just *are*. From that
direction, necessity presents an acute challenge requiring reduction or
explanation. The aim becomes one of providing some account in terms
of contingent or empirical facts for the real or apparent force of necessity – maybe facts about the operations of the mind on 'ideas', or facts
about the use of language. When that approach is turned on its head, the
assumptions in it are made explicit. Spinoza takes what he considers to
be necessities as clear and primary, as a corollary of the intelligibility of
nature. Necessities are for him in the end *causa sui*: their own sufficient
causes. Since a necessity is something for him that has a cause, the
problem for him is what he sees as contingency – the prospect that there
might be things which are not caused or which might lie outside a unified
system of causality. He takes necessities to be brute facts in the sense that
they are ultimately self-explanatory in a strangely literal way, and he
relates contingencies to them. 'Brute facts' are explained through self-
causality. We end up with a result that *more* is explained – contingencies
in terms of necessities, and necessities in terms of the self-explanatory
order of nature. But perhaps that is hardly surprising, given the underlying assumption that everything ('in nature') must have a cause.

The status of universal causality will be discussed in the next chapter.
For now, it is important to look at some of the ramifications of the
reading offered here, since these differ from the assumptions of many of
Spinoza's commentators. There are two logical corollaries that must be
considered: the consequences for the notion of possibility and the

---

[48] *Ethics* II, 10, Corollary, Scholium = G II 93–4.

grounding of necessity in necessary propositions. Then we can get back to a wider view of how things happen in nature.

A coherent story about possibility is needed in a technical sense to complete any account of modality. In Spinoza's case the interest goes beyond a technical detour, in two ways. We shall see in the next chapter how it relates to his attitude towards scepticism: he needs hard support for his thinking on the relevance of what 'can' be conceived or imagined. In Chapter 10 we shall see a link with his views on the eternal existence of part of the mind.

It might be thought, though, that his view of possibility leaves little to be said. *Ethics* I, 33, seems to extinguish any likely interest – 'Things could not have been produced by God in any other way or in any other order than is the case' – so we are mistaken in ever believing that a situation now 'might' be different from what it is. If that could be so, it would suggest that the whole order of nature – the past – might not have been what it was.

A thing is impossible if its 'essence or definition involves a contradiction' or if 'there is no external cause determined to bring it into existence'. Much later, possibility is defined:

I call individual things possible in so far as, in attending to the causes by which they should be brought about, we do not know whether these causes are determined to bring them about.[49]

The definition suggests that future situations are only possible to the extent that we do not know what they are. (It does *not* suggest, of course, that we are fatalistically powerless to alter the future: among the causes that will bring about the future are decisions I make now, based partly on what I have been able to discover about how I arrived where I am.)

This all looks uninteresting, though: just a typical set of conclusions that might be expected from any hard-line determinist. Yet, in reality Spinoza's conclusions about possibility were far from uninteresting, and were linked to some of his most central thinking on knowledge and on the nature of science, with important implications for divine causality.

To appreciate that, we need to ask why – for what purpose – anyone might want or need an account of possibility. Here are three alternative sorts of reason:

---

[49] *Ethics* IV, Definition 4.

(a) *Semantic*: to explain, elucidate or justify our uses of language about possible things, situations or events. We may feel that we can *say* 'It is possible that I might be (or might have been) an astronaut' – so what does that *mean*? Is there a possible situation that it represents? Or even a possible world for (or in) which it is true?

(b) *Psychological* or *conceptual*: to explain, elucidate or justify our *thoughts* or *imagination* about possibilities. I can imagine myself as an astronaut – so am I imagining a possible astronaut? Or a possible-astronaut?

(c) *Ontological*: to allow for the *existence* of non-actual but possible objects, events or constructions. An infinite number of triangles can be constructed in a circle. Are these possible triangles? In what sense, if any, do they exist?

(a), (b) and (c) might be thought to overlap in various ways. Someone might believe, for example, that I can't think about possible situations unless I can describe them satisfactorily to myself, so (a) becomes fundamental to (b); or that the existence of possible objects explains or justifies the use of language about possibility, so that (c) becomes fundamental to (a). Anyway, Spinoza's position is reasonably plain. He had no interest at all in issues such as (a), very little in those like (b), but he did offer some theorising – or at any rate, some terminology – to deal with (c).

It is not hard to see why this was. For him, what a person can *say* or can *imagine* had no connection with what can be so. To be able to portray a situation, or not to be able to portray it – in words or in mental imagery – was of no interest to him. He would not deny that we can talk meaningfully – or think – about a lot of things, or many situations, that are not actual: no one could deny that sensibly. But we see no trace of any suggestion that he might need possible objects, or even 'possible worlds', in the manner of Leibniz, to explain or justify any use of language about possibilities or any capacity we might have to imagine them.

In his earlier work, the view about what we can think – rather than *say* – was less clear. In the *Treatise on the Emendation of the Intellect* the emphasis was placed on the psychological question, what is it to feign (*fingere*) something that is not the case? His reply is similar to Wittgenstein's assertion that 'We cannot think anything unlogical, for otherwise we should have to think unlogically.'[50] The idea was that we cannot properly conceive a non-existent or impossible thing. If we think that we do conceive a thing which we believe to be possible ('by its very nature, neither its existence nor its non-existence implies a contradiction') then we are in

---

[50] *Tractatus Logico-Philosophicus*, 3.03.

fact only assembling imagery rather than conceiving a true idea. If we think we are conceiving something impossible, such as a square circle or a non-existing God, then we are still more fundamentally mistaken. We *think* we conceive a 'simple idea', but in reality, if an idea is simple 'it would be clear and distinct, and consequently true'.[51] The implicit thought must have been very like Wittgenstein's: in some way we cannot represent to ourselves a thing (state of affairs) that is contradicted by the necessary structure of nature (logic). Possibility was therefore construed in Spinoza's early thought partly in terms of a priori psychology.

He did not say why, or how far, he shifted from this early view, but his approach in the *Ethics* was different. The element of a priori psychology vanished: that is, any attempt to tell us what we can or cannot conceive, the attempt to analyse simple or complex thoughts and the interpretation of possibility in terms of human imagination or conception. He continued to think that an inadequate or false idea cannot be properly conceived by the mind;[52] but what he said about possibility no longer had a solely psychological basis. In the *Ethics* he seemed to get down to a metaphysical or ontological problem – (c) above – what is it for there to be other possible states of affairs? The most thoroughgoing determinism does not imply anything about the status of non-actual possibilities. We can still speculate counter-factually, in any instance, that the whole of history *might* have been different, so that one outcome followed rather than another. What about the order of things that did not occur? Can that be seen as a *possible world*?

This takes us towards what we must consider to be a positive account of possibilities, contained, unfortunately, in one of Spinoza's most cryptic passages. *Ethics* Part II, Proposition 8, touches on the 'ideas of non-existing individual things or modes'. The illustration, typically, is geometrical, where 'an infinite number of equal rectangles are contained in a circle, but none of them can be said to exist except in so far as the circle exists'. The ideas of these infinite, non-existent rectangles are said to be 'comprehended in the infinite idea of God'.

The interpretation of this which comes to mind looks like Leibniz: infinite possibilities do not really exist in the actual world but only as thoughts which God might have (or *does* have). So we may not quite have possible worlds, but there may be *ideas* of possible worlds in God's mind – God's mind, not mine, because both Spinoza and Leibniz knew that there will always be possibilities beyond the capacity of my enumeration.

---

[51] §§ 53, 64; pp. 245, 249 = G II 20/1–2, 24/30–31. [52] *Ethics* II, 40 and 43.

Whatever Spinoza could have meant by an idea in the infinite idea of God, it cannot have been much like the domain of divine choice that Leibniz was trying to evoke. Again, 'infinite idea of God' is one of Spinoza's terms for his infinite modes. Obscurely, in a letter of 1665, he had written that – 'in Nature there . . . exists an infinite power of thinking, which in so far as it is infinite, contains within itself the whole of Nature ideally'[53] – but this kind of language is likely to hinder rather than help our understanding. In some way, following the arguments in the last chapter, we can probably say that infinite modes were meant to allow for infinities in a sense that differed from the unqualified infinity of God as substance.

In the most ordinary sense, the point may only be that there can be infinite constructions and hence there can be infinite thoughts related to them. But that leaves the interpretation of *can be* where we started: how is that sort of possibility to be construed?

Spinoza is well known for running together necessity and what he called causality – this has been discussed – but a corollary which has not been so well noted is the conflation of modal (or 'logical') possibility and practical possibility. Still less well noted has been the direction of that conflation. There is no scope in his thought for any distinction between what can be conceived as possible – some might now wish to say 'logically' – and what is causally or practically possible. And in fact that is obvious. If the laws of nature are seen as universal and necessitating, then whatever can be the case can only be the case within them. To 'be possible' cannot be to exist or subsist in some shadowy propositional or conceptual world of possibilities, but is simply to be an available outcome within a framework of nature and its action. Using Spinoza's kind of example: if there are two movable, non-parallel straight lines on a plane, there are infinite possible points of intersection. If the lines are parallel, then no intersection may be possible. This is one way in which possibilities may be seen without the need for possible worlds or for a regress of possibilities each calling for explanation. The possible points on the lines may be seen as those which *can be* constructed in the nature of plane space. One point may be actual, others will be actual if the construction is differently executed. Spinoza would like this applied outside geometry. If the antecedent causes – the causal histories – had been different then he might have been born in Paris rather than Amsterdam; but whatever the antecedent causes he could not have been

<hr>

[53] Letter 32; L 194 = G IV 173/18–19.

born on Sirius. Possibilities become what is possible – what *can happen* – in a literal way.

If this is right, 'logical possibility' is squeezed out of the picture. Logic meets metaphysics or ontology. We may not like this, being accustomed since the writings of Hume to imagining kettles which can fail to boil over fires and billiard balls which can fly off at odd angles. But Spinoza's position is probably nearer to pre-philosophical common sense, in that some philosophers would suppose it to be *logically possible* to fly unaided to the moon.

We may wish to say that we can represent to ourselves situations which are not possible in nature but which do not 'involve a contradiction', as both Spinoza[54] and Hume would put it. But in the absence of some very specific assumptions about meaning, the fact that we *can think* or *can say* things about situations implies nothing about the existence or potential existence of those situations. Spinoza would not deny the capacity of the imagination to picture unlikely states of affairs, or the capacity of language to express them: 'For many more ideas can be constructed from words or images than from merely the principles and axioms on which our entire natural knowledge is based.'[55] What he may have done was to offer a framework which emptied those capacities – to construct ideas from words and images – of significance.

It is a curious irony that the limit of possibility for Hume – who was supposed to be an empiricist – was discovered a priori: by thought-experiment, finding out what could or could not be imagined. For Spinoza, the dissolution of logical possibility meant that the way to find out what is possible could only be to see what can happen in the world, by means of demonstration and experiment, not by imagination or story-telling.

This line of interpretation may help with the rescue of Spinoza's compressed thinking on possible objects and possible thoughts. It does not remove all the difficulties in his treatment of possibility. Translating back into his terminology, we may say that the nature of the extended world – the infinite mode of 'motion and rest' – will allow for an infinite range of outcomes within nature. Matching these outcomes will be an infinite range of ideas that go to make up the 'infinite idea of God'. A possible idea may be one which is deducible from other ideas, just as a possible thing is one which can be caused within a framework of physical law. In this way, the 'infinite idea of God' can be read unmystically as

---

[54] *Ethics* I, 33, Scholium.   [55] S 71 = G III 28/23–5.

being the range of thoughts which is, as some might wish to say, logically available[56] (although 'logically' adds nothing here). Given an identification of possible ideas with the ideas of possible things, we get back to the view that there can be ideas of things that are possible, but not of things that are not. But demystification will only go so far. This reading does little to advance an understanding of Spinoza's view that part of the mind is eternal, which appears in *Ethics* v, 23 and which is said there to have some grounding in the thinking in Part ii, Proposition 8, which has been the starting-point for this discussion. We shall need to return to that in Chapter 10.

CONCRETENESS

Spinoza's thinking on possibility takes us back again to his concrete, non-propositional, non-linguistic approach. In fact, we can see this in relation to both possibility and necessity. Take, for example:

(i) $a_1, a_2, a_3 \ldots$ cause b

where $a_1, a_2, a_3 \ldots$ and b will be what he would call *res particulares*: individual things. Now (i) may be read as:

(ii) $a_1, a_2, a_3 \ldots$ necessarily cause b

in the sense we have been discussing, because $a_1, a_2, a_3 \ldots$ exist as the cause for b, and that constitutes necessity (by *Ethics* i, Definition 7). So (ii) says no more than (i).

We can *say* or *think* –

(iii) $a_1, a_2, a_3 \ldots$ might not cause b

– if we like, but this will not be *true*. Spinoza could show no sign of caring that (iii), for example, might need a possible world or a possible state of affairs by which its meaning might be explained or supported. His thinking about counterfactual suppositions has no bearing on their meaning or their meaningfulness.

If we take a propositional version of (ii) –

(iv) it is necessary that $a_1, a_2, a_3 \ldots$ cause b

– where this is taken to be the same as –

(v) the proposition[57] that $a_1, a_2, a_3 \ldots$ cause b is necessarily true

– then we can see where a divergence between Spinoza and conventional modern thinking will begin to open up. Because, simply, (v) tells us that a

[56] A strongly 'logical' reading can be found in Elhanan Yakira, 'Ideas of Nonexistent Modes: *Ethics* II Proposition 8, its Corollary and Scholium' in Yirmiyahu Yovel (ed.), *Spinoza on Knowledge and the Human Mind* (Leiden: Brill, 1994).

[57] Or sentence or statement: this is not an argument where any difference matters.

proposition – something said, thought, written or whatever – must be true. Hence, if some explanation for necessity is felt to be needed, *what* is needed is an explanation why a proposition must be true. Part of such an explanation will have to be some account of how the proposition is true: how it says truly what it does say. But (ii) does not lead down that difficult path. There is no need to explain the necessity in it, because it only tells us that (i). The necessity in it consists only in that b has a cause in a_1, a_2, a_3...

This is very abstract. We can see how it works by starting again with a practical example. Take

(i) the fire ... makes the water boil[58]

Now Spinoza would think that

(ii) the fire ... must make the water boil

is the same as (i) (in nature, the fire makes the water boil) and he would think that

(iii) the fire ... might not make the water boil

is simply false. The fact that we – or Hume – may be able to form a mental image of the water not boiling on the fire would make no impression on Spinoza at all. This is partly because he had no interest in our capacity to tell ourselves false stories, but partly for a more important reason.

Someone who thinks that

(ii) the fire ... must make the water boil

means the same as

(v) the proposition that the fire ... makes the water boil must be true

will also think that this means

(vi) the proposition that the fire ... makes the water boil cannot be false

and may want to say that (vi) has something wrong with it because we can (no doubt thanks to Hume) imagine the fire not making the water boil, and hence, one might think, the possible falsity of a proposition that the fire makes the water boil.[59] And if a proposition can be imagined to be false, it cannot be necessarily true.

The underlying logic, again – now in schematic outline – might seem to be

---

[58] Where 'the fire' indicates the heat of the fire and an endless set of other physical conditions. 'The water' is short for some particular lot of water in a container on the fire (plus many other conditions).

[59] 'We'd know what was being described – what it would be like for it to be true – if it were reported for example that a kettle of water was put, and kept, directly on a hot fire, but the water did not heat up' G. E. M. Anscombe, 'Causality and Determination' (1971), *Collected Philosophical Papers*, vol. II (Oxford: Blackwell, 1981), p. 134.

(i) *a* causes *b*
(ii) *a* necessarily causes *b*
so:
(iv) it is necessary that *a* causes *b*
which means:
(v) the proposition that *a* causes *b* is necessarily true
but:
(vi) if the proposition that *a* causes *b* is necessarily true it is not possible
that the proposition that *a* causes *b* is false
and:
(vii) we can imagine the falsity of the proposition that *a* causes *b*
so:
(viii) it is possible that the proposition that *a* causes *b* is false
so (by (vi)):
(ix) the proposition that *a* causes *b* is not necessarily true (= not-(v))
so:
(x) not-(ii)

Leaping from the schematic to the particular – if we put 'God exists' for
'*a* causes *b*', we can see how this argument might be meant to work
against Spinoza. But his presumed attitude should be clear enough. (vii)
is irrelevant, and certainly does not entail (viii); but that does not matter
anyway, because the move from (i) and (ii) to (iv) or (v) is a mistake.
Necessity has to be understood not in terms of propositions which must
be true, but in terms of things which have causes. We *can say* (iv) if we
like, if it is taken to mean (ii), but not if it is taken to mean (v).

 We may seem to have strayed a long way from Spinoza's text, and a
long way from his thinking about how God acts; but we have not.

 We saw earlier that his assertions about universal causality were
framed in terms of the existence of things, not the truth of propositions.
The sense of this should now be clearer. Assertions translated out of
Spinoza's terms into terms of truths, propositions or necessarily true
propositions can lead to paradoxes or absurdities: all propositions are
necessarily true, for example, but some are not, or some are less so than
others.[60] Since we are dealing with the central machinery by which
nature is said to operate, this should matter.

 To stress that Spinoza's thinking was about things and their existence
may rescue it from anachronism, but is still some way from clarifying it

---

[60] Curley, *Spinoza's Metaphysics*, Chapter 3.

completely. After all, the reason why Curley, for example, sought to translate what Spinoza said 'into talk about truths' and to develop 'a general account of necessary truth that will accord with Spinoza's intentions'[61] can only have been that talk about the existence and acting of things must have seemed even harder to justify, explain or defend.

But is that so? The contrast between –

(ii) *a* necessarily causes *b*

– and –

(v) the proposition that *a* causes *b* is necessarily true

– is not, as it might seem to a logician, a conventional contrast between *de re* and *de dicto* formulations. In fact, 'necessarily' turns out to have wholly different senses in the two cases.[62] Rather, the contrast is nearer to one frequently underlined in the work of Donald Davidson, between 'the analysis of causality' and the 'logical form of causal statements'.[63] Davidson has remarked that

it is sentences (or statements or propositions), or the relations between them, that are properly classified as contingent or logical; if causal relations are 'in nature', it makes no sense to classify them as logical or contingent[64]

and this is exactly the point that applies to Spinoza. For him, causal relations could not be 'logical'. The necessity in causality was nothing like the necessity by which propositions are said to be necessarily true. In – 'For each single existent thing there must necessarily be a definite cause for its existence'[65] – 'must necessarily' adds nothing to the force of the assertion. The necessity consists only in the existence of a cause for each thing. Spinoza takes immanence seriously and literally. Necessity is not embodied in nature like a set of 'logical' regulations applying within it. It is how things are and how they act.

LAW

This also goes for his views on natural law. As we might expect, the law of nature is the same as the law of God:

the universal laws of Nature according to which all things happen and are determined are nothing but God's eternal decrees which always involve eternal truth and necessity.[66]

[61] *Ibid.*, p. 88.
[62] A point well made, with a different example, in Hughes, *The Nature of God*, pp. 28–30, 187.
[63] 'Causal Relations' (1967), in *Essays on Actions and Events* (Oxford: Clarendon Press, 1982), p. 161.
[64] 'Reply to P. F. Strawson', in B. Vermazen and M. Hintikka (eds.), *Essays on Davidson* (Oxford: Clarendon Press, 1985), p. 224.   [65] *Ethics* I, 8, Scholium 2.   [66] S 89 = G III 46.

But despite some extremely confident assertions about the universality of law –

> our approach to the understanding of the nature of things of every kind should . . . be one and the same; namely, through the universal laws and rules of Nature[67]

– laws actually play a curiously low-key rôle in the *Ethics*.

Law and *nature* are the same – *leges, sive natura*:[68] the way in which something exists and acts is its nature, best identified with its 'proximate cause'. In the *Ethics*, Spinoza chose to express himself almost entirely in terms of *nature*, rather than *law*. A clue as to why this was so can be seen in the *Theological-Political Treatise*, where the whole subject acquired a theological slant, startlingly at odds with the austere treatment in the *Ethics*. We see a characteristic preference for an explanation from a geometrical case. In the chapter *Of the Divine Law* we learn that:

> in respect of God our affirmation is one and the same, whether we say that God has eternally willed and decreed that the three angles of a triangle should be equal to two right angles, or that God has understood this fact.[69]

And we find that divine law applies to people and their behaviour as it does to triangles. Yet Spinoza was forthright about the metaphor contained in *law*: a law suggests a lawgiver[70] and any anthropomorphic thoughts must be extinguished completely:

> We therefore conclude that it is only in concession to the understanding of the multitude and the defectiveness of their thought that God is described as a lawgiver or ruler, and is called just, merciful, and so on, and that in reality God acts and governs all things [*omnia dirigere*] solely from the necessity of his own nature and perfection . . .[71]

He also wanted to make a point about Jewish law. (And we do not know whether this was a consequence of his views or if it was the motivation underlying them.) In Chapter 9 we shall look in detail at the puzzlingly oblique uses he made of the figure of Christ. One such use was in relation to law. The teaching of Christ, he wrote, 'took the form of eternal truths, not of prescribed laws' – freeing people from bondage to the law, 'while nevertheless giving further strength and stability to the law, inscribing it deep in their hearts'. That sounds not unlike the Epistle to the Romans, which was indeed cited with approval on this point,[72] but

---

[67] *Ethics* III, Preface.   [68] Letter 32; L 192 = G IV 170/13.   [69] S 106 = G III 63/7–10.
[70] See *Summa Theologiæ* 1a. 2æ. 93, 1.; Suárez, *De Legibus*, I, I, 2.   [71] S 108–9 = G III 65/28–32.
[72] S 108 = G III 65/9–14; S 97 = G III 54/21–7.

Spinoza's perspective was far from conventional. Law as externally binding was, unsurprisingly, to be over-ridden; but the law was to be internalised to an extreme degree, in how things are and how they act, not in any set of rules explaining how and why they behave as they do.

FROM METAPHYSICS TO PHYSICS

Taken together – and of course they could not be taken in any other way – Spinoza's views about what exists and how it works provided a basis for science. In the *Ethics*, this was primarily what used to be called *moral science*. The title of the *Ethics* tells us the point of the work, and in the brief Preface to Part II the author reminds us that he is going to pass on only to 'those things that can lead us as it were by the hand to the knowledge of the human mind and its blessedness', although 'infinite things' follow in the widest sense – in 'infinite ways' – from the metaphysical conclusions of Part I.

Although his focus is ethical, at the beginning of Part II of the *Ethics* Spinoza still steps aside to give 'a brief preface concerning the nature of bodies' – a set of axioms, lemmas and postulates that offer a sketch of a kind of proto-physics. This, and his offhand introduction to it, is curious. We might expect, from the point of view of any understanding of his understanding of Descartes, that the transition from metaphysical principles to the groundings of real science would be an exceptionally delicate step, to be handled with exceptional care. Yet this does not seem to be so. We are just told that we need to know something – a 'few things', *pauca*[73] – about bodies because we need to know about minds, presumably because a proof of a large part of the *Ethics* 'as everyone knows must be based on metaphysics and physics';[74] but almost no elucidation is offered on how we step from abstractions or generalities (about substance, essence, attributes and so on) to practical facts. To anyone worried about 'religion and science', the rabbit may seem to have been pulled from the hat rather too quickly. In theological terms this is a vital question. If God is the sort of God who can make things happen, we can ask exactly *how?*

Spinoza's approach was not obscure or mysterious, and there is nothing too difficult about it – though his insouciance towards palatable exposition is well illustrated by his lack of desire to emphasise or underline what he said on this vital point. And that is especially striking because the risk of confusion with the approach of Descartes was considerable.

---

[73] *Ethics* II, 13, Scholium = G II 97/18. [74] Letter 27; L 177 = G IV 160–1.

In rough terms, there seems to be a need to get from metaphysics to physics. The Cartesian project was based in the most familiar story in Western philosophy: Descartes had wanted to ground his science in solid foundations. Everything had to be dug up and rebuilt.[75] By the time he wrote the French Preface to the *Principles of Philosophy* in 1647, his thinking on this was as clarified as it would ever be:

These are all the principles that I make use of with regard to immaterial things, and from them I deduce very clearly the principles of corporeal or physical things, namely that there are bodies which are extended in length, breadth and depth, and which have various shapes and move in various ways. Here, in total, are all the principles which I use to deduce the truth of other things . . .

The aim was to start from 'the principles of philosophy' and to 'deduce the knowledge of all the other things to be found in the world'.[76]

Spinoza's reading of Descartes is seen in his *Descartes' Principles of Philosophy Demonstrated in the Geometric Manner*, where he tried to reframe the project in what he took to be the most transparent and well-ordered manner, without endorsing its premises, its conclusions or – vitally – its order. The result, obviously, was entirely different from the working-out of his own system where, as we saw, 'the proper order of philosophical enquiry'[77] had to begin with 'divine nature'. Descartes, thought Spinoza, began with *thought, idea, mind,* then *body. Substance* appears first, obliquely, as our idea of substance. Even more strikingly – and to be discussed at length in the next chapter – his whole treatment of Descartes set off with an immediate detour through the method of doubt, placed outside the presentation in the 'geometrical method', in a prolegomenon. Descartes, surely correctly, was portrayed as starting from his own mind – the 'mind, or thinking thing'.[78] The deduction of the knowledge of all things to be found in the world started from some concrete specifics: the author is thinking – and this is 'the unique and most certain foundation of the whole of Philosophy'.[79] So we are not really working in terms of deductions from general principles at all, or alone, but from that starting-point.

The balance between general and particular was radically altered by Spinoza. From this chapter it should be evident that how individuals exist and act is determined by the existence and action of other individuals. *How things are* depends on how other things are, in an infinite causal net. So to pick out any single factual starting-point would be a mistake.

---

[75] *Seventh Replies*, CSMK II 366ff = AT VII 536ff (the most extended use of the image).
[76] CSMK I 184 = AT IXB, 10.   [77] *Ethics* II, 10, Scholium.
[78] *mentem, sive rem cogitantem* Curley, p. 242 = G I 153/6.   [79] Curley, p. 242 = G I 153/15–16.

For practical purposes we may cite or bring in individual data – 'Man thinks', for example, or 'Of the individual parts of the human body, some are liquid, some are soft, and some are hard', or 'The human body can move external bodies and dispose them in a great many ways'[80] – but all these appear well into the development of the work, not at the beginning, and are needed for Spinoza's conclusions about human life and behaviour. They are specific but not privileged facts.

Another mistake that Spinoza might diagnose would be to start not with any specific individual existents or facts, but with generalities (or universal statements). One natural reading, perhaps, might be to think that because a particular Cartesian fulcrum had been repudiated, the only available alternative would be generalities. That this reading is not unnatural can be seen from the fact that it seems to have been followed by Spinoza's most acute correspondent, Tschirnhaus, here going straight to the point:

Most learned Sir,
I should like you to do me the kindness of showing how, from Extension as conceived in your philosophy, the variety of things can be demonstrated a priori . . . In mathematics I have always observed that from any thing considered in itself – that is, from the definition of any thing – we are able to deduce at least one property; but if we wish to deduce more properties, we have to relate the thing defined to other things.[81]

Spinoza's answer – Letter 83 – was unsatisfactory (and sadly so. 'If I live long enough', he wrote, 'I shall some time discuss this with you more clearly'; seven months later he was dead). He could only point out to Tschirnhaus that his question was based on a misunderstanding. In fact it was possible to deduce a good deal about God from the definition of a being to whose essence existence pertained. Descartes had been wrong to start with matter defined as extension. Instead 'it' must be 'explicated through an attribute which expresses eternal and infinite essence'.[82] Here, the negative point is a lot clearer than the positive one. Negatively, Descartes's introduction of 'matter' into his system was as far from Spinoza's approach as possible – we have a 'clear understanding' of matter as 'something that is quite different from God'.[83]

Tschirnhaus's question is revealing because it brings to the fore a

---

[80] *Ethics* II, Axiom 2; Postulate 2; Postulate 6.   [81] Letter 82; 1676, L 353 = G IV 333.

[82] Letter 83; L 355 = G IV 334/25–7.

[83] *Principles* II, 1; CSMK I 223 = AT VIIIA 41. The positive view is more cryptic: Spinoza's 'it' which must be 'explicated through an attribute' could, grammatically, be 'matter' – as all translators assume – or equally it could be 'the variety of things'. Anyway, what he meant, presumably, was that one of the widest possible conceptions of nature was extendedness – the attribute of extension. And 'the variety of things' had nothing to do with that.

crucial point in grasping Spinoza's system. We may think that what it contains is a set of general principles about the world which then need to be related to existing, concrete reality. That view might seem to be encouraged by the presence of wide, abstract principles and of specific empirical postulates. General rules plus particular instances, as it were, generate the results: physical truths about the world, psychological and moral truths about people.

That reading may be harmless for the consequences deduced from Spinoza's empirical postulates (and, confusingly, it would be accurate as an understanding of his view of scientific method[84]) but it is seriously misleading for the basic moves in his thinking and fatal for an accurate grasp of his connection between nature and individuals.

An instructive analogue is provided by the Cambridge metaphysician John McTaggart Ellis McTaggart, one of whose merits was an exceptional capacity for teasing out the exact premises within his thinking. He believed that –

It would be possible to consider what characteristics are involved in being existent, or in being the whole of what exists, without raising the question whether anything did exist.[85]

– and to get his system going, he thought, he needed to rely on 'perception' to show him that at least one thing did, in fact, exist.

Now this looks like Spinoza's introduction of postulates such as 'Man thinks': as if we need *something* specific. But the difference is absolute and essential. For Spinoza, there could be no question, even in theory, as there had been for Descartes and as there would be for McTaggart, that anything like 'matter' might *not* exist. Divine nature – the starting-point – was not a generalised abstraction – a concept – needing the addition of particular premises – it was what exists. What exists is presented as extended (and as thought, and in infinite other ways). Getting from that level of abstraction to useful physical principles might indeed present formidable problems – but among those problems was not any question to be answered by a premise that some object exists: that was taken for granted from the outset. This bears crucially on the Cartesian transition from metaphysics to physics.[86]

---

[84] As e.g. sketched at S 145 = G III 102/21–5: in 'examining natural phenomena' (*res naturales*) we *start* with 'those features which are most universal and common to the whole of Nature'.

[85] *The Nature of Existence* (Cambridge University Press, 1921), vol. I, p. 41.

[86] As Derrida points out, Cartesian methodology should not have been an external preliminary to science; it must be somehow part of it: 'elle est la production et la structure du tout de la science tel qu'il s'expose lui-même dans la logique', *La dissémination* (Paris: Seuil, 1972), p. 21.

Nor was Spinoza's ideal model of explanation one of general law + specific instance = result.[87] What exists or happens in nature never 'follows' in that way from some general characteristics of nature. What happens in nature depends on other things that happen in nature.

Again, all this looks remote and abstract, but it matters centrally for Spinoza's conception of relations between God and the world. Even if we grasp the equivalence of God and nature and the thoroughness of immanent explanation, it may still remain tempting to see Spinoza as deducing particular facts about things from general truths, in the style of Descartes's *Principles*. In a crucial sense that would be wrong. The factual postulates for worthwhile science in Part II of the *Ethics* were just that – factual postulates. They were not deduced from anything general. Once more, what happens in the world is caused by other things that happen in the world. To suppose that things as a whole – or as 'matter' – might not exist, even as a metaphysical premise, would be completely inappropriate, and could have no place anywhere.

HOW GOD ACTS

Where does this leave God's action?

Earlier in this chapter it was mentioned that the general outline of Spinoza's position has never been in doubt – that the real interest – and all the real theological questions – lies in how his position could or could not be made to work.

Questions about modality – the status and force of necessity, possibility and contingency – appear at a meeting-place of mathematics and theology. In a theological context they appear as problems about God's scope for choice, in forms that now seem quaintly arcane: does God create the rules of geometry? Or choose to go along with them? Or is God bound by them? Such problems may also be framed non-theologically, in terms of whether we – whoever *we* are – create mathematical truths, decide to adopt them or whether we have to discover or accept them.[88] In terms of systematic consistency it seems absurd to insist, rightly, on the immanentism of Spinoza's thinking about God while leaving God, even immanently, in thrall to 'logic'.

---

[87] As Curley believes: 'Particular events in nature will be deducible from the eternal order of nature only if we add to our description of the eternal order descriptions of prior particular events': 'Donagan's Spinoza', *Ethics*, 104, 1993, p. 126.

[88] Although it might be a good question to ask whether *we* in this context can be defined without theological presuppositions: a point to be pursued in the next chapter.

Much of the importance in Spinoza comes from his point of balance between perspectives. Most of his terminology looks theological, and the extent to which his motivation was theological is entirely unknown. But his use of that terminology was almost entirely innovative, and, viewed from a later perspective, almost entirely geared to the requirements of the new mathematicised sciences. There was to be nothing outside nature. The necessity of nature and the laws of nature's action were not to be seen as sets of regulations that bound it, so much as simply its existence and action.

Theological questions about God's freedom could hardly be asked in any recognisable sense. In a framework of what, later, might be called logic, Spinoza might be seen as an anti-theorist. His approach made necessity intelligible – made it into *what was intelligible* – with possibility and contingency to be understood in terms of it. His answer to the question, what exists? was a kind of non-answer, in that what exists is nature and nature is what exists. Similarly, his answer to why do things exist and what makes them happen? was also a non-answer, in that things exist as nature exists and they happen as they happen. That is only informative in that it tells us that no other types of explanation are to be sought. The way is opened and simplified for natural, scientific, inquiry. We are to find out in detail about what exists, what happens and what *can* happen by studying nature.

SOME IMPLICATIONS

We have seen that Spinoza may have taken for granted a whole view about modality which is of great interest and originality in itself. In any event, the implications for some traditional theological difficulties were radical and brisk. God's plan in history – divine providence – was how things happen in accordance with historical causality. Miracles, in the sense of breaches in the causal order, were not possible; and if they *were* possible they would be more of a disproof than a confirmation of God's existence. We shall come back later to some of the ramifications of these views. As corollaries of Spinoza's central metaphysics their main angle of interest is not what he thought – which is surely obvious enough – but how far, in religious terms, he took what we might see as a *reductive* view – divine providence was *no more than* or *nothing but* normal history. That is not quite so obvious, and is where the interest lies.

Part I of the *Ethics* takes seriously the question of God's physical relationship to creation: a topic that has subsequently become less pressing, quite possibly because of some of Spinoza's arguments. One reading of what he was doing is that he took some of the characteristics tradition- ally associated with God – starting with infinity or limitedlessness – and some of the terminology from past philosophy – starting with *cause* and *substance* – and he compressed them together to their extreme points. If you say that God is unlimited, how can there be anything that is not God? If the causality in nature operates as God's law, how can it ever be less than universal? And so on.

For Spinoza, the relation between historical religion and what we might call science was not a straightforward one, as we shall see in Part II of this study; but the relation between theological and physical results was entirely straightforward: they were identical. As Donagan put it, 'If nature is God, then natural science is theology, at least in its fundamental principles.'[89]

A good illustration of the sureness and subtlety in Spinoza's approach is given by his attitude towards God as first cause – as creator or initiator of nature. After all, this can be seen as one focus of connection between theology and physics.

God is said to be 'absolutely the first cause' – a corollary of the proposition in the *Ethics*[90] that infinite things in infinite ways must follow from the necessity of (the) divine nature. But that did not mean that God or nature was either first in time or was the first in all causal series or net- works. If causal networks were unlimited then there would be no point in thinking about their beginnings. 'If there is granted an infinite series of causes, all things which are, are also caused.'[91] The implications of this must be seen in a thoroughgoing way: there need be no first event or first existent. What does exist – the unlimited concatenation of things and events – can be seen as something in need of a cause – as *natura naturata*, or as 'infinite modes' – but no cause can be sought outside its own exis- tence. It can be seen as having a cause – as being *natura naturans* – only in that it is self-caused.

Maybe this looks like playing with words, but as a refusal to present a philosophical theory it allows – or makes possible – a good deal of room for physical theorising. For example:

The idea that space and time may form a closed surface without boundary . . . has profound implications for the role of God in the affairs of the universe. With the success of scientific theories in describing events, most people have come to

[89] *Spinoza*, p. 21.   [90] I, 16.
[91] Letter 12; L 107 = G IV 62/1–2. (Here Spinoza is quoting a premise which he accepts.)

believe that God allows the universe to evolve according to a set of laws and does not intervene in the universe to break these laws. However, the laws do not tell us what the universe should have looked like when it started – it would still be up to God to wind up the clockwork and choose how to start it off. So long as the universe had a beginning, we could suppose it had a creator. But if the universe is really completely self-contained, having no boundary or edge, it would have neither beginning nor end: it would simply be. What place then for a creator?[92]

Spinoza could go along with most of this; but he would not treat the final question as only rhetorical.

[92] Stephen Hawking, *A Brief History of Time* (New York: Bantam, 1990), pp. 140–1.

CHAPTER 3

God and doubt

It is generally agreed that modern Western philosophy begins with a story told by Descartes about himself:

I am presenting this work only as a history or, if you prefer, a fable . . . I hope it will be useful for some without being harmful to any, and that everyone will be grateful to me for my frankness.

His sense of certainty had been 'beset by so many doubts and errors', he wrote, that 'I had gained nothing from my attempts to become educated but increasing recognition of my ignorance.'[1] From that point, his narrative became less straightforward and more contentious. God came into it. God's existence was proved from premises which he found undeniable: 'I concluded that it is at least as certain as any geometrical proof that God . . . is or exists.'[2] God's existence and character seemed to underwrite or guarantee the rest of Descartes's knowledge.

The parallel story left to us by Spinoza is only a fragment of an early work. It sets off in an autobiographical tone reminiscent of Descartes, though even more reminiscent of a medieval confessional memoir: 'After experience had taught me the hollowness and futility of everything that is ordinarily encountered in daily life', and the source of initial concern was entirely different from Descartes's: 'and I realised that all the things which were the source and object of my anxiety held nothing of good and evil in themselves save in so far as the mind was influenced by them, I resolved at length to enquire whether there existed a true good'. The objective was not certainty but 'something whose discovery and acquisition would afford me a continuous and supreme joy to all eternity'[3] – though there seemed to be a convergence back towards Descartes when we read a few pages later that the 'supreme good' would be derived from

[1] *Discourse on the Method*, I; CSMK I 112–13 = AT VI 4.
[2] *Discourse on the Method*, IV; CSMK I 129 = AT VI 36.
[3] *Treatise on the Emendation of the Intellect*, §1, p. 233 = G II 6.

85

'the knowledge of the union which the mind has with the whole of Nature'.[4]

God appeared to have little part in the pursuit of such knowledge, though Spinoza did remark later, in passing, in a footnote, that 'although many may say that they doubt the existence of God, they have in mind nothing but a word, or some fictitious idea they call God. This does not accord with the nature of God'.[5]

The narrative of Descartes had a huge influence on the course of philosophy. In comparison, Spinoza has seemed a sidetrack. He refused to pursue the trail opened by Descartes's uncertainties. Even though his story began with himself, it was not self-centred, working from the certainty of an inner self towards supposed knowledge of an 'external' world outside it, along the path opened by the *Discourse on the Method* and the *Meditations*. In a period full of change and uncertainties, he looks dogmatic. As he conceived the existence of God, it did not seem to be open to question. And, on human knowledge: 'He who has a true idea knows at the same time that he has a true idea, and cannot doubt its truth . . . just as light makes manifest both itself and darkness, so truth is the standard both of itself and falsity.'[6]

GOD AND KNOWLEDGE

We can look at the links between God and human knowledge from two directions.

From one direction, there are questions about human knowledge of God: how, if at all, is it to fit in with other types of human knowledge – *above them*, as a sort of super-science? As *one of them*, as one sort of knowledge among others? As something *different in kind*, such as 'faith', distinct from sorts of other knowing, and to be assessed by different criteria? Or as something to be rejected altogether? These are questions that must be faced at any time when claims are made about knowledge and God.

From the other direction, we can ask about the rôle or place of God in human knowing. Does God play *no* part – in the sense that we can know what we know whether or not God is there? Is God *essential*, in the sense

---

[4] *Treatise on the Emendation of the Intellect*, §21, p. 235 = G II 8. Descartes had described 'the highest degree of wisdom' as 'the supreme good of human life'. Preface to the French edition of the *Principles*, CSMK I 183 = AT IXB 9.
[5] *Treatise on the Emendation of the Intellect*, §54, p. 245 = G II 20, note t.
[6] *Ethics* II, 43 and Scholium.

that unless there were a God we would not be able to know anything? Or can God be considered as a knower *alongside* us, in the sense, for example, that the Homeric gods were said to know or see some things, but not others, alongside mortals? These issues might seem esoteric or outdated in comparison with issues about our knowledge of God.

Thinking about the place of God in relation to human knowing, there is also the less directly theological question of a divine perspective. The question, how does – or would – the world look to God, or to an angel? while sounding intriguing, does not sound like one that would ever provoke much concern. But asking that question does force us to consider the possibility and status of non-human, and hence perhaps non-subjective, perspectives. From what do 'we' construct the perspective from which 'we' make geometrical judgments? Who are 'we'? 'Rational' humans? The ideal rational knower? From long before the time of Spinoza – from Parmenides – divine perception and judgment had been a kind of objective benchmark: God, at least, sees and judges truly, whether I do or not. Attaining to, or sharing, God's absolute perspective could be one metaphor to indicate objective knowledge or perception.[7]

Spinoza's *Treatise on the Emendation of the Intellect* shares with the works of Descartes a belief that a method[8] might be discovered to deliver and sort out truths. That belief does not appear in the *Ethics*, although there has been much speculation on whether the book's 'geometrical' presentation was meant to embody or exhibit a method for revealing truths.[9] This is not self-evident.

Definitely shared by Spinoza and Descartes, and by many other philosophers up to the nineteenth century and beyond, was a feeling that discussion about *what* can be known must be connected with some account of *how* we come to know it. That feeling led to good deal of speculative physiology and psychology and to the postulation of elaborate mental machinery for the manipulation and processing of perceptions, thoughts and (the universal term of convenience) 'ideas'. Human beings during their lives, unlike God or angels, were thought to inhabit bodies which seem to influence the process of acquiring and validating knowledge. Theories of knowledge became encrusted with accounts about how the mind and the body work together (or not) to produce

---

[7] See Edward Craig, *The Mind of God and the Works of Man* (Oxford: Clarendon Press, 1987), Chapter 1).   [8] *modus medendi intellectus*; §16, p. 236 = G II 9/10–11.
[9] For a very clear discussion see Piet Steenbakkers, *Spinoza's Ethica from Manuscript to Print* (Assen: Van Gorcum, 1994), Chapter 5.

knowledge. ('Do my eyes tell me the truth?') Part II of Spinoza's *Ethics* includes his account of how ideas in the mind are related to the body – how they come to be there.

The only non-antiquarian interest in such accounts is the question of *fallibility*, and here, too, the use of a divine benchmark appeared. If the human perceptual apparatus is, as it were, all there is, then, we might wish to say, it is the best we have, and we cannot contrast its effectiveness with anything better. If other forms of apparatus may be supposed – divine or angelic – then other possibilities arise. Humans may be said *never* to be able to discover and know about the world in contrast with God or angels, or may be said to be able to do this *some times*, or perhaps with *parts* of their intellectual apparatus – such as a 'natural light' – or only in certain states (when relevantly educated, mystically transported or after death).

This is the theological backdrop for discussions about scepticism. Am I constructed so that I can acquire knowledge reliably? Or has God made me so that on earth my knowledge is only incomplete and partly reliable? Or am I constructed so that what I know in certain ways – mathematically, perhaps – must be so?

The God of the Philosophers disparaged by Pascal had a rôle in both directions in relation to human knowledge. In one direction, the existence of such a God might be provable by means of 'rational' demonstration, naturalising theological knowledge and diminishing the virtue of faith. In the other direction, God would be brought in to underwrite or legitimise human knowing where it needed support. The interpretation of Descartes in these areas is not straightforward, but we can see how he might have opened himself to the possibility of such readings of his thought, rightly or wrongly.

KNOWLEDGE OF GOD

Whatever Descartes believed, Spinoza's position – from the direction of fitting in a knowledge of God with other forms of knowledge – was simple and clear.

Chapter 1 showed how the existence of God was to be understood: the non-existence of God was to be inconceivable, in the sense that God is nature, and it is hard to see how nature might not exist.

God's existence was *demonstrated*, for example in *Ethics* I, 11, although no one – and certainly not Spinoza – could think that such demonstrations could be personally persuasive or convincing to anyone disinclined to accept them.[10] Following the image used earlier, they were demonstrations in the sense that we can show that a clock works, and how it works, by taking it apart or by showing it running.

Furthermore, our knowledge and understanding of God and of God's existence were not obscure or complicated. In fact they were wholly transparent. God, as we saw, may not be imagined, but may be understood, in the sense that 'God's infinite essence and his eternity are known to all.'[11] That extraordinary assertion is best understood as meaning that we could not *not* understand nature. Much of this chapter will be taken with unravelling its justification, but its significance can be seen at once. God is not *hidden*, either in the sense that God's existence is a matter of decision or in that there can be anything mysterious about God's nature. And here, surely, Spinoza diverged from almost all theological tradition, Christian and Jewish.

Faith, whatever it was for him, had nothing to do with the acceptance of tenets about the existence and nature of God. Those tenets, as we have seen, may be considered to be something like the fundamentals of a natural science, and for Spinoza there could be no question of whether or not they can be believed or disbelieved. Nor, of course, could acceptance of them be a matter of value or merit.

Faith plays no part in the *Ethics*. In the *Theological-Political Treatise* it is separated from what Spinoza calls 'philosophy', which we must understand as being his amalgam of metaphysics and physics. Chapter XIV of the *Treatise* is titled explicitly enough 'An analysis of faith, the faithful, and the fundamental principles of faith. Faith is finally set apart from philosophy.' The chapter concludes, unsurprisingly, that

The aim of philosophy is, quite simply, truth, while the aim of faith . . . is nothing other than obedience and piety. Again, philosophy rests on the basis of universally valid axioms, and must be constructed by studying Nature alone, whereas faith is based on history and language, and must be derived only from Scripture and revelation.[12]

Spinoza's need was to empty faith of any content that could be judged to be true or false, so that it could be set aside entirely from the body of results to be derived from the study of nature. Even from a preliminary

---

[10] Even though Spinoza often seems the polar opposite of Pascal in matters of religion, he might have had some sympathy with the view in the *Pensées* (Lafuma §§190, 821) on the futility of metaphysical proofs for the existence of God as personally persuasive.

[11] Letter 56; L 278 = G IV 261/10–11; *Ethics* II, 47, Scholium. For shrewd commentary on the difference between *understanding* and *conceiving* God, see Beyssade, 'The Idea of God and the Proofs of His Existence', p. 187.   [12] S 226 = G III 179/30–4.

glance at his treatment, we can see that he placed himself in an unusual situation. The easy step – taken by many others – once the allegedly 'factual' content of faith has been eliminated or reduced is towards voluntarism: towards an emphasis on the significance or merit to be attached to the act of will contained in faith. But that route was closed for Spinoza. For him, willing and cognition were identical, and the notion of choosing to believe would have been unintelligible. We shall come back to this in more detail in Chapter 8.

Philosophy – science – was about truth which was attainable and which, he thought, had been attained:

I do not presume that I have found the best philosophy, but I know that what I understand is the true one [*sed veram me intelligere scio*]. If you ask me how I know this, I reply that I know it in the same way that you know that the three angles of a triangle are equal to two right angles.[13]

This is not a book on Spinoza's theories about knowledge, and there is no need now to go into his classifications of the different ways in which he thought knowledge could be obtained: accounts are given in the early *Treatise on the Emendation of the Intellect*, the *Short Treatise* and in the *Ethics*.[14] The *Theological-Political Treatise* contains no explicit account, but some stratification of knowing is presumed in its view that the sort of religion practised by the ignorant will have a different basis from the knowledge of nature possessed by the enlightened. There is much scope for debate over whether these various explicit and implicit accounts can be made to match up with each other. The only point of detail that will be pursued here – later, in Chapter 9 – is Spinoza's suggestion that Jesus was able to know or understand truth in a special way, which may or may not have represented a specific grade of knowledge.

In any event, as can be seen from the last quotation, from Letter 76, truth *was* attainable. People could get it, and know when they had it. The apparatus of perception and judgment, whatever it was, worked. Spinoza was no sceptic. He did not think humans fall short of God in that they can fail to know at all. Their knowledge might be necessarily partial, not in a sense contrasted with complete divine knowledge, but in an uncontroversially plain sense in which no one can know everything. Human knowledge was not incomplete in a sense that the whole truth ('Truth') was obscured. People really do know things. Probably this is

---

[13] Letter 76; L 342 = G IV 320/3–6.
[14] G II 9/34ff; *Short Treatise* I, I; *Ethics* II, 40, Scholium 2. The standard work remains G. H. R. Parkinson, *Spinoza's Theory of Knowledge* (Oxford: Clarendon Press, 1954).

only worth saying to anyone who might confuse Spinoza with an idealist philosopher of the nineteenth century, where any knowledge except that of the whole of nature (or the Absolute) may have been thought to have been defectively partial.[15]

RATIONALISM

Despite his habitual use of geometrical knowledge as a standard in his illustrations, Spinoza can only be seen in a tenuous sense as a *rationalist* about knowledge. Edwin Curley has presented a comprehensive and decisive case. If we take it that:

A rationalist is a person who has a program for science according to which it aspires to the condition of mathematics, where mathematics is conceived as a purely *a priori* discipline, which reasons deductively from self-evident premises to substantive conclusions about the nature of things. Experience, for the rationalist, plays no fundamental role, either in the discovery or in the verification of scientific truth

then, Curley argues, 'The view that Spinoza was a rationalist . . . is not just mildly inaccurate, it is wildly inaccurate. Experience has a much greater role to play in Spinoza's theory of knowledge than this view can allow for.'[16] We can *know* about individuals, *know* individual truths. 'Experience', in the technically philosophical perceptual sense, can be an integral element in acquiring knowledge. Even the highest form of knowing is related to a form of specific experience.[17] *What* we can know about the existence and action of things, as we have seen, is not a matter of deduction from general principles.

Nor, following the arguments in the previous chapter, was Spinoza a 'rationalist' about causal action and prediction in practice. We can never hope to grasp any full order of individual causes, past or future; so any capacity we may have to predict what is going to happen will be just as limited as we know that it actually is. This scarcely constitutes 'rationalism', however that is seen.

15] Harold Joachim offered this line in *A Study of Spinoza's Ethics* (Oxford: Clarendon Press, 1901).
[16] Edwin Curley, 'Experience in Spinoza's Theory of Knowledge', in Grene (ed.), *Spinoza: A Collection of Critical Essays*, pp. 25 and 26. Naturally, this is a matter of definition. Curley's account shortens the roster of rationalists, possibly to no members at all. An alternative, based on the importance of a priori reasoning, can lengthen it considerably, e.g., G. H. R. Parkinson's Introduction to *The Renaissance and Seventeenth-Century Rationalism* (Routledge History of Philosophy, vol. IV) (London: Routledge, 1993), p. 6.
[17] Argued at length by Pierre-François Moreau, *Spinoza: L'expérience et l'éternité* (Paris: Presses Universitaires de France, 1994), Part III.

DOGMATISM

Nevertheless, nothing has been said so far to dispel the impression that Spinoza's attitude towards knowledge was a dogmatic one. He has been seen to be making the strongest claims about the certainty and truth of his knowledge, and to be having the utmost confidence in his capacity to acquire and identify knowledge. Our knowledge of God is supposed to be certain. Equally, he was clear about the rôle of God in human knowing: 'the knowledge that we acquire by the natural light of reason depends solely on knowledge of God and of his eternal decrees'. And this was not given as the conclusion of an argument, but as a plain assertion – more as a premise – on the first page of the *Theological-Political Treatise*.[18]

We must look at his reasons. And here, the discussion narrows down to a clear and specific point. How was it that Spinoza, writing when he did, twenty years after the *Meditations*, and knowing what he did about Descartes, was able to put aside Cartesian doubt so completely, to the extent of repudiating the Cartesian starting-point, from what *I know* within myself?

Richard Popkin put it neatly, if severely –

Unlike Descartes, who had to fight his way through scepticism to arrive at dogmatic truth, Spinoza simply began with an assurance that his system was true, and anyone who didn't see this was either truth-blind (like color-blind) or was an ignoramus[19]

– and the evidence to support such a verdict is not hard to see. In brief, Spinoza, who was extremely well acquainted with the work of Descartes, dismissed the doubts of the *First Meditation* in little more than a few words. Even a very sympathetic commentator could think that Spinoza had not 'really struggled with doubt as for example Descartes did'.[20]

Historically and philosophically this matters. The epistemology of Descartes presented a challenge to philosophers for three centuries. Spinoza seemed to ignore that challenge, or at least he seemed to produce no interesting response. This must have been one of the main factors which placed him outside the mainstream of the European philosophical canon.

Most of the remainder of this chapter will be taken up with Spinoza's

---

[18] S 59 = G III 15/19–20. (The translator has added 'of reason': the Latin is just *lumine naturali*.)
[19] Popkin, *The History of Scepticism*, p. 245.
[20] H. G. Hubbeling, *Spinoza's Methodology* (Assen: Van Gorcum, 1967), p. 35.

response to Cartesian doubt: his view of what we can know about nature. At the end, we can return to look at his assumptions about intelligibility: what nature enables us to know.

It was not Spinoza but Descartes who wrote:

The fact that an atheist can be 'clearly aware that the three angles of a triangle are equal to two right angles' is something I do not dispute. But I maintain that this awareness of his is not true knowledge [*scientia*], since no act of awareness that can be rendered doubtful seems fit to be called knowledge. Now since we are supposing that this individual is an atheist, he cannot be certain that he is not being deceived on matters which seem to him very evident . . . And although this doubt may not occur to him, it can still crop up if someone else raises the point or if he looks into the matter himself. So he will never be free of this doubt until he acknowledges that God exists.[21]

So God had an apparently unavoidable place in human knowing.

Descartes himself was well aware of the problems that could be created by his thinking in this area, as we know from his responses to charges of circularity in the *Objections and Replies* to the *Meditations* and from his late *Conversation with Burman*. I prove that God exists by means of clear conceptions; but my clear conception is validated by God's existence. Descartes's attitude is not our concern now. But we should note what Spinoza took Descartes's attitude to be. In the *Prolegomenon* to the *Principles of Philosophy Demonstrated in the Geometric Manner* he referred to remarks by Descartes about the uncertainty of memory. He represented Descartes as relying on the validity of immediate, continuous, clear perception:

although God's existence cannot come to be known through itself, but only through something else, we will be able to attain a certain knowledge of his existence so long as we attend very accurately to all the premises from which we have inferred it. See *Principles* I, 13; *Reply to the Second Objections*, 3, and the *Fifth Meditation*, at the end.[22]

In effect, that would be an insistence that clear and distinct conception cannot be trumped or outflanked while it is being used.

Spinoza went on to mention, perhaps ironically, that 'this answer does not satisfy some people' and offered an alternative, to be considered later

---

[21] *Second Replies*, CSMK II 101 = AT VII 141, Descartes quotes from Mersenne.
[22] Curley, p. 236 = G I 147.

in this chapter. The disentangling of his own position from his view of Descartes's position in this early work cannot be decisive; but his approach is interesting. He saw that immediate intuition alone as a guarantee of knowledge *did* present problems. He did not say that they were insoluble, but he did see a point in offering another line of support. He would not do this if he thought that clear and distinct perception was the only way of dealing with doubt. More bluntly: dogmatism was not enough.

It scarcely seems credible that the author of the *Principles of Philosophy Demonstrated in the Geometric Manner* could have misunderstood Descartes so badly as not to have seen the force of hyperbolic doubt. The pages headed *Liberation from all Doubts* in his *Prolegomenon* portray the force of Descartes's point as fairly as anyone could wish.

In reality, Spinoza felt more strongly than Descartes about the fallibility of the senses and of the imagination. Whereas Descartes made use of the factual evidence familiar to any reader of ancient scepticism, Spinoza produced a fully worked-out psychological–physiological theory to explain the weaknesses of sense-perception and imagination. Descartes's subsequent vindication of *scientia* through the beneficence of God would leave a cautious reader puzzled as to why God did not trouble to finish his task by underwriting sense-perception and imagination as well as rational judgment. The theory of error, designed to cover this inexplicable failure by God, rested on a flimsy and undefended dichotomy between things taught by nature and other things 'which in reality I acquired not from nature but from a habit of making ill-considered judgments; and it is therefore quite possible that these are false'.[23] It is not surprising that some commentators have wondered whether Descartes even really believed this sort of thing himself.[24]

Spinoza's classification of knowledge *left* sense-perception and imagination as inadequate, if taken alone. An important factor in his attitude to doubt was his acceptance of the standard sceptical line on sense-perception. For him, the traditional paraphernalia of dreams and illusions were not to be put aside as unfortunate aberrations. They were welcomed as support in his scorn for empiricism. He had no wish to instate guarantees (divine or physiological) for the accuracy of what we see, hear or picture to ourselves. He had no thought that the deliverances of sense-perception *could* have been the sole or unsupported basis for a

---

[23] *Sixth Meditation*, CSMK II 56 = AT VII 82.
[24] The most well-known example is Hiram Caton, as in *The Origin of Subjectivity* (New Haven: Yale, 1973).

coherent, non-chaotic understanding of the world, though they could contribute to such an understanding.[25] In this sense he, not Descartes, was 'plus sceptique que les sceptiques'. Because for him sense-perception was never where we should start in a knowledge of nature,[26] unreliability in sense-perception (or in imagination linked to it) had no crucial significance.

We can imagine some sort of response to scepticism about sense-perception along the lines that a consistent ('clear and distinct') picture of physical reality would not be available – walking through walls in dreams and bent sticks in optical illusions may not fit a coherent account of physical reality. Maybe it is significant that this line of thought is *not* found in Spinoza.[27] His attitude looks both too brief and too dogmatic: 'after demonstrating that the human body exists just as we sense it, we may not doubt experience'.[28] And that attitude, of course, must be part of the cause of the poor reputation of his theory of knowledge. Many subsequent philosophers worried about sense perception *a lot*. In so far as Spinoza had a response to Cartesian doubt, it was not a rejection of the possibility of either perceptual error or the capacity of the imagination to represent non-actual situations.

His attitude towards extreme doubt about rationality looks even more liberal. It can seem as though his approach was to agree enthusiastically with Descartes about the efficacy of clear and distinct conception but then to ignore Descartes's suggestion that clear and distinct conception might itself be liable to failure – or open to suspension – in ways that could not be conceived. This, we have seen already, is an incorrect reading, but we should not think that it is a surprising one. But in fact Spinoza's attitude was not that the prospect posed by extreme doubt needed an answer. In the *Ethics* he seemed to believe that the prospect could never arise; that there was no real problem to be answered. The view of Kant that scepticism might be 'a resting-place for human reason', to be overcome by subsequent arguments,[29] would have had no appeal. Extreme scepticism was, literally, an unattainable position, even for the sake of argument.

We need to see why this was.

---

[25] See, at length, C. De Deugd, *The Significance of Spinoza's First Kind of Knowledge* (Assen: Van Gorcum, 1966), also Amihud Gilead, 'The Indispensability of the First Kind of Knowledge', in Yovel (ed.), *Spinoza on Knowledge*.   [26] *Ethics* II, 10, Corollary, Scholium, to be discussed later.

[27] Though maybe it is in Berkeley: *Principles of Human Knowledge*, I, §§29–34.

[28] *Ethics* II, 17, Corollary, Scholium, referring back to II, 13, Corollary.

[29] In so far as this applies to reason rather than perception, Hubbeling thought Spinoza *commended* doubt about perception: *Spinoza's Methodology*, p. 35. Kant: *Critique of Pure Reason*, A761.

Some of Spinoza's own explanations, it has to be said, are not compelling. For example, he denies that 'we have free power to suspend judgment. For when we say that someone suspends judgment, we are saying only that he sees that he is not adequately perceiving the thing. So suspension of judgment is really a perception, not free will'[30] – and his explanation for this was short and not convincing alone: we can imagine something non-existent, but if we try to conceive it clearly – or even, perhaps, to think hard about it as if it *did* exist – we will see that our idea is 'inadequate'. Very surprisingly, the chosen example was not of something impossible (a square circle or a never-ending circular staircase) but just of something that happens not to exist and which is not even biologically impossible (so to speak), or totally unlikely: a winged horse. No laws of nature that Spinoza could have imagined at that time actually ruled out winged horses, and he could have seen stranger things through his microscope at any time. The 'free power of suspending judgment' is of virtually no interest in such examples.

At least three better lines of argument were available to him. We can look first at their underlying rationale and then at whether this gives an accurate view of his contribution.

THE DEMON

The use of the deceiving demon by Descartes, or the supposition of the non-benevolent action of God, was *essentially* non-natural or supernatural, not incidentally. Descartes was unable to represent to himself the possibility that he was mistaken while perceiving clearly. By natural means it was impossible, but by supposing a supernatural intervention he could portray or construct a possibility that it might have been possible. Putting his point in extreme terms – which is surely what he intended – anyone, using the most concentrated clear and distinct perception, might see something as true; but it would still be possible to represent the possibility of deception by the intervention of some agency that, *ex hypothesi*, could not be represented.

That position should be distinguished from two weaker ones mentioned by Descartes in his *Second Replies*.

First, he had no interest in the idea that clear and distinct perception – the best we can manage, as it were – could be systematically in error – it

---

[30] *Est igitur judicii suspensio reverâ perceptio, non libera voluntas; Ethics* II, 49, Corollary, Demonstration, Scholium.

might *never* be right – and that truth was really only accessible to 'God or an angel'.[31] His attitude – 'the evident clarity of our perceptions does not allow us to listen to anyone who makes up this kind of story' – might have struck some of his medieval predecessors as a little brisk.

Secondly, there were his unconvincing appeals to the weakness of memory. His genuinely powerful logical point was the introduction of second-order, possible error. A thought that we might be systematically or randomly forgetting steps in our arguments or calculations has the air of a desperate attempt to leap out of the Cartesian circle. That type of argument did not impress Spinoza.

It is important to see *why* Descartes's demon had to be an essentially non-natural device. The whole force of clear and distinct conception derived from the thought that it was the best we can do. This itself was a belief that rested on factual assumptions about the constitution of humanity – *we* are all made up in roughly the same way, within reasonably well-appreciated limits. The sense of Descartes's arguments suggests a picture of the best-equipped, most clear-sighted mind, concentrating to its best ability in the most ideal circumstances and then conceiving a truth to be true.[32] Even then – we are asked to suppose – it can be conjectured that some other agency might be producing an error, although there is no way for us to represent what that error might be. (If we could, of course, we *would* represent it.) So doubt becomes possible, and hence obligatory. The whole argument rests on a notion of limited natural capacity and then the supposition of its non-natural suspension. Every philosophy student's first lesson is that the demon was only an artificial device introduced to make a point; but it is as well for the student to go on to ask two further questions: what was the point? and why did Descartes need to resort to such bizarre means to make it? Starting with the familiar notion of known capacities, he posited superhuman capacities that were by definition beyond our access. At first sight this only seems open-mindedly liberal: maybe we can't think of everything; why not try the supposition that there are some things we can't conceive? Isn't it only dogmatism to deny that?

We should see where Descartes's position took him: towards an assumption of some plane of sense or explanation that was unintelligible

---

[31] *Second Replies*, CSMK II 104 = AT VII 146. The argument is discussed interestingly in S. Gaukroger, *Cartesian Logic* (Oxford: Clarendon Press, 1989), pp. 63–9.

[32] And buried beneath that assumption may be another one, still more threatening to Descartes's case, that an objective form – 'our judgment' – is presupposed by subjective clear perception, since what 'I' perceive clearly is what a rational person would perceive.

or inaccessible by definition. This is much more than the modest thought that reason could fail. It was a permanent possibility that however much our natural capacities were refined, something beyond might overrule or impede them. That view presupposed, as we shall see shortly, a definite position on the nature of possibility. It also presupposed other positions on the inclusiveness of nature and on the completeness of explanation. What Descartes needed for his argument was a natural order *defined* as finite and a God by definition not limited by any canons of explanation accessible to us. As Sherlock Holmes put it shrewdly, in *The Devil's Foot*: 'if the matter is beyond humanity it is certainly beyond me . . . we must exhaust all natural explanations before we fall back upon such a theory as this'.

THE POSSIBILITY OF DOUBT

Secondly: Descartes's supposition was that he *could* represent to himself *the possibility that* even his *best* perceptions *might* be mistaken. He supposed that he could suspend his judgment about his perceptions. (And that he could conceive ideas clearly without making judgments about them.) Supposition for him could consist only of some form of representation to himself of a possibility. But what room was there for that in his metaphysics, or even his psychology? His fallible imagination had already been trumped in the method of doubt by the presence of clear and distinct perceptions. Those perceptions in turn could not be trumped again by imagination: that would have been circular. On the other hand, his supposition could not be strengthened into a clear and distinct conception. It was, after all, as a counterfactual, false, and should have been obvious as such. So the supposition should have been ruled out of court.

Despite this, maybe Descartes could make use of some wholly different form of representation, outside the confines of his metaphysics? But that would be another way of stating the former point – that his demon had to be an essentially, not incidentally, non-natural device. A conception that is not possible naturally might be possible non-naturally. Superficially, that might not seem too bad an outcome. Non-natural possibility, viewed in a generous light, looks not too different from some later notions, like thoughts in the infinite mind of God, or truth in other possible worlds. Having satisfied himself that truth seemed to be available through the best natural apparatus – clear and distinct conception – why *couldn't* Descartes postulate non-natural circumstances in which that apparatus *might* fail?

Quite apart from the problems just mentioned, that escape was barred. To see this, we need to focus once again on the notion of possibility. For Descartes, as for many philosophers, it was closely allied to a notion of representability or intelligibility: 'It seems very clear to me that possible existence is contained in everything which we clearly understand, because from the fact that we clearly understand something it follows that it can be created by God.'[33]

This sense of possibility was an ancestor of the later idea of *logical* possibility. And possibility seen in terms of representability allows no access to higher-order, 'possible' possibility: how might the possibility of a higher-order possibility be represented? Not, obviously, in terms of imagination. Imagination is no touchstone for truths even at the most basic level where clear and distinct perceptions are supposed to work. I may, for example, be totally unable to *imagine* how the theorem of Pythagoras could apply to some shapes of right-angled triangles; but I know that it does.

Nor, more seriously, will clear and distinct perception do what Descartes would need. The story he would need to tell would be that he *could* conceive of God possibly conceiving the possible falsity of something he (Descartes) himself clearly conceived to be true. And this would not work.[34] The problem illustrates the weakness of a link between possibility and representability and, just as badly for Descartes, the difficulty in dissociating clear and distinct perception from visual imagination while at the same time relying on visual metaphors to explain it.[35]

Spinoza could be on firmer ground. But not because of his theory about affirmation or judgment that might look to be his overt response: he suggested that suspension of beliefs was contradictory where we really affirm them to be true.[36] We can see what that meant, and it had a value, but it also looks as though it could do rather more than he wished, such as ruling out counterfactual suppositions in geometrical proofs by *reductio ad absurdum*.

More interestingly, it was his views about possibility, discussed in the

---

[33] Letter to Mersenne, 1640 CSMK III 166 = AT III 274: *Il me semble bien clair qu'existentia possibilis continetur in omni eo quod clarè intelligimus, quia ex hoc ipso quod clarè intelligimus, sequitur illud à Deo posse creari.*

[34] The issue was aired, none too decisively, in Descartes's letter to Mesland of 2 May 1644; CSMK III 235 = AT IV 118–19.

[35] A contradiction much exploited by Descartes. Contrast his letter to Mersenne of July 1641 (CSMK III 186 = AT III 395): 'whatever we conceive without an image is an idea of the pure mind', with, most strikingly, *Rule Nine for the Direction of the Mind*: 'We must concentrate our mind's eye . . . to acquire the habit of intuiting the truth clearly and distinctly' (CSMK I 33 = AT X 400).

[36] *Ethics*, II, 49, Corollary, Scholium. John Cottingham argues that, in any case, Spinoza did not differ from Descartes as much on this point as he thought: 'The Intellect, the Will and the Passions: Spinoza's Critique of Descartes', *Journal of the History of Philosophy*, 26, 1988.

previous chapter, that could be helpful. He did not, as we saw, tie possibility to what could be imagined or conceived. What was possible for him was what could follow from – or simply happen in – a particular state of affairs. The most plausible form of understanding is in geometrical terms – there are an infinite number of *possible* chords of a circle; it is *not possible* to trisect an angle with compasses and a ruler. As we saw, this view of possibility is much nearer to a prosaic view of *what is allowable* or *what can happen* than a view of logical possibility in terms of *what can be represented*.

The relevance of this should be plain. What happens (and what is true) in accordance with nature will be conceivable by clear and distinct perception. What is possible – what can happen or what can be true – will not be determinable by the use of our imaginations. It will be determined by calculation or experiment. This is why Descartes's demon can be ignored. The possibility presented by it would be an illicit one. The reason why we need not raise the possibility that clear and distinct perception *might* itself be thrown into doubt is not just dogmatism. It is because Spinoza can place a construction on *might* – on the nature of this modality – which makes it of no significant interest. I can of course *imagine* the demon making chaos of rationality; but there is no worthwhile link between *that* sort of imagining and what can happen or what might be true.

Such a line of thinking need not be seen just as an assertion that there are rules of mathematics or physics which are so immutable that we can't even suspend our belief in them for the sake of argument. It can be seen more constructively as offering some understanding of a notion of possibility outside the cul-de-sac offered by any analogy with representability. To make the demon threatening, an inference is needed from 'Descartes can represent to himself the operation of the demon' to 'The operation of the demon is possible', and Descartes could have no support for that inference.[37] Spinoza might have had access to a view of possibility that ruled it out.

REASONS TO DOUBT

Thirdly, a general case can be made by considering the *reasons for doubt* in Descartes's arguments. The method of doubt did not rely upon a use of

---

[37] Its modal logic can be seen in one of Descartes's most famous arguments: 'the fact that I can clearly and distinctly understand one thing apart from another is enough to make me certain that the two things are distinct, since they are capable of being separated, at least by God' (*Sixth Meditation*, CSMK II 54 = AT VII 78).

equipollence familiar in ancient scepticism: there are reasons for *a*, reasons against *a* (or for *not-a*), so we would do well to suspend our belief in *a* (and *not-a*). Descartes used the strong principle that doubt is advisable where any possibility of doubt can be introduced. This was far stronger than the thought that we should doubt only if there are more reasons to doubt than not to doubt. Applied to sense-perception, and to the judgments said to be derived from it, this strong principle can be persuasive. There will seldom be more reasons to doubt my senses than not to doubt them; but there may often be *some* reason to doubt them. Hence the appeal of the image of rotten apples in a basket used by Descartes.[38]

There is no need to comment on the use of this line of argument with sense-perception. Spinoza seemed to have accepted it in that his caution about empirical knowledge went well beyond Descartes. The point of interest is the application to rationality, or to clear and distinct perception.

Plainly, there are *not* more reasons *for* the likelihood of the machinations of a deceiving demon than there are reasons *against* them. If the issue were a balance of probabilities there would be no problem. The suggestion is that *any* likelihood is a threat. This looks a good argument. Using a modern parallel, I do not need a 50:50 possibility that there is a virus in my computer before I get worried. *Any* possibility at all is bad news: I have to check to find out.

But this does not work with reason itself. Clear and distinct perception is presented by Descartes as the best natural means for the detection of truth. Suspension of belief in it needs to be rational, in the minimal sense of being persuasive for *some* reason, in the vaguest sense. If I am very worried about the fate of this writing on my word-processor, I may check my computer for viruses every day, in case someone has stolen into my home to introduce one overnight. If I do this every hour, while continuously in the room with my (new, un-networked) computer, my behaviour is ill-supported to the point of neurosis: if someone asks for an explanation of my behaviour I can't give it. And the point about the demon is much stronger than that. Descartes gave every reason to believe in his clear and distinct perception. He would not introduce doubt there – in analogy with the doubt he had applied to sense-perception – because of the possibility of occasional errors – since this, for him, was ruled out *ex hypothesi*. So doubt had to consist of the suspension of credence in the whole apparatus.

---

[38] *Seventh Objections and Replies*, CSMK II 324 = AT VII 481.

What was the support for this? We have seen that Descartes had to
appeal to non-natural reasons and to a representational notion of
possibility. To make credible his suspension of belief in his clear and distinct perception he needed to offer *some* kind of persuasion to weigh in
the balance against his overwhelming confidence in his rational apparatus. (A non-natural suspension of belief places a burden of proof on
anyone who wants to show why it is worth considering, not why it is not.)
The criterion of persuasiveness to be applied was not evident, and was
certainly less a priori than Descartes hoped. Just as, factually, for
instance, there are people for whom neither his *cogito* nor the arguments
from dreams will work at all,[39] so it must be a matter of context (not logic)
to say what counts as adequate persuasion. Popkin mentions the likely
origin of the demon in the witch-hunts of the 1630s.[40] This is not just an
irrelevant detail. To get *some* support for his suspension of belief,
Descartes had to have *some* form of explanatory context or narrative.[41]
No reason at all would have had no persuasive power.

There is one obvious reason why Spinoza would reject this. His correspondence shows us how little any appeal to supernatural agencies
would have had for him: this will be pursued in Part II. Many now might
agree, to the extent that it is hard to envisage the mental world in which
Descartes's imagery could have had any influence. We may still try,
though, to modernise the explanatory context. Hypnosis, mental or
neurological illness, perhaps, might derange my rationality at any time;
perhaps it is doing so now.[42]

But there are two important things wrong here. First, both Descartes
and Spinoza would agree – and so would we, in a different idiom – that if
my present conception is rationally disordered, then even if I don't
realise this, it can't be clear and distinct. This is not simply a reversion to
crude intuitionism, but a reminder that clear and distinct conception
must incorporate some attention to minimal consistency of beliefs. Such
consistency may fall far short of the demands of a coherence theory of
truth. There is also the associated thought[43] that 'the evidence of truths'
can be prior to their 'epistemic credentials'. *No one* wants to posit the

[39] People not capable of the required level of rational reflection, for example, and (more unclearly)
    people who have never experienced a dream.   [40] *History of Scepticism*, p. 180 and note 38.
[41] Here, rationality is narrowed to the possibility to tell any kind of explanatory story, however far-
    fetched.
[42] Peter Unger, for instance, thinks the demon can be modernised in much this way: *Ignorance*
    (Oxford: Clarendon Press, 1975), pp. 7–8. Bernard Williams apparently agrees: *Descartes*
    (Harmondsworth: Penguin, 1978), p. 56.
[43] Well argued by Martha Bolton, 'Spinoza on Cartesian Doubt', *Noûs*, 19, 1985, p. 392.

possibility of a (deluded) clear and distinct perception that 3 + 2 = 6. The whole point about clear and distinct perception, after all, is that it has *passed* a test of what we might call superficial rationality.[44]

Secondly, there is the much more telling point that an argument will not project from perception to rationality. It is not hard to persuade me – if I am due to be a witness in court, for example – that my perceptual judgments may be less than 100 per cent reliable, and that dogmatism about them is inadvisable. Any doubt will do. In Cartesian terms, suspending belief in sense-perception still leaves me with rational judgment. Suspending belief in rational judgment leaves me with nothing, to the extent that this suspension itself is not operating rationally. And then the facile objection – but why not suspend judgment *irrationally*? – betrays its own mistake. The answer is: because there is no reason to do so.[45]

The logic here – and the logic available to Spinoza – can be misleading. It is not pragmatic, in the sense that being rational, or just consistent, works better than being non-rational. And it is not circular, in the sense that it is rational to be rational. The point, in minimal terms, is that if you purport to be rational at all, then you need some reasons to suspend that rationality. These reasons need not be demonstrations or even reasoned arguments, but they do need to be *some* sort of considerations that have some power that is persuasive by criteria you claim to accept:

Those who deny to themselves a faculty for sound reasoning cannot claim to prove their assertion by reasoning. And if they claim for themselves some supra-rational faculty, this is the merest fiction, and far inferior to reason.[46]

This is very far from 'rationalism' in a pejorative sense.

SPINOZA'S CASE

Three lines of argument have been outlined that Spinoza might have used to block Cartesian doubt: from the non-naturalism of extreme doubt; from the type of modality it implied, and from considerations

[44] Some go further, holding that a divine guarantee was meant to apply 'to all, and only, those beliefs that satisfy our best possible criterion of truth, which, according to Descartes, is the test of clear and distinct perception': Maudmarie Clark, *Nietzsche on Truth and Philosophy* (Cambridge University Press, 1990), p. 52.
[45] This echoes a view attributed to Descartes by Harry Frankfurt. The argument is said to be 'an attempt to show that there are no good reasons for believing that reason is unreliable': 'Descartes' Validation of Reason', *American Philosophical Quarterly*, 2, 1965, p. 155.
[46] S 123 = G III 80/20–22.

about the reasons why doubt should arise. All three have the same tendency: not that extreme doubt can be answered, but that it can or should
never occur.

How clearly can we find these arguments in Spinoza? We need to pay
attention to three texts in particular: *The Treatise on the Emendation of the
Intellect*, the *Prolegomenon* to the *Principles of Philosophy Demonstrated in the
Geometrical Manner* and the end of Part II of the *Ethics*.[47]

We need to notice a development in Spinoza's viewpoint. In the
Treatise, he seemed uncertain about the possibility of doubt. He differen-
tiated real doubt in the mind (*vera dubitatione in mente*) from 'what we commonly see happen, when someone says in words that he doubts,
although his mind does not doubt'. But he then went on to say that 'all
doubt is removed' when we see that an idea is clear and distinct. In particular, knowledge of God, of the kind that we have of the nature of a
triangle, is sufficient to 'remove every doubt we can have concerning
clear and distinct ideas'.[48] What he meant was maybe that we can *believe*
we can have doubts about clear ideas, or *say* this, but if we think about
them we will realise that we cannot. Doubt can at least be supposed, if
only in an illusory form. His presentation of Descartes's argument in the
Prolegomenon makes it hard to see whether he still maintained that view
there.[49]

Later, in Part II of the *Ethics*, the position was different: doubt could
not arise because the suspension of clear and distinct ideas is not available. As we have seen, Spinoza denied 'that we have a free power of suspending judgment'.[50] The difference is a fine one, a matter of clearing an
ambiguity, but it is significant. The impression is that even a mistaken
possibility of doubt was removed. It was a mistake to think we can even
pretend to suspend belief in clear and distinct ideas. If an idea is really
apprehended then it is apprehended as clear and distinct.[51] If it is apprehended as clear and distinct then the supposition of its falsehood is not
available. So there is no room for doubt. What Spinoza may have been
doing was not ruling out doubt by intensified dogmatism, but focusing
his thought in the areas that have been mentioned: how could hyperbolic
doubt fit into the view of nature he had developed? What could its place
be? Not in nature; so, for Spinoza, nowhere. This is an important conceptual point in discussing the possibility of doubt. Alan Gewirth

---

[47] A little was said in the *Short Treatise* II, xv, §§3–4, but that added nothing.

[48] §79, p. 254 = G II 30.

[49] Although a remark at the end of his argument, about to be discussed, suggests that he had seen its
weakness: G I 149/14.   [50] *Ethics* II, 49, Corollary, Scholium; G II 134/11.   [51] *Ethics* II, 43.

claimed that Descartes showed the 'logical impossibility of general doubt'.[52] But if doubt was logically impossible, how was Descartes able to make use of it? And how could it have been at all tempting? If something is completely impossible it should be completely ruled out, not half-discussed.

Next, we should consider the arguments used for the 'Liberation from all doubts' in the *Prolegomenon* to the *Principles of Philosophy*. As seen earlier, Spinoza stated a problem in entirely Cartesian terms:

Since God's existence does not become known to us through itself, we seem unable to be ever certain of anything; nor will we ever be able to come to know God's existence. For we have said that everything is uncertain so long as we are ignorant of our origin, and from uncertain premises, nothing certain can be inferred.[53]

'To remove this difficulty, Descartes makes the following reply', he said, and went on to give a fair representation of Descartes's unhappy evasions about the fallibility of memory. But, 'since this answer does not satisfy some people', Spinoza then gave another reply. As Curley comments, that reply was 'at least consistent with Cartesian principles'.[54] Spinoza, in effect, put the Cartesian case as well as it could be put. A clear and distinct idea of God – not a knowledge of God's existence – is enough to remove the possibility of doubt.

But the final lines of this important text took a jarring step into Spinoza's direct speech and then added a significant turn to his argument:

we have a clear and distinct idea of a Triangle, although we do not know whether the author of our nature deceives us; and provided we have such an idea . . . we will be able to doubt neither his existence, nor any Mathematical truth.[55]

So, not only is the idea of God enough; the idea of a triangle will do just as well.

It is not the *origin* of our clear and distinct ideas that matters.[56] The whole notion of God as a supernatural guarantor 'supremely good and veracious' is wholly out of keeping with Spinoza's metaphysics. Rather, the point of Spinoza's apparent afterthought to his exposition of Descartes must have been that knowledge of *any* clear and distinct idea

---

[52] 'The Cartesian Circle', *The Philosophical Review*, 50, 1941, p. 394.   [53] Curley, p. 236 = G I 146.
[54] Curley, p. 236, note 8.   [55] Curley, p. 238 = G I 149/11–15.
[56] This is the case argued by Willis Doney, 'Spinoza on Philosophical Scepticism', in M. Mandelbaum and E. Freeman (eds.), *Spinoza: Essays in Interpretation* (La Salle: Open Court, 1975).

is enough to remove the possibility of a general suspension of reason. Far from being consistent with Descartes's opinions, this would be inconsistent with them (or at least with some of them, since it would be over-generous to suggest that they are consistent). Spinoza's thought was that a real understanding of anything – that is, of any part of nature, for example, geometry – will be inconsistent with the kind of anomalies entailed by the supposition that 'the author of our nature deceives us'.

The disentangling of Spinoza's views from his exposition of Descartes will always remain open for debate. We can turn to the *Ethics* for a better picture.

Even there, his discussion of doubt could have been more explicit. The order of his thinking ought to strike us first. His earlier exposition of Descartes not only opened in a Cartesian spirit, but it had a preface, wholly supplementary to the main argument, dealing with doubt. Its opening words could not have been more direct:

> Before we come to the Propositions themselves and their Demonstrations, it seems desirable to explain concisely why Descartes doubted everything, how he brought to light solid foundations for the sciences, and finally, by what means he freed himself from all doubts.[57]

It is not easy to believe that those words could have been written by anyone who had not seen the importance that could be given to philosophical doubt. But then, speaking for himself in the *Ethics*, Spinoza dealt with doubt only at the end of Part II. This could only mean that he did not share the view of Descartes that doubt has to be removed before philosophy can begin. We have seen his own view on 'the order of Philosophizing'.[58] The error of some previous philosophers (who must be taken to include Descartes), as we have seen, was that 'they believed that [the] divine nature which they should have contemplated before all else – being prior both in cognition and in Nature – they have taken to be the last in the order of cognition'. And that view is well reflected by the order of the *Ethics*. God or nature comes first, the mind second: 'our intellect and knowledge depend solely on the idea or knowledge of God, and spring from it and are perfected by it'.[59] Doubt, far from coming first, could not even be fitted into nature.[60]

---

[57] *Descartes' Principles of Philosophy*, Curley, p. 131 = G I 141.   [58] *Ethics* II, 10, Corollary, Scholium.
[59] S 110 = G III 67/27–9.
[60] An echo of Don Garrett, 'Truth and Ideas of Imagination in the *Tractatus de Intellectus Emendatione*', *Studia Spinozana*, 2, 1986, p. 71.

THE PRIORITY OF KNOWLEDGE

What we see in the *Ethics* is the construction of a framework in which extreme doubt will not fit. That is not to say, implausibly, that doubt was just defined out of existence. Perception, supposition, imagination, conception and doubt had their places in an understood picture of nature, both logically and psychologically. What was possible was seen as what could be related to that picture. To wonder about imagined possibilities was therefore pointless.

This was not solely a matter of an ordering of priorities – as if it were possible to decide to give preference to an understanding of nature over a knowledge of nature (of metaphysics over epistemology) or not, according to taste. It was more a matter of setting a framework in which doubt had some meaningful content. The capacity of Descartes to tell himself stories could not be questioned. You can tell stories about goblins or werewolves; but it is as well to conduct some further inquiries before being frightened by them. The logic of a step from an imaginary narrative to a genuinely disturbing possibility was never made explicit by Descartes. For Spinoza, that step would not work at all.

The secondary priority given by Spinoza to questions about knowledge is not irrelevant, even though it cannot be cited on its own without circularity in support of his case against Descartes. *How things are* was to be discussed before asking *how we know*. This was not some anachronistic preference for medieval dogmatism, as Popkin's critical remarks seem to suggest. But the principles underlying Spinoza's choice of perspective are not easy to identify. His repudiation of a method of doubt meant that he had no reason to start a view of the world from his own consciousness. Descartes had written that 'We must begin with the rational soul, for all our knowledge resides in it; and after considering its nature and effects, we shall proceed to its author.'[61] In contrast, Spinoza's implicit order of thought, in the most abstract terms, was: nature exists – people exist in nature – people have various sorts of knowledge.

Maybe only a philosopher would think that such an order needs further comment. By the end of Part II of the *Ethics*, Spinoza felt able to assume that knowledge is possible, in the sense that he had fitted together a story about a working perceptual and cognitive apparatus which, as part of nature, could deliver and validate truths. He was not begging the question by taking this for granted in Part I of the *Ethics*, because he was

---

[61] *The Search after Truth*, CSMK II 405 = AT x 505.

never able to ascribe any force to a possible failure in knowledge. It was not as though doubt was possible until it had been dispatched at the end of Part II. It was never possible; it never had been possible.

Nevertheless, strong claims about God or nature were made at the beginning of the *Ethics*, and we can ask about their basis, even if we do not want to adopt an egocentric, Cartesian perspective. We might suspect, for example, that even if there are no suppressed assumptions about what we can *know*, there might still be some assumptions about our *understanding* of nature. Spinoza seemed to take for granted that we are constructed so that we can understand how things are, and that nature is constructed so that it can be understood. In principle, nothing is to be mysterious. Nothing is to be, in principle, beyond our comprehension. Once again: 'our approach to the understanding of the nature of things of every kind should . . . be one and the same; namely, through the universal laws and rules of Nature'.[62]

Einstein is supposed to have said that the most incomprehensible thing about nature is its comprehensibility.[63] Some of the most acute commentators on Spinoza have commented that the intelligibility of nature is the basic principle in his thought. Alexandre Matheron has called it the *leitmotiv* of the *Ethics*. Stuart Hampshire has said that the question from which Spinozism begins is 'What must we suppose if Nature as a whole is to be regarded as completely intelligible?'[64]

We might imagine that these thoughts reveal a significant chink in the armour of Spinoza's system, opening another channel for scepticism: even if *knowledge* is satisfactorily fortified, maybe our *understanding* could fail in some radical way? Couldn't there be facts about nature that we will never be able to understand because of our limited mental powers? Couldn't there be entire ways of understanding nature that we can neither know nor understand? Anyone who wants to refer to the infinity of God, for example, might be very likely to have this sort of thinking in mind – that there is something about God which is beyond our comprehension. Yet Spinoza, it seems, from the outset, assumed exactly the opposite. Isn't that the ground level of his dogmatism?

His views about intelligibility can be pieced together fairly easily.

---

[62] *Ethics* III, Preface.
[63] G. N. Schlesinger, *The Intelligibility of Nature* (Aberdeen University Press, 1985), p. xiii.
[64] A. Matheron, *Individu et communauté*, p. 9; Hampshire, *Spinoza*, p. 218; also Gueroult, *Spinoza* I, p. 12.

Things are known or understood through knowing their 'causes' – 'The knowledge of an effect depends on, and involves, the knowledge of the cause.'[65] There is only one, connected, system of causes. Or rather, there can be no separated, discrete causal systems, either outside or within nature.

These premises or assumptions stemmed from no single starting-point, but were embodied in the opening propositions of Part I of the *Ethics*. That fact may seem strange, given the attention lavished by Spinoza on his geometrical presentation. We might wonder, for example, why an apparently crucial assumption is mentioned only in passing, rather than as a fundamental axiom: 'For each single existent thing there must necessarily be a definite cause for its existence' and 'For every thing a cause or reason must be assigned either for its existence or for its non-existence.'[66]

The impression is that nature is intelligible in the sense that everything must have a cause or reason; that nothing can be uncaused because nothing can be outside a single system of causality. Which hardly sounds satisfactory. In fact, it sounds both dogmatic and circular. John McDowell notes that

If we identify nature with what natural science aims to make comprehensible, we threaten, at least, to empty it of meaning. By way of compensation, so to speak, we see it as the home of a perhaps inexhaustible supply of intelligibility of the . . . kind we find in a phenomenon when we see it as governed by natural law.[67]

Yet if being 'governed by natural law' and being intelligible are, as in Spinoza's case, so close together as to be inseparable, there seems to be a problem.

INTELLIGIBILITY: THE ASSUMPTIONS

We can find three lines of thinking in Spinoza which are relevant in response to that thought.

First, his thinking about infinity[68] shows that he had a clear grasp of what he wanted to consider as intelligible and what he did not. In one way, much of nature was *not* intelligible to us, as a matter of fact. Chains or networks of causes or explanations are endless; our understanding is

[65] *Ethics* I, Axiom 4. [66] *Ethics* I, 8, Scholium 2; I, 11 Demonstration 2.
[67] *Mind and World* (Cambridge: Harvard University Press, 1994), pp. 70–1.
[68] In Letter 12, *On the Infinite*, and in Part I of the *Ethics* – mostly 15, Scholium.

limited; so we can[69] only understand limited proportions of what is happening and why. That should not be controversial. What Spinoza refused to regard as mysterious was the fact of an infinite series. There may be an uncountable number of points between two curves. That, to him, seemed to be a graspable and unmysterious image of the infinite. What he sought to do was to find a useful sense for the idea of something *without limit*. His reliance on a mathematical metaphor was clever, in that an uncountable collection of points is an intelligible image both for something we can grasp clearly and for something unmysterious which we cannot.

Similarly, his doctrine of the infinite unknown attributes (discussed in Chapter 1) was a matter-of-fact expression of the thought that we can understand nature in some ways, but that there may be other ways of understanding it which we have not yet understood. This boils mystery down to the truism that we do not know everything.

Secondly, the notion of nature as cause of itself may have had some relevance here. Things are either caused or self-caused. The question, why are things as they are? will always be answerable in terms of natural science – causes should always be available, although there can be no guarantee that any specific series of causes can ever be within someone's grasp. A question such as, why is it raining today? can be answered to some degree of detail. The infinite, necessarily missing, causal detail is not unintelligible: there is just far too much of it. The question, why is everything as it is? though, has no answer; not because it strays into a zone of mystery, but because nature as such is supposed to be its own cause. The only constructive sense we can give to that idea is that no external – that is, non-natural – cause is to be sought.

A third assumption is contained in the identity of *cause* and *reason*: another of Spinoza's terminological compressions that carry so much theoretical weight in his philosophy.

We have seen in the previous chapter that he started not from the truth of what might be said about nature, but from nature. His interest was in 'the analysis of causality' rather than with 'the logical form of causal statements'.[70] We can see some of the reasons for this, but we may feel less confident about how far he was able to get away with it.

He gave no account of any difference in sense between *causa* and *ratio* which might help us, and no account of the similarity in sense which we

[69] As we have seen, Spinoza's thinking on modality removes any distinction between *can* 'in practice' and 'in principle'.
[70] Cited from Davidson, 'Causal Relations'; see Chapter 2 above, p. 75.

must understand from *causa, seu ratio*. His preference for concreteness and for the priority of proximate causes[71] may have reinforced his view that *causa* and *ratio* are the same: as if, on some basic level, it could be possible to say why things exist or happen by simply identifying and enunciating chains of causes.[72] It seems natural to read his views, in modern terms, as at least a strong preference for a particular causal explanation, or a wish to reduce all forms of explanation to the listing of causes. Yet in modern terms, it seems natural to point out that explanations are not, after all, causes. Causes *make things happen* while explanations *say* why they happen. *Making happen* and *saying* are different. Things happen and we understand how they happen (partly or fully).

One modern way round this difference might be to argue that some (fundamental) forms of explanation are completely transparent, thus abolishing the gap between what happens and what may be said about it.[73] But that perspective is some way from Spinoza's and we should hesitate about associating him with it. It seems unavoidable that *causa* is a metaphysical, ontological notion and *ratio* is an unavoidably epistemological one. An explanation must always explain to *somebody*, if only 'in principle'; the wish for 'transparency' is surely an attempt to get around this.

A possible reading is that *causa* and *ratio* will be, along familiar Spinozist lines, the same thing taken in different ways. His view may have been that these two cannot be separated. Explanations will be available in the same sense as causes exist.

INTELLIGIBILITY: THE CONCLUSIONS

The feeling that there may be some entire perspective on nature that we have *not* grasped, or could not grasp, or that our whole understanding of nature might be defective in some large-scale way, beyond our comprehension, can be seen as a relic of a superstition that *everything* could be different. And that superstition could be rooted in turn in a feeling that nature – all there is – is *not* all there is – there may be *something* else. Yet that feeling is based not on an interesting paradox, but on a

---

[71] 'We ought to define and explain things through their proximate causes', S 101–2 = G III 58/19–20.

[72] This point is not elucidated at all by reference to earlier theories of *emanation* (Wolfson, *The Philosophy of Spinoza*, vol. I, pp. 373–5), since an emanation is no more an explanation than a cause. Perhaps a more useful historical analogy is in the Platonic *aitia*, which serves both as cause and explanation as a result of an origin in a notion of (moral) responsibility.

[73] See David-Hillel Ruben, *Explaining Explanation* (London: Routledge, 1990), pp. 160–8, for discussion.

simple confusion. The removal of the possibility of an external 'cause' for nature is the same as the removal of an external perspective on it. Without an external perspective, the allegedly remarkable fact that 'we' can understand nature looks a good deal less remarkable. 'Our' understanding is the only understanding that we understand, after all, so the threat that nature might be understood in some wholly different way is deprived of content.

Ernest Gellner pointed out that philosophical theorising in this territory faces in two directions. One way, there is the imagined intellectual threat of 'orderless chaos'. The other direction is towards magic, the possibility of rival, unrelated forms of understanding, explanation and control.[74] Gellner believed that there can be no proof to insure against chaos. Spinoza's approach supports that view. The possible assault on intelligibility threatened by Descartes's demon was seen as non-existent. Spinoza did not try to argue against Descartes, but instead provided a context in which the demon could not threaten.[75] Gellner's other direction is more real and more serious. The existence of a single, unified order of causality or explanation excludes 'magic', in that all explanations, in the end, will be expected to cohere without remainder. This needs some support.

Axiom 5 of Part I of the *Ethics* – 'Things which have nothing in common with each other cannot be understood through each other.' – is a principle of great logical force. A discrete, separated causal series – for example, as in magic – would be simply unintelligible: the means by which we understand – the grasping of causes or reasons – could make no contact.[76] Part I of the *Ethics* unravels the corollaries. The underlying thought must be exactly analogous to the case against Descartes's demon, if you *think* that you can conceive a detached order of causes then consider how that possibility is to be represented. You may *imagine* magical causality easily enough – stories can be told – but if you claim to be able to understand or conceive it, in what form can a narrative be assembled without inconsistencies?

---

[74] *Legitimation of Belief* (Cambridge University Press, 1974), pp. 124–7.

[75] In maybe too tidy a contrast, Harry Frankfurt concludes that 'Descartes substitutes the order in himself for the chaos in the world. Spinoza substitutes the order of the universe for the chaos within himself': 'Two Motivations for Rationalism: Descartes and Spinoza', in A. Donagan, A. N. Perovich and M. V. Wedin (eds.), *Human Nature and Human Knowledge* (Dordrecht: Reidel, 1986), p. 60.

[76] A later version: 'speakers of different languages may share a conceptual scheme provided there is a way of translating one language into the other', Donald Davidson, 'On the Very Idea of a Conceptual Scheme' (1974), in *Inquiries into Truth and Interpretation* (Oxford: Clarendon Press, 1984), p. 184.

The fate of the God of the Philosophers was a curiously ironic one. Spinoza took more seriously than anyone the assumption that God exists infinitely and that God stands in a relation of causality or explanation to what exists and happens. The consequence was that physics becomes possible. Nature can be understood. How and why things happen is not to be understood by anything external – even by anything as external as divine laws. Nature will be intelligible and we will be able to understand it. Nothing will be hidden or mysterious.

God becomes naturalised, but nature also becomes divine. We must return (in Chapter 6) to ask in which direction the identification of God with nature is to be understood. It is easy to assume that Spinoza must have preferred one direction to the other. At different times, admirers and critics have assumed both alternatives with equal certainty and enthusiasm.

PART II

The God of Abraham, of Isaac and of Jacob

Come, ᶜlet us reach an understanding,ᶜ – says the LORD.
(Footnote: ᶜ – ᶜ *meaning of Hebrew uncertain.*)

(Isaiah, 1: 18 (JPS))

CHAPTER 4

Final causes

NATURAL THEOLOGY AND RELIGION

Whatever we desire and do, whereof we are the cause in so far as we have the idea of God, that is, in so far as we know God, I refer to religion.[1]

Despite this apparently clear statement, for Spinoza, the connection between God, or knowledge of God – natural theology – and the human practice of religion was not simple or direct. Religion was seen as a human activity in society and in history, in terms of morality, social order and ritual. In the *Ethics*, where God appears from the first page, and where God's existence is allegedly proved, religion is scarcely mentioned. Where it is mentioned, this is sometimes in a startlingly naturalistic way:

By disapproving of wrong actions and frequently rebuking their children when they commit them, and contrariwise by approving and praising right actions, parents have caused the former to be associated with painful feelings and the latter with pleasurable feelings. This is further confirmed by experience. For not all people have the same customs and religion [*Nam consuetudo, & Religio non est omnibus eadem*]. What some hold as sacred, others regard as profane; what some hold as honourable, others regard as disgraceful. So each individual repents of a deed or exults in it according to his upbringing.[2]

In the *Ethics*, we read that everything concerning 'the true way of life and religion'[3] is supposed to be proved in only two propositions, to be found in Part IV –

37: The good which every man who pursues virtue aims at for himself he will also desire for the rest of mankind, and all the more as he acquires a greater knowledge of God

---

[1] *Ethics* IV, 37, Scholium I = G II 236/17–19.
[2] *Ethics* III, Definitions of the Emotions, 27, Explication = G II 197/16–24.
[3] *omnia, quæ ad veram vitam, & Religionem spectant*: IV, 73, Scholium = G II 265/17–21.

and –

46: He who lives by the guidance of reason endeavours as far as he can to repay with love or nobility another's hatred, anger, contempt, etc. towards himself.

In contrast with the *Ethics*, in the *Theological-Political Treatise* a good deal was said about religion, but not much about the nature of God. There, Spinoza's main aim was to differentiate religion, custom, practice and ritual from what he called 'philosophy'. He tried to present the difference in stark terms:

I am . . . astonished at the ingenuity displayed by those . . . who find in Scripture mysteries so profound as not to be open to explanation in any human language, and who have then imported into religion so many matters of a philosophic nature that the Church seems like an academy, and religion like a science, or rather, a subject for debate.[4]

And, even more bluntly, in a letter:

High speculative thought, in my view, has nothing to do with Scripture. For my part I have never learned, nor could I have learned, any of God's eternal attributes from Holy Scripture.[5]

He might have liked to align some clear dichotomies: on the one side, nature, God, knowledge, truth, philosophy; on the other, history, custom, practice, obedience, piety, faith, religion. But an exact alignment would have led to an uninteresting and indefensible position. The view that we can choose what to believe or how to act quite regardless of how things are ('in nature') is an extreme one that has never been occupied seriously. Spinoza's wish was to diminish the element of philosophic knowledge in religion, not to nothing but to a bare minimum – 'I do not go so far as to maintain that nothing whatsoever of a purely philosophic nature is to be found in Scripture's teaching . . . But this much I will say, that such affirmations are very few, and of a very simple nature'[6] – though, as we shall see in Chapter 8, this reservation created painful tensions for him. In the *Ethics*, a knowledge of how things are was said to be the basis for living 'by the guidance of reason', and that seemed to leave not much room for a choice of alternatives. True virtue is 'nothing other than to live by the guidance of reason'.[7] It is not clear how reason might offer *varied* forms of guidance.

But for now, the subject is the practice and history of religion.

---

[4] S 214 = G III 167/25–30.   [5] Letter 21; L 158 = G IV 133/4–7.
[6] S 215 = G III 168/5–9; the 'simple affirmations' are listed at S 120 = G III 77/24–9 and at S 212 = G III 265/25f.   [7] *Ethics* IV, 37, Scholium 1 = G II/28.

The aim of the *Theological-Political Treatise*, stated on its title page, was to show that 'freedom to philosophise can not only be granted without injury to Piety and the peace of the Commonwealth, but that the Peace of the Commonwealth and Piety are endangered by the suppression of freedom'.[8] Spinoza's explicit advocacy to further that aim was not particularly convincing, and it contains far less of interest than the questions asked on the way towards it. What is the basis, if any, for claims of knowledge in religion? Sacred writings, direct personal revelation, miracles? What should be the approach to rival religious claims? As we have just seen, his hope was to say as little as possible about the metaphysical background in the *Theological-Political Treatise*: this suited his rhetorical strategy, but it also matched his philosophical position, that the philosophic contents of religion should be minimised. It is believed that Parts I and II of the *Ethics* existed at least in draft before the *Treatise* was written, and it is certain that many of the main metaphysical conclusions of the *Ethics*, if not the finalised arguments, are to be found in Spinoza's earlier works. So the metaphysical foundations were there, however deeply they may have been buried.

FINAL CAUSES AND RELIGION

An apparent anomaly in his work, fitting comfortably neither into the careful polemics of the *Theological-Political Treatise* nor into the geometrical development of the *Ethics*, is the lengthy Appendix to Part I of the *Ethics*, which deals with teleology – purpose in nature – the Aristotelian notion that nature may act for 'final causes', that explanations may be sought in terms of ends as well as in terms of preceding causes. The argument of the Appendix was not needed for Part II of the *Ethics*, and if it were needed logically for Parts III or IV we might wonder why it was not placed nearer to them: perhaps because it forms an extended corollary to the conclusions about the 'nature and properties of God' reached in Part I. But however it fits into the logic of the *Ethics*, it is an indispensable preliminary to any discussion about religion. Spinoza's target is 'the widespread belief among men that all things in Nature are like themselves in acting with an end in view' taken with a theological slant: 'Indeed, they hold it as certain that God himself directs everything to a fixed end; for they say that God has made everything for man's sake and has made man so that he should worship God.'[9]

---

[8] Also see S 51–2 and 292 = G III 7/24–7 and 240/28–32. [9] *Ethics* I, Appendix = G II 78/3–6.

This bears on religion in the widest way. No story can be told truly about nature which ascribes to it a purpose, destination or significance. Why things are as they are, and why they act as they do, can never be explained in terms of a providential plan, and can never be referred to some future state of fulfilment, culmination or return. What happens ('within nature') cannot be referred to the future destiny of nature as a whole, but only to what has happened beforehand.

This chapter will look in detail at the justification for these conclusions, and at how generally they are to be understood. But we need to see why they occur as a first step in a discussion about religion. 'Final causes' are scarcely mentioned in the *Theological-Political Treatise*,[10] and the direct case against them is never mentioned there, but their repudiation is essential to its case. Nature is to be stripped of intrinsic significance including, centrally, any significance that could be derived from a discovered religious account of its creation or direction.

This is only one area where we need some caution in accepting Spinoza's claim that affirmations 'of a purely philosophic nature' can be 'very few, and of a very simple nature' in scripture's teaching.[11] It certainly seems to be a 'purely philosophic' presupposition about nature that it cannot be acting in accordance with any divine design or intention. Any narrative about final salvation or an end to history can be seen as human,[12] but it can have no basis in how things are ('in nature'). This is the complete disenchantment of nature. Spinoza's approach assumes that however we are to understand narratives about divine intentions in creation and history, it cannot be in any physical sense. That seems to exclude any form of natural eschatology, although, as we will see, the real interest lies in what we understand by *natural* here. It may not be too contentious in a sense connected with astronomy or particle physics. It becomes more delicate when we come to ask how the series of events in human history can be regarded, in the same way, as being without any intrinsic end or purpose.

FINAL CAUSES: SOME ARGUMENTS

Spinoza launches into his Appendix on final causes in a businesslike way. There are to be three parts to his case. First: an account of *why* people have believed that 'all things in Nature are like themselves in acting with

---

[10] S 125 = G III 82/6.   [11] See above, note 6.
[12] Not *nothing but* human, since the natural is also the divine; this delicate balance will be studied in more detail in Chapters 9 and 11.

an end in view'. Second: there is to be a demonstration of the falsity of this belief. Third: there will be a demonstration of some resulting misconceptions about morality. The second part, which must be logically crucial to the rest, is disappointingly condensed. The impression is unavoidable that Spinoza preferred to expand at length on why people held mistaken beliefs about final causes, and what the bad effects were, rather than to discuss their justification. (But we should not forget that the link between *cause* and *reason* (considered in Chapter 3) made the question *why* people hold a belief into an extremely wide one, encompassing history, psychology and logic.)

Anyway, his case against final causes opens with what looks like plain bluster – 'There is no need to spend time in going on to show that Nature has no fixed goal and that all final causes are but figments of the human imagination. For I think that is now quite evident from . . .'[13] – and he refers back to his general conclusions about nature in Part I of the *Ethics*. Nevertheless, he does go on to elaborate his case. To begin, two arguments which he describes as self-evident:[14] the doctrine of final causes 'turns Nature upside down, for it regards as an effect that which is in effect a cause, and vice versa'; and again, it 'makes that which is by nature first to be last'. It is just as well he chose not to rely on these arguments, because they both beg the question badly. If there *were* final causes, they *would* re-order causes and effects, so that is hardly an impressive point to make against them. Two further arguments, relating to God's perfection, are given a little more attention. Spinoza brings up a scholastic argument that if God were to be said to have purposes or ends that could only be because God is lacking something, which is absurd. The way in which this is framed might be intended to have some force for Spinoza's presumed readers, but it seems oddly out of place as one of his own arguments. He might express what he wanted to say by pointing out that the notion of *God's purposes* was paradoxical, but the explicit logic of that might have been too glaringly subversive. Perhaps as a result, his point seems muted. There is one further argument from perfection again, unhappily, circular: according to propositions 21 to 23 of Part I, he says, the immediate effects of God are supposed to be more perfect than remote effects; but final causes suggest that ends will be more perfect than means; which is a contradiction. Yet there is no reason why final causes could not have been excepted from the assumption that immediate effects are more perfect. Or, worse, it might be thought that God's

---

[13] *Ethics*, p. 59 = G II 80/2–5.   [14] *per se manifesta sunt* G II 80/15.

purposes, if they existed, were actually a disproof of the principle that immediate effects are more perfect than remote effects, thus undermining a good deal of Spinoza's logic.

These arguments of Spinoza were feeble and there is no point in lingering over them. If we are charitable to him, we can conclude that he used them only to spell out something not at all unfamiliar to any thinking person at that time: that the notion of *God's intentions* contained theological difficulties. But in his own terms, and in terms of any degree of logical rigour, his case was advanced hardly at all.

In fact, his initial confident assertion that his case had been proved already was indeed his best support, although we may be able to guess why he did not choose to elaborate on it. If the premises of Part I of the *Ethics* are accepted, then the figure of an anthropomorphic God is surely excluded. Even an assumption of God's infinity, taken as seriously as Spinoza took it, would rule out any portrayal of a God making plans, having intentions, directing nature or wanting anything to happen. These would be ruled out at surely as a portrayal of a God having a beard and living in the sky. And it was Spinoza's contention that a belief in an anthropomorphic God was a consequence of an ignorance of causes resulting in a projection of human qualities on to God. This might have been the reason that he devoted so much space to *why* people wanted final causes in comparison with the space given to direct argument against them.

It is obvious that he wanted to reject an anthropomorphic deity as far as he could, and it may be that a repudiation of final causes was part of that rejection, but his reasoned justification for rejecting final causes may not be so obvious. If we accept the equivalence of God and nature, and if we accept the universality and connectedness of 'causal' explanations, it may not be clear *why* we should not think about the ends in nature. You can explain fully how a clock works by taking it apart and showing how each part works with each other part, but your explanation may be thought to be missing something if it does not mention that a clock is constructed to tell the time.

FINAL CAUSES: THE SCOPE OF THE CASE

This takes us towards some controversial territory: the question of how widely the rejection of final causes was meant to apply. Was it to nature as a whole? To all individuals in nature? Including or excluding human beings? And human history? Jonathan Bennett, in a careful analytical study, concluded that Spinoza wanted to reject final causes completely. And since human beings frequently ascribe ends and intentions to themselves, this seemed to present problems. We often cite reasons in the future, which do seem to explain our present actions.[15] In reply to this, Edwin Curley drew a distinction between the explanation of human actions, where intentions and ends do certainly play a part, and a wider case about divine purpose. And Bennett has agreed to this, conceding that 'Spinoza really did want to attribute thoughtful teleology to humans, and denied it only for items – such as the universe – that don't have thoughts about the future.'[16]

On the face of it, this difference of opinion among commentators may seem irrelevant to the general validity of Spinoza's case against final causes. But it does matter a good deal in showing that the case is more complicated than it seems, and that we need to appreciate exactly where its force applies. More specifically, if religion is based in history, if history is human and if final causes have a genuine place in the description of human activities, then final causes have a genuine place in religion.

Spinoza does refer to human intentions and ends, and indeed an essential element in his argument is to claim that people *believe* that 'all things in Nature *are like themselves* in acting with an end in view'. People project their own experience of intentions, ends and purposes on to things in the world and then on to the world as a whole. It seems to follow that ends cannot be irrelevant to the explanation of their own activities. Yet, in Part IV of the *Ethics*, much of the psychological analysis seems to depend on Spinoza's frankly anti-teleological definition: 'By the *end* for the sake of which we do something, I mean appetite', where 'appetite' is linked to 'man's essence, from the nature of which there necessarily follow those things that tend to his preservation, and which man is thus determined to perform'.[17]

In fact, a distinction or contrast between human and non-human explanation is a confusion. Spinoza tells us plainly that 'Nature has no fixed goal' and that 'all final causes are but figments of the human imagination';[18] and this should give us the clearest pointer towards his position. Of course we use teleological explanations all the time, both for our own actions, the actions of others and, most strikingly, but not always

---

[15] Bennett, *A Study of Spinoza's Ethics*, pp. 213–30.

[16] E. M. Curley, 'On Bennett's Spinoza: The Issue of Teleology'; J. F. Bennett, 'Spinoza and Teleology: A Reply to Curley' (p. 53); both in E. M. Curley and P.-F. Moreau (eds.), *Spinoza: Issues and Directions* (Leiden: Brill, 1990).   [17] *Ethics* IV, Definition 7 and III, 9, Scholium.

[18] *omnes causas finales nihil, nisi humana esse figmenta*, *Ethics*, p. 59 = G II 80/3–4.

with care, in biology. But such explanations are not correct; we *imagine* them and, in this way at least, our imagination leads us astray. Spinoza deploys a mischievous crescendo of examples, from the plausible to the ridiculous – 'eyes for seeing, teeth for chewing, cereals and living creatures for food, the sun for giving light, the sea for breeding fish'[19] – and his point is surely that *all* these are equally misguided. We may well believe that we, or other people, or other parts of creation, are guided by ends – and, as Bennett shows, such beliefs can be anatomised in some detail – but we are mistaken. Such explanations are just wrong (or *inadequate*, in technical language). The distinction between human and non-human final explanation is just a matter of being less or more obviously wrong. We need to consider how we really are, and how our thoughts and actions are really to be explained, against our inadequate understandings of them and of ourselves. When Spinoza says there are no final causes in nature it cannot make sense to think of a distinction between human and non-human nature, or part of nature against nature as a whole: 'those who do not understand the nature of things, but only imagine things . . . are firmly convinced that there is order in things (*ordinem in rebus*), ignorant as they are of things and of their own nature'.[20]

And it must be at the level of nature as a whole – God or nature – where his case derives whatever force it has. To provide support, he points us towards Proposition 16 of Part I of the *Ethics*: 'From the necessity of [the] divine nature there must follow infinite things in infinite ways (that is, everything that can come within the scope of infinite intellect).'

He wants causal explanation – explanation by prior, not final, causes or reasons – to be exhaustive. A corollary of Proposition 16 suggests just that: it is said to follow 'that God is the efficient cause of all things that can come within the scope of infinite intellect'. If 'efficient' causality is exhaustive, there can be no place for 'final' causality.

A BETTER ARGUMENT?

But maybe that still looks either circular or just dogmatic? – Final causes cannot exist because all causes are prior, or 'efficient'.

A reprise of the main case is given in the Preface to Part IV of the *Ethics*, and this seems to expose the underlying logic more clearly than the hints in the Appendix to Part I:

---

[19] *Ethics*, p. 58 = G II 78/30–2.   [20] *Ethics*, p. 60 = G II 81–2.

For we have demonstrated in Appendix, Part I that Nature does not act with an end in view; that the eternal and infinite being, whom we call God, or Nature, acts by the same necessity whereby it exists. That the necessity of [his] nature whereby [he] acts is the same as that whereby [he] exists has been demonstrated (I, 16). So the reason or cause why God, or nature, acts, and the reason or cause why [he] exists, are one and the same. Therefore, just as [he] does not exist for an end, so [he] does not act for an end; just as there is no beginning or end to [his] existing, so there is no beginning or end to [his] acting. [*Ratio igitur, seu causa, cur Deus, seu Natura agit, & cur existit, una, eademque est. Ut ergo nullius finis causa existit, nullius etiam finis causâ agit; sed ut existendi, sic & agendi principium, vel finem habet nullum.*] What is termed a 'final cause' is nothing but human appetite in so far as it is considered as the starting-point or primary cause of some thing.[21]

Once again, the notion of infinity seems central, to the extent that Spinoza seems to rely on the Latin *infinitus* – where infinite things follow in infinite ways from God – as a basis for concluding there can be no final cause, *finis causa*, that God can have no end, *finis*, in acting. As a point on its own, that might seem as question-begging as it is possible to be: God is endless, so God has no ends.

One way to interpret the case is by reading it downwards from the pointlessness of nature. Given the unboundedness of nature, Spinoza thought, there can be no external reason why nature exists and acts. (In so far as it is appropriate to mention explanation, we can only mention *self*-explanation, which is, effectively, no explanation at all.) From this it does indeed follow that nature has no end, or no ends: because that would be just the sort of external explanation that Spinoza most wanted to exclude – an answer to a question such as, why does everything exist? Then, just as nature as a whole has no end, so also we may find conditions on the sort of final explanations we may give within nature, for the existence and action of individuals. Not, as we might imagine, that such explanations may tend to terminate unsatisfyingly – we might have to stop giving reasons, at some metaphysically interesting point – but that they would *never* terminate: they would be endless, without ends, because they would always be potentially infinite. The argument seems to be an important one, but it is one that has rarely been noticed.[22]

Its use comes out in one of Spinoza's better-chosen examples. A stone falls off a roof and kills a man. Why?

---

[21] *Ethics*, p. 153 = G II 206–7: one of the most obvious passages where 'he' could as well be 'it'.

[22] The force of the case is more general than against only teleological explanations, since it bears on terminated causal series in the past as well as in the teleological future.

in order to kill the man; for if it had not fallen for this purpose by the will of God, how could so many circumstances (and there are often many coinciding circumstances) have chanced to concur?

– and here is a classic final explanation. It is no good saying that it was a windy day. Why was it windy? Because the sea had been rough. But why? Why was the man walking that way? Because he had been invited by a friend? Why?

for there is no end to questions . . . And so they will go on and on asking the causes of causes, until you take refuge in the will of God – that is, the sanctuary of ignorance.[23]

The logic of the illustration is easy to misread. The point cannot just be that 'there is no end to questions' because Spinoza strongly *agrees* that the explanation for any individual event has to be endless. The mistake is not so much in asking endless questions – who knows? one might find out something interesting along the way – as in imagining that there *is* an 'end' to the answers. The true explanation for why the stone fell on the man's head is actually endless because all causal series in nature are endless. Final causes would be non-infinite causes, cutting short inquiry in crude ignorance, or, less unkindly, in *imagined* solutions.[24] This must be the point about human intentions and wishes. I may believe that the reason for my action is a 'final cause' in the form of an intention refer-ring to the future, but my belief has to be understood in terms of my inability to see backwards to the beginning of the chain of causes which makes me act as I do, including the causes which make me believe that my action is explained by an intention.

Support for this reading is to be found towards the end of the *Ethics*.[25] As the mind comes to understand that all things are determined by an infinite chain of causes it becomes less passive, or prey to emotions. (And this provides a good idea of the integration in Spinoza's thinking: the case against final causes is rooted in his view about divine causality, and that in turn is used as a basis for his psychological theory.[26])

Spinoza's willingness to move between physical and human explana-tion is surely not in doubt. It comes out most explicitly in one of his most-

---

[23] *Ethics*, pp. 59–60 = G ɪɪ 80–1.

[24] A view supported, presumably with opposite intentions, by Bacon in his essay *Of Atheisme*: 'while the minde of man looketh upon second causes scattered, it may sometimes rest in them, and goe no further: but when it beholdeth the chaine of them, confederate and linked together, it must needs flie to Providence and Deitie'.   [25] v, 6, Demonstration.

[26] Alexandre Matheron has done much to elucidate such interconnections: see, for example, *Individu et communauté*, pp. 102–12.

quoted illustrations, again using a stone – this time, a stone in flight through the air. The stone's motion is explained by an initial impact (and *that*, if we ask, will be explained by something else, and so on). We are offered a direct analogy with the stone and a human action. If the stone could think, it 'will surely think that it is completely free, and that it continues in motion for no other reason than that it so wishes. This, then, is that human freedom which all men boast of possessing, and which consists solely in this, that men are conscious of their desire, and unaware of the causes by which they are determined.'[27]

This illustration is not used to make any point about final causes, but it does show plainly how widely Spinoza wanted his views on explanation to apply: with equal force in a human and in a physical context.

The specific application of his views tended to be oblique, like much of the argumentation in the *Theological-Political Treatise*. There are three areas where final causes were important in the background: in the case against miracles, on the place of purpose in history and in Spinoza's dislike of what he considered to be superstition.

MIRACLES

The most obvious and least interesting of these is with miracles. From Chapter 2 it can be seen that miracles, as breaches of natural law and of the universal intelligibility of nature, are not possible. Although that would certainly be an important conclusion in religious terms, the force of Spinoza's case was entirely dependent on his wider views about law, necessity and intelligibility.[28] The specific arguments used about miracles in the chapter about them in the *Theological-Political Treatise* are striking mostly for showing more of his metaphysical hand than is revealed explicitly in the rest of the book. It is here, for example, that the equivalence between God and nature is suggested most boldly.[29]

Spinoza gave a teleological diagnosis for belief in miracles. The early Jews, he thought, to refute or impress the neighbouring Gentiles

boasted of their miracles, from which they further sought to prove that the whole of Nature was directed for their sole benefit by command of the God whom they worshipped. This idea has found such favour with mankind that

---

[27] Letter 58; L 284 = G IV 266.
[28] For clear analysis see G. H. R. Parkinson, 'Spinoza on Miracles and Natural Law', *Revue Internationale de Philosophie*, 31, 1977, and E. M. Curley, 'Spinoza on Miracles', in E. Giancotti Boscherini (ed.), *Proceedings of the First Italian International Congress on Spinoza* (Naples: Bibliopolis, 1985).   [29] S 124 = G III 81/16–19.

they have not ceased to this day to invent miracles with view to convincing people that they are more beloved of God than others, and are the final cause of God's creation and continuous direction of the world.[30]

Interestingly, this passage contains three layers of teleology. Miracles are alleged to have intrinsically teleological functions. First, overtly, by confirming or reinforcing beliefs of special election, then secondly by exhibiting the teleological pattern in nature; and then thirdly and indirectly by showing how mistaken human intentions can operate. There is no doubt that final causes are at work: people *sought to prove* that nature was directed for their benefit and *invented* miracles to assist their beliefs. These are teleological explanations of human activities, but, of course, thinks Spinoza, misguided ones.

HISTORICAL PURPOSE

More generally, there was the place of purpose in history. Plainly, Spinoza did not wish to deny that people had discerned various patterns in the evolution of history, and had produced various accounts that had included reference to divine plans and intentions. Equally, he believed that such accounts must have been, in a way, mistaken. On this, in the *Theological-Political Treatise*, his views were as elusive as they were pervasive. There can be very little question that he wished to deny that God can organise events anthropomorphically, either on a small scale or on a grand scale with a view to creating patterns of meaningfulness in human history. Yet he felt his case could be made without spelling that out explicitly; perhaps because of an over-optimistic wish not to be seen as being too confrontational towards Christianity. His interpretation of what he called 'God's choosing' (*Dei electio*) could scarcely be seen as straightforward:

since no one acts except by the predetermined order of Nature – that is, from God's eternal direction and decree – it follows that no one chooses a way of life for himself or accomplishes anything except by the special vocation of God [*nisi ex singulari Dei vocatione*], who has chosen one man before others for a particular work or a particular way of life.

He then went on, with this opaque elucidation at hand, to see 'why it was that the Hebrew nation was said to have been chosen by God before all others'.[31] We shall return to this in detail in Chapter 7.

---

[30] S 125 = G III 82/2–7.   [31] S 90 = G III 46/16–22.

SUPERSTITION

Temperamentally, Spinoza had the greatest possible scorn for what he considered to be superstition. Uncharacteristically, he reached for the blunderbuss rather than the scalpel. The diagnosis in the Appendix to Part I of the *Ethics* is a sweepingly wide one: *all* the prejudices he plans to discuss originate in a belief in final causes, and that belief in turn is traced to a number of factors, all deeply negative, including fear, ignorance, insatiable greed, blind cupidity and folly.

Much of what he says about superstition is routine. To be expected from any religious reformer is a view that superstition is a contaminant in religion: 'Happy indeed would be our age, if we were to see religion freed again from superstition.' Religion has wisdom for its foundation, where superstition has ignorance. Superstition is hostile to reason, true knowledge and true morality.[32] Writing to Albert Burgh, a young acquaintance who had become a Catholic and who had been unwise enough to urge him to take the same step, Spinoza was unrestrained. Whatever it was that distinguished the Roman church from others it was something superfluous 'and consequently is constructed merely from superstition'. Those whom he called 'the Pharisees' 'have remained steadfast over some thousands of years with no government to constrain them, solely through the efficacy of superstition'. And Islam is described bluntly as a superstition.[33] He was not the first or last to portray the elements in religions which he did not like as superstitious, as opposed to a core of *true religion*, but that was standard polemics rather than systematic theorising.

This is not edifying. The prospects for a general theory about superstition cannot be expected to be good, and some sweeping remarks about fear and ignorance may be as much as we might expect from anyone. Spinoza's correspondence in 1674 with Hugo Boxel on the existence of ghosts and spirits reveals what we might consider today to be a robust common sense, but it contains no philosophical or methodological interest on the subject.[34]

Although the diagnosis of final causes as a root of superstition is too wide, that should not make us forget the radicalism of Spinoza's prescription. Taken only as a methodological recommendation, the policy of continuing to search for causes – rather than taking refuge in the 'sanctuary of ignorance' – had as much leverage as some of his more

[32] S 204 = G III 158/13–15; Letter 73, L 333 = G IV 307–8; Letter 54, L 270 = G IV 253/33–4; S 73 = G III 29–30.　[33] Letter 76, L 341, 342, 343 = G IV 318/11, 321, 322/11.　[34] Letters 51–6.

purely metaphysical doctrines. The handling of the story of the stone
falling from the roof on to the head of the passer-by shows a mind insis-
tent on inquiry. If the reading here is correct, the methodological
message must be to go on seeking causes.

THE 'NATURAL'

We might wonder, though, whether this is not question-begging, because
it might be thought that the underlying message of the story is to go on
seeking *natural* causes, where *natural* is assumed to mean non-theological,
and where, still further in the background, something unstated is
assumed about the border between theological and non-theological
causality. It is acceptable, we can see, to say that the wind blew, taking
part of Spinoza's explanation, because 'on the previous day the sea had
begun to toss after a period of calm',[35] but not because a spirit moved on
the face of the deep. More convincingly, the story can prompt us to
protest that no explanation is offered of the event that actually needs
explaining. We may accept that the stone fell because of an endless series
of physical causes, and that the passer-by happened to be where he was
because of another series of causes – all perfectly 'natural' – but still feel
that we need to explain *the coincidence* of the stone's falling and the man's
location. After all, *that* is the interesting event: if the stone had missed the
man, the story would have had no interest to anyone. We can easily
imagine some embroidery for the story: the man is on the way to an his-
toric meeting – because the stone falls it does not take place – the subsequent history of the world is different – how remarkable . . .

Spinoza surely cannot have been unaware of that line of objection: he
chose his own illustration of a superstitious story, and it is obvious where
it could lead. No answer is indicated. But at least two kinds of answer
seem to be available to him.

First, he would not need to deny that the coincidence of the falling
stone and the man's location was itself an event in need of explanation.
In some contexts, it might be. We can think of some further embroidery:
the man is a prominent politician on his way to his meeting – there is
known to be a conspiracy – his enemies have been seen on nearby
rooftops – someone had suggested that he walked along that road rather
than another one . . . But all that can be investigated, too. The *facts in the
case*, legally, should be capable, even for the most superstitious person, of

---

[35] *Ethics*, p. 60 = G II 81/5–7.

establishing the relevant differences between an accident and an intentional action. Spinoza's story, as originally stated, assumes rightly, not circularly, that intention has been ruled out of the story. If it has not, the story becomes a very different one.

A second answer would be to note that what is characteristic about a 'natural' causal story is the fact of its potential endlessness. That does not mean than any infinite narrative is better than any closed one. But it does suggest that a narrative which closes in a terminus may not be acceptable as 'natural'. What Spinoza *wants* is continuing inquiry. We can see from Part I of this study that he has elaborate metaphysical ramifications to prop up that understanding of individual causality. One line of thought relies on the soundness of a distinction between an open and a closed narrative. But it is not hard to think of difficulties: why was the Greek fleet blown off course? . . . because Poseidon was angry . . . because he had fallen out with Athene . . . over the favour of Zeus . . . because of family rivalries . . . because of their regrettable Olympian upbringing . . . and so on, as far back into mythology as patience lasts. Here seems to be one type of endless theological, or at any rate non-natural, explanation. To deal with this, Spinoza could not appeal to distinctions between *types* of causality (corporeal, mental, intentional, natural) without begging the question. Nor, of course, could he make a distinction between 'natural' and 'divine' causality. Perhaps he could rely on some idea of explanation that would be infinite *in principle*, as opposed to being simply *ad hoc*; but that leads to the murky waters surrounding the characterisation of an adequate scientific or explanatory theory.

In practice, the most likely possibility is that he and his scientific friends were building up a consensus of what could be accepted as a 'natural' explanation. His contribution, had it been recognised, was a valuable one. The most practical yardstick might well have been the openness of any explanatory story, as opposed to a termination in arbitrary premises. At any rate, that could be one reading of how this issue developed in the half century after his death, which saw a gradual disengagement of theology from concepts such as *force*, where the boundary of the 'natural' was not at all self-evident. But the practical development of science and the theoretical justification for it were not equally impressive. So far as we can speculate on Spinoza's views about the causality of individuals, they would have run into problems less certainly than views that relied on general laws or theories. But, either way, the rocks under that water were still three centuries in the future.

CHAPTER 5

Hope and fear

FALSE RELIGION

Spinoza's onslaught on final causes contained an emphatically negative diagnosis for the causes of false religion. Ignorance about real causes in nature fed fear about the unknown future. Superstitious delusions were the result. That diagnosis, and the distinction upon which it was based, was surely commonplace: 'the chief distinction I make between religion and superstition is that the latter is founded on ignorance, the former on wisdom', though Spinoza could add an unexpected twist to suit himself:

And this I believe is the reason why Christians are distinguished not from other people by faith, nor charity, nor the other fruits of the Holy Spirit, but solely by an opinion they hold, namely, because as they all do, they rest their case simply on miracles, that is, on ignorance, which is the source of all wickedness, and thus they turn their faith, true as it may be, into superstition.[1]

There is no point in lingering over this negative diagnosis. Even as a piece of prejudiced, a priori anthropology, it contained some truth: we can hardly argue with the fact that indisputable superstition is more prevalent among the indisputably ignorant. But that does not support a conclusion that less overt superstitions might be less prevalent among the less ignorant. Superstition may be a more valuable term for polemical abuse than for fine analysis, and that may be the best way to see it in Spinoza.

The question why people make mistakes in any field may not be amenable to general treatment. Far more interesting than an aetiology of mistaken religion must be any account of the causes of true or valid religion. What Spinoza said about the general causes of superstition hardly weakens his wider position; though it hardly strengthens it, either.

---

[1] Letter 73, 1675; L 333 = G IV 307–8.

His thought about the positive background to religion is a different matter: it must be central to his thought.

WHY RELIGION?

The underlying general question – never presented by him in such explicit terms – must be, why do people need or want religion? And that branches rapidly into a maze of problems that extend into many areas of philosophy, psychology, politics and anthropology. Which people do we mean? Everyone alike? People in 'our society'? The stupid, the clever, the enlightened, the illuminated, all equally? Or differently? *Should* people want religion (accepting that mostly they have done, as at least one point that is relatively uncontroversial)? Is a desire for religion of human origin, and, if so, a matter of human choice? Or does God choose, or decide who is to have a desire for religion? (Leading to a further maze of problems about free will and grace, much debated in the seventeenth century.) And which religion do we mean? Are we generalising about traditional, untheological polytheisms as well as about the well-systematised monotheisms known to Spinoza? How far can we expect our inquiries to affect future behaviour? Perhaps, for example, revealing some causes for the desire for religion might do something to modify that desire?

Spinoza's position, in outline, can be sketched easily enough. He assumes that religious practice – in the sense of ceremonies and divinely reinforced ethical codes – will be an unavoidable presence in human society. To him, practised religion is a natural phenomenon which has to be neither praised nor condemned in itself, but whose causes or explanations can – must – be understood. To see this much alone is important. Because so much of what he says about religion is critical in spirit, one might imagine that he is inherently anti-religious. There is no support for such a view. Here, for example, we see the opposite: 'Whoever reflects . . . will find nothing in what I have said that is at variance with God's word or true religion and faith, or can weaken it; on the contrary, he will realise that I am strengthening it.'[2] There is no need to take this as ironic.

It is obvious, in temperamental terms, that some forms of religious life and practice were more to his taste than others: he chose to live for some time among people who could be seen today as being of a quakerish, anti-ritualistic spirit. His dislike of theological dogmatism was hardly

---

[2] S 205 = G III 159/6–9.

disguised, and there was no shortage of examples of it for him to find in most of the religious traditions he knew. These biographical facts do not mean that he wished to condemn religious practice as such. His approach was detached and anthropological – people act in certain ways: *why?*

We should remember two aspects of any reply that he could give to that question. Both make his attitude seem disconcerting to most tastes. These are areas where his radicalism is still not fully appreciated. There was his merging of the notions of *cause* and *reason*. And there was his repudiation of teleology – final causes – just discussed.

The *causes of religion* and the *reasons why* people have wanted to act religiously were not distinguished because he had no way to distinguish them. The answer to the most general question – why have most people sought religions? – in the most general terms, was perfectly simple and straightforward for him: because they were brought up like that in societies which existed like that. And, still at this extremely general level, this is one reason why there can be no real element of condemnation in his approach. How people are, how they have acted and how they will go on acting, have causes which we can seek to understand, but we might condemn them as usefully as we might try to condemn the weather or the tides. This detachment probably caused more alarm and outrage to Spinoza's critics than any other aspect of his work.

The rejection of final causes placed restraints on his approach. In response to questions about why people have wanted religions, a whole class of answers[3] may be teleological: people have wanted religions, have engaged in religious practice, behaved according to religiously reinforced moral codes because God has made them like that, for reasons connected with a plan for history or human destiny. Individual people may have sought religion – or not – because God has chosen – or not – to inspire them with a desire for it, or a desire to seek such a desire. Or, more mildly, human beings have been constructed so that it is a desire which they do, or can, have. Very typically, a narrative about desire for religion may be a central part of a narrative about the purpose of human life or about a purpose for existence generally. And, of course, that may promise a line of exhaustive and comprehensive explanation.

From all this – including characteristically religious narratives of

---

[3] *Positive* answers; as we have seen, Spinoza seemed to think that all negative desires for religion were rooted in final causes connected with fear, hope and ignorance.

salvation or redemption as human or divine aims – Spinoza barred himself by his repudiation of teleology. People may have been religious for reasons connected with accounts of the aims or purposes of human life or history, but those accounts cannot have been *correct*, because human life or history, intrinsically, has no aims or purposes.

The resulting approach to the history of religions will be studied in Chapter 7. For now, we should concentrate on Spinoza's thinking about religious motivation. His thoroughgoing ruling, 'By the end for the sake of which we do something, I mean appetite',[4] applies as much to religious ends as to any others. The 'final goal' (*finis ultimus*) for the man guided by reason is the same as the 'highest desire' (*summa Cupiditas*).[5] We may think we are acting towards an end of redemption or salvation. We may think that is how God wants us to act. In fact, our desires and actions are being caused by certain appetites, for which we may seek the explanations, but for which justification in terms of ends will be inappropriate.[6]

THEORY AND BEHAVIOUR

In thinking about the motivations underlying religion, it is essential to keep in mind Spinoza's desire to separate actual human behaviour from philosophical or theological beliefs about the structure of nature. This was certainly not the same as a separation of values from facts – far too many aspects of his thought would have prevented that possibility. It was more an identification of what mattered in *religion* with moral practice, in the most down-to-earth sense. His view is not caricatured by the shortest summary: it does not matter so much what people believe, or say they believe, as long as they act well.[7] Behind that are some less unsophisticated assumptions: theological beliefs, in practice, have very little connection with moral behaviour, one way or the other; people may not change their views, but they can be persuaded to behave well; so there is no real need for a critical approach to orthodox religions – they are not going to change, and what matters is how people act, anyway.

All this, of course, was deeply shocking, and Spinoza's views in this

---

[4] *Ethics* IV, Definition 7.   [5] *Ethics* IV, Appendix, 4 = G II 267/10.

[6] 'the love of God is man's highest happiness and blessedness, and the final end and aim [*finis ultimus, & scopus*] of all human action', according to Chapter IV of the *Theological-Political Treatise*, S 104 = G III 60/30–1. Are we to take this as an interesting slip?

[7] 'it matters not [*nihil . . . refert*] how the practice of these virtues [justice and charity] is revealed to us as long as it holds the place of supreme authority and is the supreme law', S 281 = G III 229/15–16.

area too are among those which were most alarming to his contemporaries. The Preface to the *Theological-Political Treatise* announces that 'the moral value of a man's creed should be judged only from his works'.[8] Later, in Chapter xii, there is a pointed reference to Isaiah, 'where he teaches the true way of life as consisting not in ceremonial observance but in charity and sincerity of heart, calling it God's Law and God's Word without distinction'.[9]

Far worse than this was Spinoza's Erasmian attitude towards the virtuous of other religions. He disliked what he saw as the dogmatism of Islam.[10] Nevertheless:

As for the Turks and the other Gentiles, if they worship God by the exercise of justice and by love of their neighbour, I believe that they possess the spirit of Christ and are saved, whatever convictions they may hold in their ignorance about Mahomet and the oracles.[11]

We shall have to come back to the 'spirit of Christ' (in Chapter 9), but the impression is unavoidable that the Muslims' opinions are not considered relevant if they behave well; and despite their opinions they *can* behave well.

Spinoza refers favourably to what he calls a 'religion universal to the entire human race, or catholic religion', which is the same as 'Divine Law', and 'The expression is also used metaphorically (*metaphorice*) for Nature's order and destiny (because in reality this is dependent on and follows from the eternal decree of the divine nature).'[12] The 'basis of the whole structure of religion', we see, 'is in essence this, to love God above all, and one's neighbour as oneself'.[13] Spinoza seems to reach this position independently of his metaphysical views, and independently of his thought about the basic 'dogmas of the universal faith' which he distils two chapters later in the *Theological-Political Treatise*. His idea seems to be that 'charity and sincerity of heart'[14] have nothing at all to do with beliefs. 'Honesty and sincerity of heart,' he says, 'needs godly and brotherly exhortation, a good upbringing, and most of all, a judgment that is independent and free.'[15] There seems to be no moral theory at all sup-

---

[8] S 55 = G III 11/6.
[9] S 209 = G III 162/19–22. Isaiah 1:11–17: '"What need have I of all your sacrifices?" Says the LORD . . . "Learn to do good. Devote yourself to justice; Aid the wronged".'
[10] See Letter 76; L 342 = G IV 322/9; S 51 = G III 7/2–5. Henri Laux argues that Islam, for Spinoza, was the 'religious archetype of servitude' – a kind of historical extreme: *Imagination et Religion chez Spinoza* (Paris: Vrin, 1993), p. 239.   [11] Letter 43, 1671; L 241 = G IV 226/1–4.
[12] *religio toti humano generi universalis, sive catholica*, S 208–9 = G III 162/15–26.
[13] S 211 = G III 165/12–13.   [14] S 209 = G III 162/21.   [15] S 159 = G III 116–17.

porting this view. Regardless of theory, some characteristics are to be prized: 'we cannot know anyone except by his works. He who abounds in these fruits – charity, joy, peace, patience, kindness . . . he, whether he be taught by reason alone or by Scripture alone, is in truth taught by God, and is altogether blessed.'[16]

In this sense, the answer to the question, why be religious? is a purely practical one: to be religious is to live well, and to live well can be to be brought up well in favourable surroundings.

This may seem unsurprising, and of little philosophical interest. Spinoza might agree, in that, quite unusually for a philosopher, he did not want to say that a correct philosophical understanding was necessary for right behaviour. It is relevant, though, in terms of his attitude to conventional, current religious positions other than his own. We can assume that authors who write books would prefer their readers to accept their conclusions. So it is natural to assume that Spinoza might have liked his readers, in short, to accept Spinozism, and to become Spinozists. After all, since the *Theological-Political Treatise* contains its own summary of 'the dogmas of the universal faith',[17] we might well imagine that the author would like all his readers to accept and follow these.

Yirmiyahu Yovel does assume that. The overall aim of the *Treatise*, he says, is 'to establish mental and institutional mechanisms that will transform the imagination into an external imitation of reason, using state power and a purified popular religion as vehicles of a semirational civilizing process'.[18]

In other words, it would be better if people became Spinozists, or acted like Spinozists, by 'semirational' means. The implication, presumably, is that such an outcome would be more desirable than that they might continue in *un*purified 'popular religion'.

This is quite important, because it does suggest that Spinoza would have liked people to stop being Jews, or Catholics or Protestants and to become Spinozists, if not rationally then semi-rationally. Which in turn suggests that he must have been quite critical of current religions, maybe hoping to replace or supersede them in some way.

That reading may be understandable, but it is not supported by anything that Spinoza said. In fact, he regarded religion as a matter of practice, and its existence in society and in history as something that was not

---

[16] S 123 = G III 80/24–30.

[17] Including the 'dogma' that 'Worship of God and obedience to him consists solely in justice and charity, or love towards one's neighbour', S 224 = G III 177/33–5.

[18] *Spinoza and Other Heretics*, p. 130.

going to go away. Different societies had their own religions for different historical causes or reasons. Diversity was intrinsic and, maybe, not undesirable: 'as men's ways of thinking vary considerably and different beliefs are better suited to different men, and what moves one to reverence provokes ridicule in another . . . everyone should be allowed freedom of judgment and the right to interpret the basic tenets of his faith as he thinks fit, and . . . the moral value of a man's creed should be judged only from his works'.[19]

There is no trace of a view in Spinoza that things would be better if religions went away, or that a tidied-up rational religion could or should, in practice, replace historical religions. To read him along those lines is to see him as an eighteenth-century rationalist, which he certainly was not. One of the stories about him in an early biography is that 'his landlady asked him whether he believed she could be saved in the religion she professed. He answered: Your religion is a good one; you need not look for another, nor doubt that you may be saved in it, provided, whilst you apply yourself to piety, you live at the same time a peaceable and quiet life.'[20] We might take this more seriously than by seeing it as patronising condescension, in the manner of Voltaire sending his servants from the room when he discussed religion. Spinoza did not take religion, in practice, to be something that could be invented, by him or anyone else. It was a social and historical reality.[21]

CONSISTENCY

There is an important proviso, whose fuller significance we shall have to weigh up in looking at his views about choice in religion in Chapter 8. Religious faith requires 'not so much true dogmas as pious dogmas, that is, such as move the heart to obedience, and this is so even if many of those beliefs contain not a shadow of truth', and this is what we might expect, given the schism opened between faith and 'philosophy' – but, crucially:

provided that he who adheres to them knows not that they are false. If he knew that they were false, he would necessarily be a rebel, for how could it be that one who seeks to love justice and obey God should worship as divine what he knows to be alien to the divine nature?[22]

---

[19] S 55 = G III 11/1–7.　　[20] Cited by Leon Roth, *Spinoza* (London: Benn, 1929), p. 13.
[21] For those who believe that Spinoza wanted to 'naturalise' religion it would seem to follow that religion is a more, not less, permanent feature of human society: but this is a conclusion that has seldom been drawn.　　[22] *quod a divina natura alienum scit esse*; S 223 = G III 176/18–24.

This allows for uninformed faith – 'Scripture condemns only obstinacy, not ignorance' – but not inconsistency. Faith is not dependent upon a knowledge of any set of facts about nature, but if any claims *are* made about truths, they should not conflict with anything known to be true about nature. Living in truth was not obligatory, but living in known untruth was disallowed. Since Spinoza chose to say very little about divine nature in the *Theological-Political Treatise*, the problem that could arise was not so evident there; but that was hardly the case in the *Ethics*, which contained a great deal about how nature is, what people are like, how the mind relates to the body and so on. All this was known as *true* philosophy, as we shall see in Chapter 8.[23]

Furthermore, the 'true way of life and religion' described in the later parts of the *Ethics*[24] threads back inexorably through earlier geometrical proofs (via Part IV, 37) to Part IV, 24: 'To act in absolute conformity with virtue is nothing else in us but to act, to live, to preserve one's being (these three mean the same) under the guidance of reason, on the basis of seeking one's own advantage.' By the end of Part V, this had become 'the first and only basis of virtue',[25] of 'prime importance to piety and religion', regardless of anything proved about the eternity of the mind.

These views can be traced back still more deeply into the system, where 'seeking one's advantage' is tied to the definition of *good* as 'that which we certainly know to be useful [*utile*] to us',[26] and where *acting* and *preserving one's being* are technical terminology relating to the notion of *conatus*, or the striving with which everything is said to persist in its existence.[27] In other words, 'the true way of life and religion' is rooted in how we are – in our nature – in 'divine nature'. As Spinoza had said tersely in the *Short Treatise*: 'man, so long as he is a part of Nature, must follow the laws of Nature. That is [true] religion. So long as he does this, he has his well-being',[28] and in the *Theological-Political Treatise*: 'our supreme good and perfection depends solely on the knowledge of God'.[29]

If we are seeking what we might call *reasons* for a 'way of life and religion', Spinoza's approach leads us – but maybe not him – into some confusion. *Bad* causes or reasons for a way of life may include ignorance of one's nature, false beliefs or superstitions about fate or destiny or

---

[23] Letter 76; L 342 = G IV 320/3–4. The editors of Spinoza's letters (note 379) rightly point out that 'truth' here does not suggest completeness.   [24] IV, 73, Scholium.

[25] *Primum, & unicum virtutis . . . fundamentum*, V, 41, Demonstration.   [26] *Ethics* IV, Definition 1.

[27] *Ethics* III, 7.

[28] *de mensch, zoo lange hy een deel van de Natuur is, zoo moet hy de wetten van de Natuur volgen, het welk de godsdienst is. En zoo lange hy zulks doet, is hy in zyn welstand*: Curley, p. 129 = G I 88/23–6.

[29] S 103 = G III 60/2–3.

misunderstandings of one's position in relation to others. They may also include a faulty upbringing, disadvantageous surroundings or an inappropriate political framework. Presumably going out of his way to choose the most outrageously provocative example, Spinoza remarked in a letter that Nero's matricide 'in so far as it contained something positive, was not a crime'. After all, Orestes had killed his mother too, and he was not considered to be as bad as Nero: 'What then was Nero's crime? Nothing else than that by that deed he showed that he was ungrateful, devoid of compassion and obedience.'[30]

The identification of *good* causes or reasons was more complicated. The trouble is that so much that Spinoza said about motivation was so negative. Strikingly, even right at the last pages of the *Ethics*, where we might expect something rather more positive, he strayed back into a final condemnation of the multitude, driven by lust, ignorance and fear into misguided beliefs about the burdens of virtue and about dreadful punishments after death. Even the very last assertion, that 'blessedness [*beatitudo*] is not the reward of virtue, but virtue itself'[31] seems to acquire a negative tinge: the power to keep lusts in check arises from blessedness itself; the wise man, 'in so far as he is considered as such, suffers scarcely any disturbance of spirit . . .'.

TWO FALSE TRAILS

At this point, in thinking about Spinoza's more positive account for religious motivations, it is possible to go off on two trails which do not get us to the roots of his views. Both are of interest in themselves, or in other contexts, but neither can help us here. These are his classification of differing types of knowledge and his apparent stoicism. Each needs a brief discussion.

We have seen that Spinoza classifies ways of knowing, ranging through imagination to intuitive knowledge. The 'blessedness' that is its own reward at the end of the *Ethics* is said to consist in a 'love that arises from the third kind of knowledge'. This is intuition.[32] He appears to support a Platonic alignment between grades of knowledge and grades of knower. The wise man uses intuition.[33] The multitude stumble in ignorance, lightened, at best, by imagination. There is an unavoidable elitism here. Knowledge is difficult. Most people cannot share it.

---

[30] Letter 23, 1665; L 166 = G IV 147/8–14 = 25–32.   [31] *Ethics* V, 42.
[32] Characterised at *Ethics* II, 40, Scholium 2.
[33] The view that Christ may have been especially privileged in this way is discussed in Chapter 9.

A good deal can be said about the way in which knowing is graded or classified, and how this corresponds to types of knowers: By what means are the multitude supposed to be 'saved', for example?[34] What, politically and educationally, are supposed to be the implications of the idea that only a few can attain wisdom? How can virtue, as it seems, be related to intellectual capacity?

These are significant questions in important areas, but they get us no nearer to a conclusion on the basic issue of religious motivation. *Why*, after all, should anyone, wise or not, act religiously, following a life of piety or virtue? The classification of kinds of knowledge tells us why some people might *not* want to do this but not, in itself, why anyone should. *Not*, of course, to achieve any end, such as salvation or, more crudely, some reward after death. That would represent the most deluded teleology. Spinoza does assemble the machinery for an answer: the higher grades of knowledge contain more 'adequate ideas', which put the knower into a more 'active' state, which is a good thing. But why should anyone want to know in the first place?

Then there is the influence from stoicism. Historically, this is undeniable. The portrait at the end of the *Ethics* of the wise man – checking his lusts, without disturbance of spirit, 'conscious by virtue of a certain eternal necessity of himself, of God, and of things', and possessing 'true spiritual contentment' – looks as though it comes straight from a manual of stoic ethics. Again, there is much scope for debate. Spinoza himself repudiated stoicism on the grounds that 'the Stoics thought that the emotions depend absolutely on our will, and that we can have absolute command over them'.[35] One of the most important claims in the *Ethics*, that 'It is impossible for a man not to be part of Nature',[36] can be read in two different senses. Negatively, in the stoic sense that emotions – external influences – are bad, and should be minimised: 'To be ruled by passion is, in Spinoza's estimation, the natural lot of humanity; but its ubiquitousness does not prevent this condition from being a pathological one in which we fall short of our true nature.'[37] But there is also another sense that is more positive. Spinoza believed that the stoics made the emotions subject to the will. He could not accept that. We are not made in that way. That is not our nature. How we are – our nature – nature – is that we are part of nature as we are, with the drives that we have, having the power that

[34] The standard treatment of these questions is Matheron, *Le Christ et le salut des ignorants*.
[35] *Ethics* v, Preface. We shall return to this in considering religion as therapy in Chapter 10.
[36] Part IV, 4.   [37] James, 'Spinoza the Stoic', p. 298.

they have.[38] As an aspect of nature that, surely, cannot be pathological. In any event, even if we could have ends, to aim to be something other than what we are would not be one of them.[39] And even if the stoic view were correct, and were applicable to Spinoza, there would still remain a question of *why* a knowledge of nature, including our own human nature, was so desirable. Not, again, to achieve any end.

GRANTED WE WANT TRUTH: WHY NOT RATHER UNTRUTH?[40]

In the *Theological-Political Treatise*, despite the scorn for the multitude (particularly scathing at the end of the Preface, for example), there is an anti-elitist, anti-legalistic emphasis on 'the natural light that is common to all'[41] in the interpretation of the scriptures. The author prefers 'the natural and universal ability and capacity of mankind', implicitly, to the subtle readings of theologians[42] and the imposition of ecclesiastical authority. In practical terms, maybe only 'very few' will achieve wisdom, but Spinoza cannot intend to restrict this field politically. The elitism is intellectual. Some get to know more than others. 'Intellectual or exact knowledge of God is not a gift shared by all the faithful, as is obedience.'[43]

The problem he created for himself was one of accounting for the motivation behind knowledge. There was a set of apparatus embellished with elaborate terminology: we become more *active* (or less *passive*) – and more *free* – as we understand our *affects* or *emotions* – as we acquire more understanding of nature – more *adequate ideas* – increasing our state of activity – through our *conatus*, or drive to exist and *act* which we share with every part of nature. All this was intensely reductive, in that the untidy world of the emotions became narrowed into a few simple channels. There were to be three 'basic emotions':[44] desire, pleasure and pain, in terms of which other were to be understood. Desire was related directly to *conatus* – drive or striving[45] – and *conatus* was fundamental: it is described in characteristically reductionist, nothing-but terms as 'nothing but the actual essence of the thing itself'.[46] Everything that exists has a drive to persist in its being, as part of its individuality.

---

[38] A similar line, not surprisingly: 'the Bedlamite hope that, *because* you know how to tyrannize over yourselves – Stoicism is self-tyranny – nature too can be tyrannized over: for is the Stoic not a *piece* of nature?' Nietzsche, *Beyond Good and Evil* (1886), trans. R. J. Hollingdale (Harmondsworth: Penguin, 1990), I, 9.   [39] In this case, by altering the balance of power between mind and body.
[40] Nietzsche, *Beyond Good and Evil*, I, I.   [41] S 160 = G III 117/17–18.
[42] For a wider perspective see John Milbank, *Theology and Social Theory* (Oxford: Blackwell, 1990), pp. 18–20.   [43] S 215 = G III 168/28–30.   [44] *Ethics* III, 59, Scholium; G II 189/2–3.
[45] *Ethics* III, 9, Scholium.   [46] *nihil est præter ipsius rei actualem essentiam; Ethics* III, 7.

In his earlier writing, in the unfinished *Treatise on the Emendation of the Intellect*, Spinoza had given a focal importance to the acquisition of a nature exemplifying 'the union which the mind has with the whole of Nature'. To bring this about, it was necessary 'to understand as much about Nature as suffices for acquiring such a nature'. This amounted to a declaration in favour of the need for knowledge. But it was expressed in terms of 'the end for which I strive' – a teleological explanation which he could hardly employ in his more perfected work.[47]

Plato resorted to mythological narrative in the *Symposium* and the *Phædrus* to portray the desire for knowledge or understanding. Aristotle produced the blunt statement that 'All men by nature desire to know.'[48] Descartes commented that the desire for knowledge 'which is common to all men, is an illness which cannot be cured, for curiosity grows with learning'.[49] Maybe Spinoza's reliance on *conatus* is not very different as an explanation of why knowledge is wanted. What might be different is that the load to be borne in his system was a considerable one. The preferred route to religion or virtue is through an understanding of our nature, and we are supposed to *want* this understanding because that is how we are. To which it seems sensible to object, what about those people who do not seem to be interested in getting more knowledge or understanding? Particularly, as we might well suspect, if such knowledge is to be seen in terms of a certain, specific sort of grasp of nature, now seen as *scientific*.[50] Any anthropologist will confirm that the forms of human curiosity can be as culturally varied as the forms of any other human desire. Scripture may not condemn ignorance. Can it condemn a lack of curiosity?

Conatus, in this context, may be seen most charitably as a kind of non-explanation or self-explanation. We want to know because we exist with a desire for knowledge: any explanation of Spinoza's thinking on this point can tend to sound circular. *Ethics* v, 25, for example, tells us that the 'highest *conatus* of the mind and its highest virtue is to

---

[47] *Hic est . . . finis, ad quem tendo*; p. 235, §14 = G II 8/27. Later, this is turned, more consistently, into *desire*; S 90 = G III 46/29, as it is in the *Ethics*: IV, Appendix, 4 – 'the final goal, that is, the highest Desire' (*finis ultimus, hoc est, summa Cupiditas . . .* G II 267/10).   [48] *Metaphysics* A, 980ª.
[49] *Search after Truth* CSMK II 402 = AT x 499.
[50] An unusually clear declaration: 'when you come right down to it the reason that we did this job is because it was an organic necessity. If you are a scientist you cannot stop such a thing. If you are a scientist you believe that it is good to find out how the world works: that it is good to find out what the realities are': J. Robert Oppenheimer, Speech to the Association of Los Alamos Scientists, 2 November 1945, in A. K. Smith and C. Weiner (eds.), *Robert Oppenheimer: Letters and Recollections* (Stanford University Press, 1995), p. 317: 'this job' was the construction of the Hiroshima and Nagasaki bombs.

understand things by the third kind of knowledge' (i.e. intuition).[51] Pierre Macherey remarks that this kind of knowledge 'lets the mind go to the extreme of the power of thinking which is in it',[52] but that sort of gloss only tends to confirm the thought that Spinoza is engaging in rhetorical hyperbole: the best kind of knowing must be associated with the best virtue and must stem from the noblest motivations. It would be interesting to see some examples. Here, any feeling of uncertainty may result from some lack of confidence that we feel in a Platonic scale of types of knowledge: 'Since our intellect forms the better part of us, it is evident that we should endeavour above all to perfect it as far as we can, for in its perfection must consist our supreme good.'[53]

We might wonder whether there is any reason at all why we might want to accept this. One can think of extraordinary and undeniable feats of intuition – insights of Ramanujan in number theory, for instance – and one might be willing to accept that these somehow exemplify the highest powers of the human mind; but it is not clear what that achieves. That it takes the finest minds to think the finest thoughts? Where does that get us? Nor is it obvious in such a case that motives or drives – *conatus* – are particularly relevant. A priori psychology seems to part company completely with reality.

WHY BE RELIGIOUS?

In the end, we get a confusing and inconclusive picture of motivation. People may have engaged in religious practices for various reasons. Spinoza flattens together all aspects of religious behaviour, from ritual to morality. That in itself was a critically reductive step. The appraisal of behaviour takes precedence over the accuracy of beliefs. He is clear that he admires people who behave well, even if they are said to adhere to mistaken beliefs. It seems he might prefer to leave praiseworthy practice as it is, rather than to attempt improving argument.

Quite possibly his position had some basis in a sceptical view that there is not much observed connection between moral behaviour and religious profession, and to that extent it matters less what people say they believe than how they act. This appears in a negative way:

---

[51] *Summus Mentis conatus, summaque virtus est res intelligere tertio cognitionis genere.*

[52] *Introduction à l'Éthique de Spinoza: La cinquième partie, les voies de la liberté* (Paris: Presses Universitaires de France, 1994), p. 137.   [53] S 103 = G III 59/29–32.

if a man reads the narratives of Holy Scripture and has complete faith in them, and yet pays no heed to the lesson that Scripture thereby aims to convey, and leads no better life, he might just as well have read the Koran or a poetic drama . . .[54]

If that is so, it might explain why the connections he made between beliefs and action are not straightforward. We are given models of wrong beliefs, which can lead to false religion, and we are given a model of what Spinoza considers to be the truth, which can act as a grounding for a right way of life. Wrong beliefs, in general, he was inclined to ascribe to specifically negative factors such as fear, ignorance and (as he saw it) hope, all of which were tied to mistaken beliefs about ends or purposes. A prescription was recommended: reduce fear and hope by under-standing these mistaken beliefs. Similarly, acceptance of the truth, as portrayed in the *Ethics*, would imply a reasonable life which was the same as a life of virtue and which was its own reward.

It is the underlying story about motivation where the complications set in. The ignorant or deluded may behave well, despite their beliefs. But Spinoza did not think that people should (or even, maybe, *could*) hold beliefs that they know to be inconsistent with a true account of how things are. Plainly enough, he thought that things are as they are shown to be by him in the *Ethics*. If that account is accepted, virtue is meant to follow. This may not be for everyone; after all, Spinozism is not easy to understand. Many may be better as they are. But, once again, what is supposed to make people *want* to understand? The abolition of teleology creates a problem for religious motivation. The system is meant to be self-propelling. Knowledge of nature – of our nature – can lead to virtue because we will correctly understand our interests as part of our nature, and we *want* such knowledge because our nature also includes a positive drive towards *activity* – an accumulation of truths and a diminution of falsehoods. We want knowledge not because truth is attractive – that would be teleology – but because the positive side of our nature has a drive towards it.

Like much of Spinoza's philosophy, this is radically simplifying. We may think that a way of life, a religion, is based on all sorts of human needs, wishes, hopes or desires. It is certainly based on an historical and social position. People can and do act well without what he sees as true beliefs. But if they cultivate the positive part of their natures they will seek true beliefs about themselves and about their location in

---

[54] S 122 = G III 79/16–20.

nature.[55] The *reason* or cause to do that is to be simplified to a basic drive or *conatus*.

Why be religious? means the same as, why live a life of piety and virtue? With suitable research, we will see that this is our nature, it is in our interest. And why should we want to pursue such research? Because that, too, is our nature, in our interest. How do we know that? Because that is how we are. We cannot look further.

---

[55] A properly ordered society, of course, will help: if a man 'dwells among individuals who are in harmony with man's nature, by that very fact his power of activity will be assisted and fostered': *Ethics* IV, Appendix, 7.

CHAPTER 6

The meaning of revelation

As to your fifth argument (namely, that the prophets made manifest the Word of God in that way), since truth is not contrary to truth it only remains for me to prove . . . that Scripture, as it stands, is the true revealed Word of God. A mathematically exact proof of this proposition can be attained only by divine revelation. I therefore said, 'I believe but do not know in a mathematical way, that all things revealed by God to the prophets [as necessary for salvation are set down in the form of law . . .']. For I firmly believe, but do not know in a mathematical way, that the prophets were the trusted counsellors and faithful messengers of God.[1]

This comes from a letter of 1665 written in Dutch by Spinoza to Willem van Blijenbergh, a grain broker with an interest in theology. Spinoza tried to prevent the appearance of a Dutch translation of the *Theological-Political Treatise*,[2] no doubt for reasons connected with what he had said in its Preface: 'I know how deeply rooted in the mind are the prejudices embraced under the guise of piety. I know, too, that the masses can no more be freed from their superstition than from their fears.'[3] But a translation appeared anyway. Blijenbergh, in 1674, went on to compose his *Truth of the Christian Religion and the Authority of Holy Scripture, Stated Against the Arguments of Ungodliness, or a Refutation of that Blasphemous Book Called Tractatus Theologico-Politicus. In which with the help of natural and Philosophical reasons, and using Arguments from Holy Scripture, the truth and necessity of the Christian Religion is proved as well as how Soul- and Earth-Destroying is the opinion of our Author.*[4]

How are we to take what Spinoza said in his letter of 1665? If we break it down into separate elements, some parts might not be too

---

[1] Letter 21; L 158 = G IV 133/8–17 with quotation in square brackets from Letter 19; L 135 = G IV 92–3.   [2] Letter 44.   [3] S 56 = G III 12.

[4] For historical detail see W. Van Bunge, 'On the Early Dutch Reception of the *Tractatus Theologico-Politicus*', *Studia Spinozana*, 5, 1989, and H. J. Siebrand, *Spinoza and the Netherlanders* (Assen: Van Gorcum, 1988).

surprising. Divine revelation and prophecy, for him, were plainly different from mathematical proof, so it is not unexpected that he might want to point to the difference. A distinction between belief, or faith, and knowledge seems commonplace. The notion of divine revelation, of God revealing the Word, or having messengers, looks puzzling to anyone who has read the *Ethics*. Yet the sincerity of the whole appears genuine enough. Spinoza did not *need* to tell Blijenbergh that he believed the prophets were the faithful messengers of God. Even if – as seems very likely – he was following his own advice to accommodate his meaning as far as possible to his reader's level of understanding,[5] we can still ask what he *did* mean.

The opening words of the *Theological-Political Treatise* tell us that prophecy or revelation – taken to be the same – is 'the sure knowledge of some matter revealed by God to man'. The remainder of the book, in the minds of many of its readers, goes on to generate some unease about that pronouncement. Before we look at the arguments, we should ask why the subject might matter. It touches importantly upon both the theory of knowledge and on assumptions about meaning. From a post-Humeian perspective we can imagine readily that revelation might be categorised out of existence as a channel of valid knowing. From a twentieth-century, post-positivist perspective we can imagine that the deliverances of revelation and prophecy are to be understood in different or special ('religious') *senses*, possibly immunising them to some extent from criticism.

EVIDENCE?

In eighteenth-century terms, we can see why the subject mattered. Hume's suave assurance that 'a wise man . . . proportions his belief to the evidence'[6] was a milestone on a slippery slope, some way downhill from an acceptance of an assumption that 'religious beliefs' or 'faith' stood in some relation to 'evidence' or even 'proof' which supported them. From there, a further slide downhill was unavoidable: can the truths of religion be proved by logic, or by the evidence of revelation and miracles? Let us consider the evidence . . .

It is worth seeing how far Spinoza was from that slope: in fact, he was nowhere near it. Prophecy, for him – as with the ceremonial practice of

---

[5] *Treatise on the Emendation of the Intellect*, p. 236, §17 = G II 9/23–7.
[6] *Enquiry Concerning Human Understanding*, x, 1.

religion and as with a pious and virtuous way of life – was nothing to do with philosophical truth: that is to say, with truth at all. For him, as we saw in Part I of this study, the existence of God was hardly even a question for persuasive proof, though it was for geometrical demonstration. God's non-existence was inconceivable. So no 'evidence' could be relevant. If Spinoza were to be judged – in eighteenth-century terms – as trying to undermine the validity of prophecy or revelation, that could hardly be in terms of prophecy or revelation as evidence for God's existence, because he never contemplated that prophecy or revelation *were* evidence for God's existence. If we judge him in those terms then what he said to Blijenbergh is bound to seem insincere or devious.

Instead, it could be that his aims were different: that he wanted to support or endorse prophecy and revelation, as he claimed, but in the rôle he identified for them: to buttress not faith in the sense of adherence to a set of truths, but religion in his sense of social and historical practice. In the *Theological-Political Treatise*, at the end of a chapter intended to show 'that neither is theology ancillary to reason nor reason to theology' he returned to drum in his point again: 'Before I continue, I wish to emphasise in express terms – though I have said it before – the importance and necessity of the role that I assign to Scripture, or revelation.'[7] And he does tell us, in fact, that it is essential that there should be revelation.[8]

SOME POSSIBLE ARGUMENTS

First, we should consider the strategy in Spinoza's case. Readers from an empiricist tradition are likely to be misled. From such a perspective, it looks as though his approach was a matter-of-fact, critical, one, relying on several weak dichotomies and executed, apparently, through some fairly blunt, if not crude, arguments. Along such lines, it is possible to dissect out two phases to his arguments, as one route into his thinking. We should try this, if only to show how easy this access route seems to be; but then we should also go on to look at the problems it leaves unresolved. Early in the *Theological-Political Treatise* – in Chapters I and II – we can find a discussion of the legitimation of prophecy. Later on, in a second phase of arguments, prophecy seems to be located in relation to philosophy or 'natural' knowing. Most of this looks plain enough in his own words.

---

[7] S 236 = G III 188/19–22.
[8] Or, rather 'should have been' – the significance of this will be discussed later: *revelationem maxime necessariam fuisse*, S 233 = G III 185/26.

PHASE I: THE LEGITIMATION OF PROPHECY

(a) First, the bundling-together of prophecy and revelation is an important assumption in itself, characteristic of Spinoza's minimalism. 'An examination of the Bible will show us that everything that God revealed to the prophets was revealed either by words, or by appearances, or by a combination of both.'[9] It is essential to his case to tidy up the subject-matter. The cloudy and archetypally mysterious deliverances of divine revelation have to be pinned down to being 'either by words, or by appearances, or by a combination of both'.

(b) A distinction is assumed between the 'natural light' (or the 'light of reason') and 'the imaginative faculty'. Something is 'told us by the prophets, not revealed through reason':[10] these seem to be straight alternatives.

(c) 'We can now have no hesitation in affirming that the prophets perceived God's revelations with the aid of the imaginative faculty alone, that is, through the medium of words or images'[11] ('with the exception of Christ':[12] more on that later, in Chapter 9).

(d) And imagination, 'unlike every clear and distinct idea, does not of its own nature carry certainty with it'. Prophecy 'cannot of itself carry certainty' because it depends solely on the imagination.[13]

(e) 'Since . . . the prophets perceived the revelations of God with the aid of the imaginative faculty, they may doubtless have perceived much that is beyond the limits of the intellect.' This is the point that was considered in Chapters 2 and 3 in connection with possibility: we can *think* or *say* all kinds of things, but that capacity tells us nothing about their possibility, and still less about their actuality. Again: 'For many more ideas can be constructed from words or images than from merely the principles and axioms on which our entire natural knowledge is based.'[14]

(f) The imaginative faculty is 'fleeting and inconstant', so the gift of prophecy has been historically uncommon.[15]

(g) And 'prophecy varied not only with the imagination and the temperament of each prophet but also with the beliefs in which they had been brought up'. 'the signs vouchsafed were suited to the beliefs and capacity of the prophet'.[16]

---

[9] S 61 = G III 17/9–11.   [10] S 66 = G III 23/14–15.   [11] S 70–1 = G III 28/3–5.
[12] S 65 = G III 21/23.   [13] S 74 = G III 30/13–15.   [14] S 71 = G III 28/21–5.
[15] S 71 = G III 29/3.   [16] S 73, 75 = G III 30/5–8, 32/17.

PHASE II: PROPHECY AND PHILOSOPHY

(h) Prophets did not 'perceive God's decrees adequately, as eternal truths'.[17]

(i) So they were different from philosophers, 'who endeavour to understand things not from miracles but from clear conceptions'.[18]

(j) Prophecy 'surpasses human understanding and is a purely theological question, revelation being the only basis for making any assertion about it, or even for understanding its essential nature'.[19]

(k) 'Nobody knows by nature that he has any duty to obey God. Indeed, this knowledge cannot be attained by any process of reasoning; one can only gain it by revelation confirmed by signs.'[20]

(l) Reason cannot demonstrate that we are saved 'simply by obedience'. This 'cannot be investigated by the natural light of reason'.

So, it seems that Spinoza concludes, it is essential that there is revelation.[21]

Parallel lines of thinking deal with the authority of scripture. Scripture is 'chiefly made up of historical narratives and revelation'. Its real authors 'taught for the most part not from the natural light common to all but from a light peculiar to themselves'. To understand it 'is by no means the same thing as to understand the mind of God, that is, to understand truth itself'.[22]

If (a)–(l), assembled like this, were to be taken as a chain of critical arguments, they would not add up to an impressive case.

The opening move, for both revelation and scripture, is a simplifying one, analogous to Descartes's agglomeration of sensation, affirmation and will into a single category of the 'mental'. The simplification is hardly convincing. 'It was only through images and words that God revealed'; 'These are the only means of communication between God and man that I find in the Bible, and so, as I have previously shown, no other means should be alleged or admitted.'[23] But he had not 'previously shown' this, except by a carefully presented selection of texts. His point is a purely prescriptive one: only words or images are to count as divine communications. Strenuous biblical exegesis is applied to assist that view.

In the background, it seems, is (b): an exhaustive dichotomy between the *natural light* (or, at least here, *clear conception*) which delivers truths about

---

[17] S 107 = G III 50/1–2. [18] S 131 = G III 88/4–5. [19] S 138 = G III 95/5–7.
[20] S 246 = G III 198/13–15. [21] S 233 = G III 185/16–26.
[22] S 141, 209, 210 = G III 98/34–5, 162–3, 163/31–2. [23] S 64 = G III 20/30–2.

nature, and the *imagination*, whose action is unreliable as far is truth is concerned but is – so it seems – essential for the reinforcement of morality: what Spinoza calls 'obedience'.

A great deal has been written about this.[24] We can, if we wish, try to align the dichotomy between imagination (in prophecy, scripture, revelation) and rational knowledge (in philosophy) in the *Theological-Political Treatise* with the distinctions between types of cognition given in Part II of the *Ethics*. Imagination is portrayed as visual imagining and is, to some extent, dependent on the powers of the body.[25] The light of nature, or clear and distinct conception, provides more reliable information. But all this, though important in other contexts, is not especially relevant to the basic weakness of the case as now presented. We would be asked to accept, a priori, that information can get to us in either of two ways – imaginatively or by the natural light of clear perception. The logical fork would then be used to tidy any recalcitrant items into line. Someone who *starts* by saying that religious information is intrinsically different – or even not quite so simple – is not answered by such an approach. It would beg the question: *can* there be knowledge vouchsafed by revelation?

NON-NATURAL KNOWING?

Spinoza was not trying to present a critique of revelation from an empiricist perspective, or anything remotely like one. That may seem obvious, yet assumptions to the contrary can be hard to put aside. For example, it is easy to overlook an important element which is implicit in his thinking. He *seems* to need a way to deny that any channel of supernatural or non-natural information might be available. Yet the orthodox distinction between the 'natural light' (which could deliver the substance of mathematics and the sciences) and a 'supernatural light' (for matters of faith) could scarcely be open to him for use as a premise in a critical argument. Descartes had declared that the 'formal reason which leads us to assent to matters of faith consists in a certain inner light which comes from God, and when we are supernaturally illumined by it we are confident that what is put forward for us to believe has been revealed by God himself . . . this is more certain than any natural light'.[26]

And that was enough for *him*, given his reluctance to stray into matters of theology: he was glad to remain silent on supernatural illumination.

[24] See Laux, *Imagination et religion, passim*, for example.
[25] See R. G. Blair, 'Spinoza's Account of Imagination', in Grene (ed.), *Spinoza: A Collection of Critical Essays.*   [26] *Second Replies*, CSMK II 105 = AT VII 148.

Spinoza represented the position of Descartes correctly in his *Principles of Descartes' Philosophy* where he wrote that angels are a subject for theology, but not for metaphysics: 'For their essence and existence are known only by revelation and so pertain only to Theology. Since theological knowledge is altogether other than, or completely different in kind from, natural knowledge, it ought not to be mixed with it in any way. So no one will expect us to say anything about angels.'[27]

Such a separation was impossible in his own thought. He was barred from any sort of knowing other than natural knowing (as he saw it) because he could admit nothing but what he saw as nature. From the *Ethics* that is clear, but the question of prophetic or revealed knowledge was hardly mentioned there.[28] On the other hand, the *Theological-Political Treatise* contains no systematic explanation of why the non-natural or the supernatural should be ruled out. The identity of nature with God looms up many times, most boldly at the beginnings of Chapters IV and VI, but its implications are not spelled out anywhere.[29]

That omission made the discussion about revelation and prophecy far more fragile than it might have been. Spinoza might have argued that because there can be nothing but nature, supernatural knowing is excluded; or, more plausibly, that his was not the kind of God who could or would impart specific items of knowledge through channels of supernatural illumination, in a non-systematic way.

His omission is usually seen as a matter of rhetorical strategy.[30] He would have had to fight on too many fronts at once if he had unveiled the God of the *Ethics* in the *Theological-Political Treatise*. But there might also have been far better reasons, connected with the characterisation of *the natural*.

In Chapter 3 we saw that one of the reasons for his repudiation of Cartesian doubt may have been a rejection of a *non-natural* suspension of judgment: a rejection of the Cartesian evil demon. But *that* line of thinking did not really require any difficult assumptions about what was 'natural' and what was not. The hypothesis of the evil demon required the supposition of some form of explanation which was detached from (and hence inaccessible to) other forms of explanation accessible to Descartes: if he could understand how the demon might be subverting

---

[27] Appendix II, XII; Curley, p. 341 = G I 275.
[28] And then in an extremely negative way, at Part IV, 54, Scholium, as Laux points out, *Imagination et religion*, p. 45 and n. 5.
[29] S 89–90 = G III 45–6 and S 124–6 = G III 81–3; though this did not conceal Spinoza's position from his contemporary readers, as Van Bunge describes, 'On the Early Dutch Reception of the *Tractatus Theologico-Politicus*', pp. 235–40.　　[30] Or by critics, such as Strauss, as insincerity.

his reasoning, after all, he could theorise a way around it, so that its threat would disappear. In that area of argument, the boundary between the natural and the non-natural could be expressed in other ways: in terms of intelligibility or, more specifically, in terms of the connected-ness of explanations.

In the case of prophetic revelations, that was not so. Why, for example, *could* there not be a different source for information, separate from intui-tion, rational knowledge or imagination: information imparted by God? As a foundation beneath his arguments, it might seem that Spinoza needed to be able to take some negative attitude towards the possibility of special supernatural insight, of the kind which Descartes had found so diplomatic to ignore. But how could he do this non-circularly?

Sometimes, like Hume later, he did tend to rely tactically on the prior or superior likelihood of non-supernatural explanation. One of his most often-cited illustrations is from Joshua, Chapter 10, where the prophet asked God to prolong the daylight so that he could carry on smiting the Amorites: 'the sun halted in midheaven, and did not press on to set, for a whole day; for the LORD fought for Israel. Neither before nor since has there been such a day, when the LORD acted on words spoken by a man.'

Spinoza's assumption in dealing with this[31] is that we do not need to resort to supernatural explanation if a perfectly sensible physical one is at hand. But this begs the question by taking for granted that we already know what a sensible physical explanation is. And any confidence on *that* point which may have built up since his time has evaporated during the twentieth century.

He hinted at a more subtle line of thinking:

> everything takes place through the power of God. Indeed, since Nature's power is nothing but the power of God, it is beyond doubt that ignorance of natural causes is the measure of our ignorance of the power of God. So it is folly to have recourse to the power of God when we do not know the natural cause of some phenomenon – that is, when we do not know the power of God. However, there is no need anyway for us now to have an understanding of the cause of pro-phetic knowledge . . . our enquiry is here confined to the teachings of Scripture, with a view to drawing our conclusions from these, as from data presented by Nature. The causes of these Scriptural teachings is not our concern.[32]

Here, the underlying principle is that where something seems to be unexplained, we should go on seeking explanations as far as possible.

---

[31] Joshua 10: 13, 14 (JPS). S 79, 127, 135 = G III 35–6, 84, 92. The text was central in Galileo's dealings with the Inquisition, as Spinoza would have known.   [32] S 71 = G III 28/11–20.

That, we know, was one of Spinoza's cardinal methodological tenets. Now, as in the case against final causes, the added presumption is that where an explanation is missing, we are to assume that one can be found, rather than appeal to 'the power of God' as an end to inquiry. In so far as the power of God can tend to be used as the 'sanctuary of ignorance', this is surely a sound pragmatic procedure. In the simplest terms, it will be good for science if we go on looking for explanations and bad for science if we give up and bring in God as a *deus ex machina* when we can't find other answers.

In addition, in the quoted passage, and assuming a knowledge of the *Ethics*, we can see that another strand of argument lends support, further beneath the surface. Any chain of causes will be endless, spreading throughout nature, and as such, as a whole, could only be intelligible in terms of the 'power of God'; but it will be a mistake to break off an endless chain of causes where our knowledge can take us no further and to say that God's action begins there. That would apply to prophetic revelation as much as to any other event ('in nature').

Maybe this is wrong: like ruling out the super-natural or the non-natural by assuming that there can be no place for it, because, again, everything can be explained in principle within nature – which is just to say that everything can be explained: scientific dogmatism.

But if one adopts Spinoza's standpoint, there is no need to draw a distinction between the natural and the non-natural, because such a contrast has no basis. The quotations assembled into arguments earlier in this chapter look like an unnecessary diversion if they are read in a spirit of later critical philosophy: as if prophetic-imaginative utterances should be seen as non-natural in contrast with the 'natural light' of true knowledge, and hence – inevitably – as less legitimate. If Spinoza is read in that way, the case does seem weak, or even circular. How do we *know*, after all, that all cognition is either through imagination or rational judgment or intuition, without any other possibility? How could we rely on that classification to exclude other forms of cognition – mystical illumination, prophetic vision, miraculous revelation – without circularity?

Yet Spinoza was not thinking like a critical philosopher, trying to discriminate valid from invalid knowledge – on the one side: natural, rational light leading to truth; on the other side: non-natural, prophetic imagination leading to error. We can see how easy it has been to read him in that way – and it may well have been the direction in which thinking moved during the century after he lived – but we should also see how faulty it is. Faulty in at least two radical ways: first, in that he never admitted *any* distinction between the 'natural' and the 'non-natural'.[33] Imagination was not non-natural or super-natural. Like anything else, it was a process to be understood (we can say a *natural* process if we like, but that adds nothing but emphasis: all processes are natural). Secondly, he did not think the prophets were *wrong* at all. A statement such as 'We can . . . have no hesitation in affirming that the prophets perceived God's revelations with the aid of the imaginative faculty alone'[34] does not seek to invalidate or downgrade prophetic revelation. And, again, we can recall the opening words of the *Theological-Political Treatise*: 'Prophecy, or Revelation, is the sure knowledge of some matter revealed by God to man.' Instead of straining to take this ironically or insincerely, we can take it seriously, in Spinoza's sense. His aim was not to make a critical separation between pretended information from the prophets and reliable information obtained rationally. Prophecy and philosophy (that is, science) did have different functions, but so far as they needed to be legitimised by their origins they were equal: *both* came from nature. 'Natural knowledge can be called prophecy, for the knowledge that we acquire by the natural light of reason depends solely on knowledge of God and of his eternal decrees' and – seen the other way – prophetic knowledge 'has as much right as any other to be called divine, since it is dictated to us, as it were, by God's nature in so far as we participate therein, and by God's decrees'.[35]

THE COMPLETENESS OF PROPHECY

Before looking at the differing functions of prophecy and philosophy, it is worth noting one aspect of the logic in Spinoza's case which has been overlooked by commentators. He regarded prophecy (and hence prophetic revelation) as being in the past, and hence complete. Not only that, but it was to be taken as completely recorded. This move in his argument was made in the first pages of the *Theological-Political Treatise*:

what can we say of things transcending the bounds of our intellect [*de rebus, limites nostri intellectus excendetibus*] except what is transmitted to us by the prophets by word or writing? And since there are no prophets among us today, as far as I know, our only recourse is to peruse the sacred books left to us by the prophets of old, taking care, however . . .

[33] Sylvain Zac, *Spinoza et l'interprétation de l'Ecriture* (Paris: Presses Universitaires de France, 1965), p. 90.   [34] S 70 = G III 28/3–5.   [35] S 59 = G III 15.

And the conclusion, as he said, was that 'our discussion must be confined to what is drawn only from Scripture'.[36] The consequences in terms of his approach are clear enough. Given his premises, he had no need to seek a critical criterion to test the validity of prophetic revelation in general (here is a prophetic claim – how do we tell that it is genuine?) because the class of prophetic revelations was to be regarded as closed. Also, to a large extent, the validation of prophecy consisted in its inclusion in the canon of scripture.[37] The logical upshot was that he could turn his attention to examples of prophecy recorded in the scriptures and, he seems to have thought, deal with them exhaustively: 'In the matter of prophecy I made no assertion that I could not infer from grounds revealed in Holy Scripture . . . In the case of prophecy I had no alternative but to compile a historical account .'[38]

The weakness is evident: there would be later claims of prophecy and there would certainly be disputes over the interpretation of scripture. But there was also some logical strength in the approach. Spinoza could make generalisations about prophecy on the basis of an exhaustive catalogue, not by using general psychological or epistemological criteria. Hence we see statements such as: 'An examination of the Bible will show us that everything that God revealed to the prophets was revealed either by words, or by appearances.'[39]

An examination of the Bible is the only support for the important claim that 'God never deceives the good and his chosen ones'[40] which in turn supports the view that 'the certainty afforded by prophecy was not a mathematical certainty, but only a moral certainty'.[41] But the principle that God never deceives the good is not suggested as a general criterion for the identification of valid prophecy (and still less in the Cartesian sense in which God could not deceive); it is more a thought about the constitution of prophecy – what the prophets have said has had moral certainty, and that is the same as the idea that God does not deceive the good.

So, logically, again: 'These are the only means of communication between God and man that I can find in the Bible, and so, as I have previously shown, no other means should be alleged or admitted.'[42]

---

[36] S 60 = G III 16/27ff. [37] S 236 = G III 185/33–186/4. [38] S 137–8 = G III 94–5.
[39] S 61 = G III 17/9–11.
[40] S 74 = G III 31/15: *Deus pios, & electos nunquam decipit.* Curiously, the text cited by Spinoza actually says the converse: 'As the ancient proverb has it: "Wicked deeds come from wicked men!"', I Samuel 24: 14 (JPS). [41] *sed tantum moralis* S 74 = G III 30/35.
[42] *nulla alia fingenda, neque admittenda*, S 64 = G III 20/30–2.

We can see from that last remark that the approach offered a temptation to extend itself beyond its proper bounds. If the textual scholarship was correct, 'no other means should be alleged or admitted' in the Bible; but that would have no bearing on the possibility of later revelations. The claim that 'there are no prophets among us today' is not one that everyone might support, especially since 'prophet' is being used in the tendentiously wide sense of anyone claiming to be in receipt of divine communication, in the loosest way. This piece of argument is more revealing about Spinoza's attitude or approach than as a contribution to thinking about religion.

THE NEED FOR REVELATION

So what was to be the function of prophecy? This is plain enough. The prophets, expressing their understanding of human nature in their own ways, will speak and act to reinforce social solidarity and morality in ways that will be intelligible in their place and time. In short – and again, Spinoza uses a single term to embrace a great deal – much of this comes under the title of 'obedience'. Again, his underlying argument looks like the use of a simple dichotomy. Factual information about nature may be complicated and difficult to discover, and will be known only to a few – the philosophers – who take the trouble. For the rest (or in the meantime) society has to function, and morality is required in terms in which it can be understood and enforced. Hence the need for prophets and for the 'laws' they may have enunciated.

And is easy enough to find Spinoza sounding like this: 'God adapted his revelations to the understanding and beliefs of the prophets, who may well have been ignorant of matters that have no bearing on charity and moral conduct but concern philosophic speculation.'[43]

In fact his case seems to be even more forceful. Reason will not be sufficient for what he calls salvation. It cannot 'demonstrate this fundamental principle of theology, that men may be saved simply by obedience'; 'we cannot perceive by the natural light that simple obedience is a way to salvation'. But 'all men without exception are capable of obedience'.[44] So prophecy or revelation is needed.

This all looks simple, although we might be rather surprised to find Spinoza straying so close to the battle-grounds of post-reformation polemics: we even find remarks such as that only revelation teaches us

---

[43] S 86 = G III 42/26–8.   [44] S 233, 236 = G III 185/16–17, 188.

that salvation comes about 'by God's singular grace which we cannot attain by reason',[45] suggesting that he may have had more relish for partisan theology than he liked to admit. But it is striking and important that he held back from the clear-cut conclusions that we might expect to be drawn from his arguments. Here, for example, is a passage which has been quoted only in part. We need to see the whole to sense the true direction of his thinking:

> I wish to emphasise . . . the importance and necessity of the role that I assign to Scripture, or revelation. For since we cannot perceive by the natural light that simple obedience is a way to salvation <annotation 31: see below>, and since only revelation teaches us that this comes about by God's singular grace which we cannot attain by reason, it follows that Scripture has brought very great comfort to mankind. For all men without exception are capable of obedience, while there are only a few – in proportion to the whole of humanity – who acquire a virtuous disposition under the guidance of reason alone. Thus, did we not have the testimony of Scripture, the salvation of nearly all men would be in doubt.[46]

Although the intention is supposed to be to emphasise the necessity of scripture or revelation, the curiously muted conclusion is that scripture has 'brought very great comfort to mankind'(*magnum admodum solamen mortalibus attulisse*). The reason is evident – Spinoza wants to allow for those who may acquire a virtuous disposition under the guidance of reason alone. So, at best, scripture or revelation is not necessary for everyone. This is not just an *ad hoc* exception (to make allowance for himself and Jesus, putting it unkindly). If we look at his annotation we see where the argument starts to unravel:

> [Note 31] 'that simple obedience is a way to salvation'. That is, it is not reason but revelation that can teach us that it is enough for blessedness or salvation for us to accept the divine decrees as laws or commandments, and that there is no need to conceive them as eternal truths. This is made clear by what we have demonstrated in Chapter IV.

What he thought he had demonstrated in Chapter IV was that the divine law, whether physical, moral or political, was the same as the law of nature. (Although it is doubtful whether he had *demonstrated* that there. It would be more accurate to say that he had imported the assumption from the *Ethics*.)

This is significant because it shows us that his argument did not have the form that we might have expected. What we do *not* see, crucially, is

---

[45] S 236 = G III 188/23–5: *ex singulari Dei gratia.* [46] S 236 = G III 188.

reliance on a distinction between fact and value: facts to be ascertained by philosophy (science), values to be asserted and reinforced by prophecy and revelation – so we need prophets because facts without values are impossible for normal life. Such a reading would be quite understandable in the light of many of Spinoza's remarks, but there are two things wrong with it.

First, there is a specific reservation which cuts across any dichotomy of fact against value in the course of this very discussion. Reason is not able to demonstrate that we may be 'saved' by obedience alone. So why rely on it? Not for no reason: that would be stupid. But if there *is* a reason 'then theology becomes part of philosophy and inseparable from it'. This dilemma is apparently accepted. So 'it is essential that there should be revelation'. But then the telling, cautious reservation:

Nevertheless, we can use judgment before we accept with at least moral certainty that which has been revealed [*nos judicio uti posse, ut id jam revelatum morali saltem certitudine amplectamur*]. I say 'with moral certainty', for we have no grounds for expecting to reach greater certainty in this matter than did the prophets to whom it was originally revealed.[47]

So, we can use 'judgment' even in the acceptance of what has been revealed. The term (*judicium*) is an unexpected one, used in the *Theological-Political Treatise* mostly in connection with freedom of religious choice and in the *Ethics* in only one place,[48] and then in connection with the impossibility of suspending judgment. Anyway, the point is that Spinoza was antagonistic to judgment in any form except as rational decision-making in the sense of an acceptance of truths. So his reservation that judgment must be prior to moral certainty is a revealing one. The impression that prophecy or morality takes over where reason stops is a misleading one.

Secondly, and more fundamentally, there can be no question of a dichotomy between value and fact in his thinking. In Note 31, just quoted, where 'it is not reason but revelation that can teach us that it is enough' to accept divine decrees as commandments, the contrast is not between the *facts* discovered by reason (philosophy, science) and the *values* pronounced in revelation or prophecy (in scripture). It is between *less* knowledge – or even ignorance – and *more* knowledge. If we see that divine laws are eternal truths then we cease to regard them as 'laws or commandments' because we have simply seen their truth.

That reading is reinforced in a later annotation, to a remark that

---

[47] S 233 = G III 185/23–30.   [48] II, 49 Scholium; G II 132–4.

'nobody knows by nature that he has any duty to obey God'.[49] The note – 34 – seems to corrode much of the thinking in the main text, and is of great interest. Here, obedience – given such focal importance as the purpose of prophecy – 'has regard to the will of him who commands, and not to necessity and truth':

> Now since we do not know the nature of God's will . . . it is only from revelation that we can know whether God wishes to receive honour from men like some temporal ruler. Furthermore, we have shown that the divine commandments appear to us as commandments or ordinances only as long as we do not know their cause. Once this is known, they cease to be commandments, and we embrace them as eternal truths, not as commandments; that is, obedience forthwith passes into love, which arises from true knowledge by the same necessity as light arises from the sun. Therefore by the guidance of reason we can love God, but not obey him . . .[50]

More plainly here than in Note 31 (see above), we see that the contrast between obedience as a source of moral value, and philosophy, is a question of less and more knowledge, not of a need for value to help us take decisions where reason will not work. We only think in terms of obedience or commandments in a state of relative ignorance. Prophecy is necessary and appropriate in a sense that not everyone can understand 'eternal truths'. It is not necessary in a sense that everyone needs it. But Spinoza's expression in his note, and in the text on which it comments, is tortuous. 'Nobody knows by nature that he has any duty to obey God. Indeed, this knowledge cannot be attained by any process of reasoning; one can only gain it by revelation.'[51] Yet, as if to counteract that, he takes 'the divine natural law whose chief commandment . . . is to love God', and is suddenly explicit: 'love of God is not obedience but a virtue necessarily present in a man who knows God aright [*qui Deum recte novit*], whereas obedience has regard to the will of him who commands, and not to necessity and truth'.[52]

So the very best way to live is not to be subject to obedience on the advice of the prophets, but to live in virtue as a result of knowledge. The necessity of prophecy and revelation has to be seen in that context. 'Obedience' may be necessary for morality and social order, and these are never underestimated: Spinoza is clear that 'salvation' is possible through an honest and decent life.[53]

[49] S 246 = G III 198/13–14. [50] S 308 = G III 264/15–25.
[51] 'knowledge' is added by the translator; there is no suggestion that we do know this; S 246 = G III 198 13–15 . . . *imo nec ulla ratione hoc assequi.* [52] S 307–8 = G III 264/12–15.
[53] *Salus* means 'health' or 'well-being' as well as salvation in a specifically religious sense: an ambiguity almost perfect for Spinozistic purposes.

His first readers did not have the benefit of the annotations to the *Theological-Political Treatise*, where, as we have seen, his sense emerges most openly, but this did not prevent them from seeing some of his points. A letter of 1671 from Lambert de Velthuysen, for example, is precise:

[the author] holds that the man who understands things aright ought to devote himself to virtue not because of God's precepts and law, nor through hope of reward or fear of punishment, but because he is enticed by the beauty of virtue and the joy which a man feels in the practice of virtue.

He therefore asserts that it is only to outward appearance that God, through the prophets and through revelation, exhorts men to virtue . . . But men of true judgment understand that there is no truth or force underlying such arguments.[54]

Spinoza's reply to this was partial and indirect. He drew attention to the supreme injunction to love God, but without explaining his own unusual understanding of that love. His response on prophecy must have been an exercise in careful wording:

I showed that God has revealed this very law to his prophets, and whether I maintain that this law of God received its authoritative form from God himself or whether I conceive it to be like the rest of God's decrees which involve eternal necessity and truth, it will nevertheless remain God's decree and a teaching for salvation.[55]

Disentangling this, we can see, crucially, that he himself did not regard his account of prophecy as *reductive*, in the sense that revelation might be thought to be *nothing but* imagination. He ascribes to it what we might call a psychological or naturalistic origin, but that for him did not at all prevent it from being 'the decree of God':

the imaginative faculty of the prophets, in so far as it was the instrument for the revelation of God's decrees, could equally well be called the mind of God, and the prophets could be said to have possessed the mind of God. Now the mind of God and his eternal thoughts are inscribed in our minds, too, and therefore we also, in Scriptural language, perceive the mind of God.[56]

And presumably this was his line on the legitimacy of revelation. We would be mistaken to think of it as 'only' psychological. If it came from the imagination of the prophets and if it led to lives conducted in accordance with virtue then it was authentic. But it is not hard to see why Spinoza's readers might have found that unsatisfactory. In reply to

---

[54] Letter 42; L 227 = G IV 209/3 ff (the letter was written in the third person, via an intermediary).
[55] Letter 43; L 240 = G IV 223–4.   [56] S 70 = G III 27/24–9.

Velthuysen's charge that, according to Spinoza, 'the purpose of the prophet's mission was to promote the cultivation of virtue among men, and not to teach any truth',[57] he made no reply; nor could he, because the charge was surely justified.

Spinoza's position on revelation and prophecy was not difficult to misunderstand, either for his contemporaries or for later readers. It seems beyond doubt that his intention was to locate prophecy where he felt it should belong, rather than to undermine it, and the account in this chapter should have shown how he tried to do that. Although he may not have wanted to diminish the standing of revelation in religion – even to put it in those terms seems badly out of line with his approach – there are at least two strands in his thinking which have an undeniably critical effect.

First, there was the flattening effect produced by treating the scriptures, revelation and the deliverances of the prophets all in the same way. In one sense, he was anxious to stress the diversity of prophecy, just as it suited his case to draw attention to the diversity of styles and genres in the Bible. The prophets and the writers of the scriptures adapted their utterances and their writings consciously or unconsciously to the minds of their audiences. But in another sense, tracing prophecy and revelation to a single origin in the imagination had a constricting effect. It may not have been meant reductively, but it certainly must have paved the way for reduction: the next step, definitely not taken by Spinoza, but all too obvious, was to say that revelation was *only* the product of the imagination.

Secondly, Spinoza may not have meant to criticise the legitimacy of revelation – on the contrary, if it was to be seen as 'the sure knowledge of some matter revealed by God to man' – but he did cut away much of its traditional support. The accusation by Velthuysen that 'the Koran . . . is to be put on a level with the Word of God. And the author has not left himself a single argument to prove that Mahomet was not a true prophet. For the Turks, too, in obedience to the command of their prophet, cultivate those moral virtues about which there is no disagreement among nations'[58] was more or less correct; and Spinoza answered it in a way that could have only inflamed his critics. He noted that

---

[57] Letter 42; L 227–8 = G IV 209–10.   [58] Letter 42; L 236 = G IV 218/25–9.

Muhammad was an 'impostor' because he took away religious freedom, but all the same, if he taught divine law and gave signs of his mission, then there would be no reason to deny that he was a true prophet. Then, as we have seen, he went on to say that Muslims would be saved if they 'worship God by the exercise of justice and by love of their neighbour', whatever their opinions.[59] The validation of revelation, as Velthuysen had seen, was moral. Much of the lengthy biblical exegesis in the *Theological-Political Treatise* was aimed to show that prophecy in the Hebrew scriptures and in the teachings of Christian writers, as far as the author went into them, was moral in character rather than 'philosophical'. It could only follow that the authenticity or legitimacy of these writings was also moral: 'the divinity of Scripture must be established solely from the fact that it teaches true virtue'.[60] Spinoza saw that as an advantage, in disentangling faith from philosophy or religion from science. With an aftersight of subsequent history it is easy to forget that he thought he was establishing the divinity of scripture, not undermining it. But, to his critics, the price was a high one.

NON-CRITICAL APPROACHES: KNOWLEDGE

From this chapter it should have emerged that Spinoza's interest in prophecy and revelation was not one based in a critical, epistemological approach. His aim was not to apply some test or criterion derived from a theory of knowledge to sort out real knowledge ('philosophy', 'truth') from pretended knowledge ('imagination', 'prophecy', 'faith'). If we judge him in that way, as we have seen, we not only distort his intentions but we also land him with some indefensible positions. He did not lean upon an assumed division between 'natural' and 'non-natural' sources of knowledge, for example. (Nor does it affect the force of his case on revelation that the physiological–psychological support for his account of imagination was, in fact, only rudimentary.[61]) And, on reflection, we might see that his approach would not be an epistemologically critical one. From Chapter 3 we saw how he felt able to repudiate the priority of questions about knowledge and certainty. That priority tended to dominate subsequent philosophy, including what came to be seen as the philosophy of religion; so perhaps it is not surprising that there may be a temptation to read Spinoza on prophecy in a critical, epistemological

---

[59] L 241 = G IV 225.   [60] S 142 = G III 99/20–21.
[61] See again Blair, 'Spinoza's Account of Imagination'.

sense. But the primacy of the theory of knowledge in philosophy is now said to be ebbing, so we may be able to get a fairer view.

If we are able to put aside preconceptions imposed by a legacy from worries about theories of knowledge, it may be more difficult to relinquish worries about meaning. Spinoza used the language of the *Ethics* in the *Theological-Political Treatise* without explanation. We have just seen how 'the revelation of God's decrees' could be seen as the 'the mind of God' and how the prophets could be said to have 'possessed the mind of God'. But the *Treatise* is full of reports such as that 'God bestowed a far greater gift of prophecy on one prophet than another', 'With a real voice God revealed to Moses', God 'forgives repentant sinners', 'It was through images and words that God revealed to Joshua'.[62] Despite the total opposition of Spinoza to any form of anthropomorphism, and despite the account of the existence and action of God in the *Ethics*, we find God speaking, bestowing, revealing and much else.

What are we to make of this? One response is to think in terms of duplicity, dishonesty or insincerity. This was the view of Leo Strauss and Julius Guttmann,[63] and it is hardly a new charge. Less severely, one might think that Spinoza said one thing while meaning another. Yovel, for example, draws attention to the importance of double language in Spinoza's Marrano background. He believes that 'metaphoric expressions' such as 'God's will' actually can be *translated* into what he calls 'systematic equivalents' such as 'the totality of things, events, and processes in the universe taken in their necessary causal connections'. The 'systematic equivalents', Yovel thinks, are 'literal' and 'rational', reflecting his opinion that Spinoza wanted to represent religion in practice as semi-rational. He thinks that 'There is a whole series of terms which serve Spinoza as metaphors, but are perfectly translatable into strict philosophical language . . . Although the literal sense of the term may be very misleading (e.g., "the will of God"), there is another, philosophical sense into which it can be translated and which constitutes its tacit new meaning.'[64]

---

[62] S 70, 78, 61, 225, 63 = G III 27/26–7, 35/13–14, 17/16, 178/4, 20/1.
[63] In Strauss, 'How to Study Spinoza's Theological-Political Treatise' and *Spinoza's Critique of Religion*; Julius Guttmann wrote that 'Spinoza pretends to be a believer in the divine origin of Scripture', *Philosophies of Judaism*, trans. D. W. Silverman (London: Routledge & Kegan Paul, 1964), p. 282.   [64] Yovel, *Spinoza and Other Heretics*, p. 146.

Here it is possible to stray into a lengthy detour. Strauss commented that 'To ascertain how to read Spinoza, we shall do well to cast a glance at his rules for reading the Bible', and then, despite some later reservations,[65] went on in some detail to discuss Spinoza's views about biblical criticism as a guide to the understanding of his philosophical writings.

Some of Strauss's thoughts are common sense. Spinoza suggests that the authors and editors of the scriptures wrote with the knowledge and prejudices of their readers in mind; and it is certainly true that this applies equally to himself. We should ask for whom he was writing, and why he chose to write as he did. Indeed, there may have been less than completely admirable reasons for some aspects of his caution. It seems obvious, for instance, that regardless of his theological or philosophical position he tried to be more circumspect in what he said about Christianity than in his treatment of Judaism.[66] And it is hard to avoid the view that this was partly because the Christian majority could cause him far more trouble than his former Jewish community. Plainly, that circumspection infuriated Strauss.

But none of this has much to do with the sense of Spinoza's own uses of language where he wrote directly about the actions, emotions or expressions of God. When he tells us that it was with a real voice that God revealed the law to Moses, this is heavily underscored: 'it is the indisputable meaning of Scripture that God himself spoke (for which purpose he descended from Heaven to Mount Sinai) and not only did the Jews hear him speaking but their chief men even beheld him (Exodus 24)'.[67]

And if, with Yovel, we feel inclined to start thinking in terms of metaphor at this point, we can recall that a metaphorical sense – 'God is fire' – is painstakingly separated by Spinoza from what he seems to consider to be a non-metaphorical sense – 'God is jealous'. There is also the scorn he poured on the metaphorical biblical interpretations he attributed to Alpakhar.[68] We are to accept that 'God is jealous' *was* believed by Moses 'however strongly we may be convinced that this opinion is contrary to reason'.[69]

The *Theological-Political Treatise* is an overtly rhetorical book, and its

---

[65] Strauss, 'How to Study Spinoza's Theological–Political Treatise', pp. 144, 162.

[66] Spinoza knew that Jews were prohibited from reading his work. Although that may not be an excuse it might be one reason for his attitude.

[67] S 62 = G III 19/3–7. The 'indisputable meaning of Scripture' is *Scriptura omnino indicare videtur*, which might be translated a little more weakly.

[68] S 143–4 = G III 100–1; S 229 = G III 181/16–30.

[69] Prophets may be 'deceived', though: Letter 78; L 348 = G IV 328/15–16.

rhetoric is of great interest in itself.[70] Spinoza's work on biblical criticism is of enormous intrinsic importance and was also, in its context,
of enormous historical value.[71] But its relevance to understanding his
own central positions on religion is doubtful. That work shows us that
he was fully aware of distinctions between the metaphorical and the
literal and between the factual, the symbolic and the allegorical, as we
might well expect from someone at his time with his degree of understanding of Jewish and Christian scriptural scholarship. But for our
purposes now the point is that, despite his sophistication about vari-
eties of meaning in the scriptures, he did seem ready to accept some
senses of terms as fundamental, without reservation: and that remains
problematic. This comes out at the end of the chapter in the
Theological-Political Treatise (xii) headed *Of the true original of the Divine
Law. In what respect Scripture is called holy and the Word of God. It is shown
that Scripture, in so far as it contains the Word of God, has come down to us uncorrupted.* He thinks that a fundamental principle – 'to love God above all,
and one's neighbour as oneself' – has been handed down uncorrupted
and

the same must be granted of all that indisputably follows therefrom and is like-
wise fundamental, such as that God exists, that He provides for all things, that
He is omnipotent, that by His decrees the good prosper and the wicked are cast
down, and that our salvation depends solely on His grace. For all these are doctrines which are plainly taught throughout Scripture.[72]

It seems undeniable that he really did wish to say, for example, that
God decrees that the good prosper and the wicked are cast down, despite
his insights into the subtleties of scriptural meaning and despite what we
know he thought, and, again, 'however strongly we may be convinced
that this opinion is contrary to reason'.

So what do we make of this?

The assumption from which Strauss starts his line of criticism – that
we can examine Spinoza's own use of language in the *Theological-Political
Treatise* along the same lines as we look at his treatment of scriptural
language – may well be badly wrong. (After all, 'To understand Scripture
and the mind of the prophets is by no means the same thing as to

---

[70] See Akkerman, 'Le caractère rhétorique du *Traité théologico-politique*'. One perplexing question,
despite what Spinoza said about his intended readership (in Letter 30), is whether he really
thought he could convince any of his contemporaries.
[71] The most recent brief assessment of it is Richard Popkin, 'Spinoza and Bible Scholarship', in
Force and Popkin (eds.), *The Books of Nature and Scripture*, also in Garrett (ed.), *Cambridge Companion*.
[72] S 212 = G iii 165/23–9.

understand the mind of God, that is, to understand truth itself.'[73])
Spinoza's approaches may have been quite different.

In his scriptural explanations, for example, we find the significant
reductive phrases 'nothing but', or 'nothing other than' (*nihil aliud*).
Expressions about the Spirit of the Lord and the Holy Spirit mean
merely[74] that the prophets were endowed with extraordinary virtue. The
choosing of the Jews referred only[75] to their temporal material prosperity, freedom and so on. God's positioning of a rainbow was 'assuredly
nothing other than[76] the refraction and reflection of the sun's rays'.
Several scriptural passages are said to indicate that God's decree,
command, edict and word are nothing other than[77] the actions and
order of nature. When 'Scripture tells us that this or that was accom-
plished by God's will, nothing more is intended than that it came about
in accordance with Nature's law and order'.[78] It is quite clear in scripture
that the Holy Spirit itself is nothing other than[79] nature's order.

In contrast, his explanations of some of his own uses of terms seem to
be strikingly *non*-reductive. He writes of the sense he attaches to the
kingdom of God: 'he who practises justice and charity in accordance
with God's command is fulfilling God's law, from which justice and
charity have the force of law and command'.[80] And we should note that
he did not phrase this by saying that God's law is nothing but the practice
of justice and charity.[81]

In the chapter on the 'vocation of the Hebrews' in the *Theological-
Political Treatise*, he does offer direct explanations for some of his own uses
of language. Interestingly, we find reductive terminology used in the
reverse direction: in his passages about scripture, it seems, the scriptural
is nothing but the natural; here, with his own uses of words, the natural is
nothing but the divine:

the universal laws of Nature, according to which all things happen and are
determined are nothing but [*nihil esse nisi*] God's eternal decrees, which always
involve eternal truth and necessity . . . the power of Nature in its entirety is
nothing other than [*nihil est nisi*] the power of God through which alone all
things happen and are determined[82] . . . by fortune I mean simply [*nihil aliud*

---

[73] S 210 = G III 163/31–2.   [74] *nihil enim aliud significant* S 70 = G III 27/18.
[75] *nihil aliud* S 93 = G III 49/29.   [76] *nulla sane alia est* S 132 = G III 89/28.
[77] *nihil aliud esse* S 235 = G III 187/35.   [78] *nihil aliud revera intelligere* S 132 = G III 89/3–5.
[79] *revera nihil aliud est* S 235 = G III 188/1.   [80] S 280 = G III 229/10–12.
[81] Shortly after, though, he does say that God has no special kingdom save through [*nullum . . . nisi*]
the medium of those who hold the sovereignty [S 281 = G III 229/21–2].
[82] Again, at S 71 = G III 28/12–13. We also find this order in the *Political Treatise*, where 'it follows that
the power of natural things by which they exist and consequently by which they act, can be
nothing other than [*nullam aliam esse posse*] itself the eternal power of God': I, 11; G III 276/20–22.

intelligo] God's direction in so far as he directs human affairs through causes that are external and unforeseen.[83]

These are selective quotations, and it might be wrong to read too much into a turn of phrase, but the reversal does look striking.[84] Many uses of what we might want to call 'religious language' are unexplained, and are certainly unreduced. God is to be understood as author of the Bible, 'because of the true religion that is taught therein'. Without qualification, God, 'by sure revelation', promised his special help to Daniel and we are 'bound by God's command to practise piety'.[85]

If we have problems here, they may come from assuming that Spinoza had a problem himself, about 'religious language'. Our problem, not his, might come from some feeling that a defensible distinction exists between religious and non-religious language (or use of language), and that such a distinction somehow matches a distinction between the non-literal and the literal (or, more vaguely, the non-natural and the natural).[86]

But just as Spinoza did not use or assume a critical theory of knowledge in his approach to prophecy and revelation, nor did he need to assume any critical theory of meaning, such as that statements about the natural world would come out as literal whereas statements about God's actions might not. At least, if we feel puzzled by his remarks about 'God's decrees' or about God speaking, revealing or forgiving, we might be puzzled because we think he could not *really mean* these things, in contrast with what he really did mean, in the *Ethics*. 'It was through images and words that God revealed to Joshua',[87] we might imagine, *must* mean something else because the God of the *Ethics* could not reveal anything to anyone through words and images.

Maybe it is necessary to formulate these thoughts in such a naive way

---

[83] S 89 = G III 46/1–24.

[84] Although it does not seem to have been noticed by even so acute a commentator as Alan Donagan, who quotes – with his italics – *'the power of nature is the divine power and virtue itself.* Moreover, the divine power is the very essence of God' [S 126 = G III 83/7–9] and then comments that 'Spinoza's theology, in short, naturalizes God', whereas the text he quotes is surely the plainest possible example of the reverse: of divinizing nature: 'Spinoza's Theology', in Garrett (ed.), *Cambridge Companion*, p. 355.   [85] S 209, 248, 284 = G III 163/4–6, 200/8, 232/32–3.

[86] An example is provided in a paper on 'Spinoza's Use of Religious Language' by A. J. Watt, who seems bemused by his own 'naturalistic or atheistic view of Spinoza's philosophy', by Spinoza's 'borrowing from the language of religion, even of devotional writing, for his own purposes', his 'altering the normal meaning of a religious expression in order to fit it into his philosophical system'. In fact, 'Spinoza's ambivalent attitude to theological statements', to Watt, 'looks at times like an invitation to hypocrisy': *The New Scholasticism*, 46, 1972, pp. 286, 299, 303, 307.

[87] S 63 = G III 20/1.

to see what must be wrong with them. There could be no distinction for Spinoza between what is natural and what is not, in terms of meaning or anything else; and while we can hardly forget that he identified God with nature, it may be easier to forget that this implied an identification of nature with God.

The thoughts that what Spinoza could 'really mean' is something literal, to do with nature, and that other, apparently different, forms of statement need to be decoded into 'natural' terms must be grievously misguided. We have seen, in any case, in the *Theological-Political Treatise* that if he had any tendency to make such translations, as Yovel thinks, it was in the opposite direction, as where the 'universal laws of Nature' are said to be 'nothing but God's eternal decrees' or where 'Nature's power is nothing but the power of God'. When he wrote about God, or divine action, he was not 'really' writing about nature. A temptation to co-opt him as a theological demythologiser[88] has to be resisted. To assume that is to make assumptions which he not only did not share but which – if he had considered them at all – he would have repudiated.

The upshot of all this may be disconcerting. Spinoza might seem to have tilled over the territory occupied so enthusiastically by later critics of revelation, but he never occupied it himself. The origin of revelation in the 'imagination' of the prophets was not meant to downgrade or delegitimise it. He had no inclination at all to distinguish between 'natural' knowledge and allegedly non-natural or supernatural revelation. Imagination, after all, like anything else, was a 'natural' process. But it was not – any more than any other human activity – 'merely' or 'only' natural, in a reductive sense. Nor was knowing: 'The knowledge that we acquire by the natural light of reason depends solely on knowledge of God and of his eternal decrees.'[89]

Still more disconcerting is Spinoza's lack of interest in any critical theory of 'religious language'. That should not be too surprising in itself, given that he lived in the seventeenth century, not the twentieth, but writers such as Yovel have tended to ascribe to him elaborate, but implied, reductive theories of meaning. Any such enterprise is not misplaced only by virtue of anachronism. We might do better to appreciate the soundness of his philosophical instincts in not starting off along tracks which subsequently proved to be so sterile. Not for him any dis-

---

[88] In the manner, most extremely, of Giovanni Di Luca, *Critica della Religione in Spinoza* (L'Aquila: Japadre, 1982), p. 73.   [89] S 59 = G III 15/19–20; 'of reason' is added by the translator.

tinction between 'religious' and 'non-religious' language. Nor for him any assumptions that theories, or sets of sufficient conditions, could be assembled to underwrite, explain or guarantee the meaning or meaning-fulness of any area of discourse. Anyone who might want to say (taking the same text, for example) that 'The knowledge that we acquire by the natural light of reason depends solely on knowledge of God and of his eternal decrees' *must mean* something 'non-religious' should be sure of a satisfactory account of how any terms mean what they do, 'religiously' or otherwise. That could take some time.

CHAPTER 7

History

Spinoza's God cannot stand outside history, directing or intervening at will. What was said in Part I of this study applies to God's causal relationship with history as much as it does to individual people or objects.[1] Equally, from Chapter 4, it should be clear that the course of history cannot be seen as containing any directed purpose or plan. So the explanation for events should never be sought in terms of divine intentions or aims.

This suggests that any discussion of Spinoza's thinking on the place of God in history ought to be short and conclusive. Divine providence is not mentioned in the *Ethics*. In the *Theological-Political Treatise* what 'the common people suppose' by 'God's power and providence' is dismissed. Rather, God's existence and providence are far better 'inferred from Nature's fixed and immutable order'.[2]

So what is left to be said about religion in history? In particular, what is to be said about Spinoza's own native religion? The history of the Jewish people has been held to reflect or embody its election by God – *Blessed are You, Lord our God, king of the universe, who has chosen us from all the peoples and who has given us his Torah.* David Novak, writing on the Election of Israel, has described this declaration as 'an elementary Jewish proposition in the legal sense . . . irreducible to any other theological proposition'. In Spinoza can we see anything more than its blunt denial? How could his God choose anything? Or make a special choice of a people? Novak takes a bleak view – 'For Spinoza, a relationship with an intelligible and scientifically legitimate God and a relationship with the Jewish people as historically constituted are mutually exclusive' – and he regards this as 'the basis of Jewish secularism and atheism it fundamentally assumes'.[3]

---

[1] Such parallels are well brought out in Matheron, *Individu et communauté*.

[2] S 129 = G III 86/19–21.

[3] 'The Election of Israel: Outline of a Philosophical Analysis', in D. H. Frank (ed.), *A People Apart: Chosenness and Ritual in Jewish Philosophical Thought* (Albany: SUNY Press, 1993), pp. 11, 15; also *The Election of Israel* (Cambridge University Press, 1995), pp. 15–16.

The bearing on Christianity would seem to be just as destructive. According to Spinoza, the nature of the natural divine law 'does not demand belief in historical narratives of any kind whatsoever'.[4] So 'the narratives of the Old and New Testaments differ in excellence from non-sacred writings and from one another to the extent that they inspire salutary beliefs'[5] – the implication, not very obscurely, being that they do *not* differ from each other, or from other writings, in virtue of being more or less informative or accurate as narratives. So it would seem to be some kind of *mistake* to see any pattern of creation, fall, salvation or redemption in history, however implicitly, and hence a mistake we might do better to avoid.

If all this is correct, Spinoza's attitude towards historical religions can only have been hostile, and of course that is how he has been understood, sometimes with resentment, by many writers.[6] And indeed it is not difficult, in support of that understanding, to find in him the equable and urbane tone of the eighteenth century –

so belief in historical narratives cannot afford us the knowledge and love of God. I do not deny that their study can be very profitable in the matter of social relations. For the more we observe and the better we are acquainted with the ways and manners of men . . . the more prudently we can live among them.[7]

– a tone guaranteed to inflame the antagonisms of his contemporaries and successors.

If we only see so far, we see him in a negative way: disparaging religions as erroneous, as desirable for the stupid, primitive or ill-informed, and as necessary for the survival of social order, but disposable for the wise, who could move on to agree with the superior philosophical religion of the *Ethics*. Historical religions, along these lines, would be reducible in anthropological or sociological terms to tribal sagas. The 'true religion' would be philosophy.[8] Slightly less starkly, some have tried to present him in a positive way as a precursor, or even founder, of secular Judaism.[9]

Negatively too, but from a more narrowly philosophical point of view,

[4] *Natura legis divinæ naturalis* . . . S 104 = G III 61/20–24.
[5] S 122 = G III 79/13–16. Spinoza does indeed use the Christian title for the Hebrew scriptures: the Old Testament.
[6] Hermann Cohen, as reported by Strauss, Strauss himself, Lévinas (see J.-F. Rey, 'Lévinas et Spinoza', in O. Bloch (ed.), *Spinoza au XX* siècle (Paris: Presses Universitaires de France, 1993)). Leo Baeck, interestingly, is reported as writing, 'we always count Spinoza, with pride, as one of us' (quoted by Albert H. Friedlander, *Leo Baeck: Teacher of Theresienstadt* (London: Routledge & Kegan Paul, 1973), p. 23).   [7] S 105 = G III 61–2.   [8] Zac, *Spinoza et l'interprétation de l'Ecriture*, p. 230.
[9] As does Yovel, *Spinoza and Other Heretics*, Chapter 7.

it might seem that Spinoza's attitude towards divine providence in history was coarsely over-simplified. He must have been aware of the detailed discussions by Maimonides, including the dismissal of one theory[10] that looked, superficially, very like his own account: a dismissal of final causes and an identification of the will of God with necessity. Maimonides had viewed that theory as absurd, without much discussion, and that, in return, may well have been Spinoza's opinion of Maimonides, who, for example, had written:

> It may be by mere chance that a ship goes down with all her contents . . . but it is not due to chance, according to our view that . . . the men went into the ship . . . it is due to the Will of God, and is in accordance with the justice of his judgments, the method of which our mind is incapable of understanding.[11]

Any distinction in causal terms between the physical sinking of the ship and the human actions of the crew would have seemed indefensible to Spinoza, as would the inscrutability of divine judgment.

He must also have been aware of the subtleties of Christian discussions, although it is not hard to imagine his reactions to some of them. Aquinas, for example, had distinguished between a universal and a particular cause, and between a 'limited responsibility' and a 'universal providence' in an attempt to determine whether everything is subject to divine providence. 'Since God is the universal guardian of all that is real, a quality of his Providence is to allow defects in some particular things so that the complete good of the universe be disentangled.' He had gone on to say that there would be 'no patience of the martyrs were there no persecution by tyrants'.[12] Quite possibly Spinoza might have regarded that remark alone as a sufficient *reductio ad absurdum*, without further need for comment.

We should look in detail at what he said: first, about the place of God in history and then about the relevance of history to religion. These are crucial areas in his attitude towards religion. If his approach was only one of more or less crude hostility then, in short, it lacks much interest and it merits little attention. If it was one of oblique or veiled hostility then perhaps it merits little respect.

GOD IN HISTORY

Spinoza's general explanation of God's choosing (*electio*) has already been quoted in Chapter 4:

[10] Attributed by Maimonides to the Ash'arites, *The Guide for the Perplexed*, trans. M. Friedländer (New York: Dover, 1956), III, 17.   [11] *Ibid.*, p. 287.   [12] *Summa Theologiæ* Ia. 22, 2.

since no one acts except by the predetermined order of Nature – that is, from God's eternal direction and decree – it follows that no one chooses a way of life for himself or accomplishes anything except by the special vocation of God [*nisi ex singulari Dei vocatione*], who has chosen one man before others for a particular work or a particular way of life.[13]

This could not be called clear or direct. The 'special vocation of God', on examination, seems to have no place at all, or no sense, distinct from 'God's eternal direction and decree' which (a few lines earlier) we have been told is the same as 'the fixed and immutable order of Nature, or chain of natural causes'.[14] In one of Spinoza's characteristic compressions of terminology, God's providence is the same as God's will,[15] and the will of God is the same as God's intellect. We see some of this compression in a passage from Spinoza's early work on Descartes where he breaks into the first person:

Ordinary people . . . have found no stronger proof of God's providence and rule [*Ghodts voorzienicheit en bestiering*] than that based on the ignorance of causes. This shows that they have no knowledge at all of the nature of God's will, and that they have attributed a human will to him, i.e., a will really distinct from the intellect. I think this misconception has been the sole cause of superstition, and perhaps of much knavery.[16]

This view is not concealed in the *Theological-Political Treatise*. By 'God's decrees and volitions, and consequently God's providence', we see 'Scripture itself means nothing other than Nature's order, which necessarily follows from her eternal laws.'[17] The argument of the chapter on miracles (VI) is that God's existence and providence are seen far better in 'Nature's fixed and immutable order' than in miracles or in events that might be thought to surpass the understanding.[18] God's actions, decisions or choices are exhibited in what happens. As we saw in Chapter 2, the law-like-ness of what happens is the same as its 'necessity', which is the same as the existence of causes. Again, God's existence and providence will be demonstrated with greater clarity and certainty by 'events which we understand clearly and distinctly through their prime causes' than through miracles which 'contravene the order of Nature'.[19]

Spinoza wanted to stress the *universality* of God's direction, or the fixed and immutable order of nature. We saw in Chapter 2 that this was rooted in his belief in the connectedness of causes (or in the inclusiveness

---

[13] S 90 = G III 46/16–22. [14] S 89 = G III 45/35. [15] Letter 19; L 132 = G IV 88/1–2.
[16] Curley, p. 326 = G I 261/6–13: the passage is from the second, Dutch, edition.
[17] S 125 = G III 82/19–21. [18] S 129 = G III 86/18–21.
[19] S 54 = G III 10/8–10. The Latin translated as 'events' here is actually 'things' or 'matters': *res*.

of God). But he did not use universality as a premise against the special election of the Jewish people. We find no argument in the form: God's laws must be universal; special election would not be universal; so special election would be outside God's laws. With good reason: such an argument would cut no ice with anyone who wanted to insist that a special election was, after all, special or exceptional.

Yovel believes that 'Spinoza rejects the very notion of election' and that history is treated as 'a natural causal system, uninformed by divine providence'.[20] In fact, it is interesting that we find no arguments at all *against* the special election of the Jewish people. What we do find in the *Theological-Political Treatise* is Spinoza trying to clarify his understanding of that election in contrast with what he takes to be erroneous understandings, and trying to clarify how others may have thought differently.

His chapter *Of the vocation of the Hebrews*[21] contains many statements that God *did* choose the Jews. Nowhere is it denied that God chose the Jews. God chose the Jews for a particular purpose, for the establishing of a special kind of society. The Hebrew nation was 'chosen by God before all others'. 'We do not mean to deny' that God ordained the laws in the Pentateuch for the Hebrews alone, nor that he spoke only to them, nor that they witnessed marvels 'such have never befallen any other nation'. Maybe God will choose them again.[22] These are not rejections of Jewish election, and they hardly sound like an account within a 'natural causal system', as Yovel says. We must consider what they meant.

One thing that they meant, uncontroversially and clearly, was that Jews had *felt themselves* to be chosen. This fact was reflected in the scriptures: 'The Hebrew nation was said to have been chosen by God before all others.'[23] Actually, Spinoza opens his argument with this 'feeling', and treats it as a phenomenon in need of explanation. People *like* to feel special or chosen. But true happiness and blessedness should not mean that people have to feel themselves *more* happy and blessed than others. He suggests that this is a sign of immaturity or ('if it be not mere childishness') it has its only source in spite and malice.

As an opening shot in his case this is of interest in itself. The logical gain is not obvious, though as a debating point it has some *ad hominem* force. Before going on to assure us that he does not mean to deny that

[20] *Spinoza and Other Heretics*, p. 179.
[21] Geneviève Brykman finds different usages of 'Jews', 'Hebrews' and 'Israelites' in Spinoza. 'Jews' is said to be more pejorative, 'Hebrews' more political and 'Israelites' more religious: 'De l'insoumission des Hébreux selon Spinoza', *Revue de l'enseignement philosophique*, 2, 1983–4, p. 3, n. 4.
[22] S 89, 92, 91, 89, 100 = G III 45/29, 48/26–7, 47/29, 45/20–2, 57/6.   [23] S 90 = G III 46/25–6.

God spoke only to the Hebrews, Spinoza starts by saying that there is no *need* for anyone, or any people, to feel specially privileged – 'Surely they would have been no less blessed if God had called all men equally to salvation'[24] – but, nevertheless, people *have* felt specially chosen. One explanation – a cause or reason – could be a certain immaturity. The Swiftian insinuation, left hanging, is that at least those who have not looked into the question thoroughly may have held their beliefs for less than wholly worthy motives. But it is not suggested that a feeling of special election was only, or *nothing but*, 'mere childishness'.[25]

The main line of Spinoza's case is not to claim that the Jews were not chosen by God – as we have seen, he stresses several times that they were – but to consider *why* they were chosen, and to show what that choice meant. The negative reasons, to him, are obvious: they were not chosen for their 'true life' – their moral superiority – or for 'any higher understanding' – because they knew more about nature. Textual evidence is adduced to show (at any rate, to his own satisfaction) that the ancient Hebrews were neither especially virtuous nor especially adept in the natural sciences. Equally, we are told what God's choice did *not* mean. Not, for example, that the ancient Hebrews received exclusive revelations. God produced both prophets and miracles for other nations. Again, textual evidence is cited. So 'in respect of understanding and virtue, that is, in respect of blessedness, God is equally gracious to all'.[26]

Also negative – in the minds of many readers, unhelpfully and bitterly negative – is Spinoza's argument that the election of the Jews was not 'eternal'. He goes into some textual contortions to show this. If, for example, the prophets *did* describe an 'eternal covenant involving the knowledge, love and grace of God, it can easily be proved that this promise was made for the godly alone'.[27] But his main point, and the one which has caused the greatest offence, was to argue that the survival of Jews and the continuation of Jewish life proved nothing about God's special choice. He speculated anthropologically on reasons for the survival of Judaism, suggesting historical and social separation, which encouraged hatred, and hence encouraged defensive solidarity; and 'the mark of circumcision' which, he said, he considered so important that he

---

[24] S 88 = G III 44/2–3.

[25] Though Spinoza returns to this thought later from a different angle: 'To the early Jews religion was transmitted in the form of written law because at that time they were like children; but later on Moses and Jeremiah told them of a time to come when God would inscribe the law in their hearts': S 205 = G III 158–9.   [26] S 93 = G III 50/4–5.

[27] S 99 = G III 55–6: perhaps a curious echo from Christian disputes over the universal efficacy of saving grace.

was convinced 'that this by itself will preserve their nation' for ever.[28] Although we do not know the exact reasons why he was expelled from his native Jewish community such views, if he held them in 1656, must have contributed.

The positive sense of God's choice, and its positive reasons, were straightforward enough: God chose the Jews 'only for the establishing of a special kind of society and state'. That sounds not unlike an intention or final cause; but at any rate, a number of non-final causes or reasons were produced as well:

> The Hebrew nation was chosen by God before all others not by reason of its understanding [*non ratione intellectus*] nor of its spiritual qualities, but by reason of its social organisation [*sed ratione societatis*] and the good fortune whereby it achieved supremacy and retained it for so many years. This is quite evident from Scripture itself.[29]

There is certainly no need to go into the scriptural arguments. (Some of these seem so far-fetched that Spinoza may well have accepted the sceptical thought that he mentions later in the *Theological-Political Treatise*: it is possible to support almost any case with a suitable choice of texts.[30]) The interest is in the *form* of explanation that is offered, rather than its content. Here, it sounds overtly causal: God chose *by reason* of the social organisation of the Hebrew nation. Elsewhere, it sounds more reductive: the choosing of the Jews 'referred only to' (*nihil aliud spectavisse*) their prosperity and so on; the Hebrews were chosen 'only with respect to their social organisation' (*non nisi ratione societatis . . . electi fuerunt*).[31] But there is no suggestion, of course, that God is irrelevant, or that once we have seen the cause or reason for divine action, God can be omitted from the narrative. Some may want Spinoza to sound like a proto-secularist, but he does not. Yovel's 'natural causal system, uninformed by divine providence' is a long way from the types of account that Spinoza actually gave, repeatedly and emphatically. For every instance where we might think he was reducing the divine to the natural, there were at least as many instances where the natural was explained in terms of the divine. The fineness of this balance, and the care with which it can be expressed, can be seen in a passage such as this – surely central for any analysis of the place of God in history:

---

[28] S 100, S 264–5 = G III 56–7, 215; the Latin says 'this Nation', though Spinoza does habitually write of Jews in the third person, never in the first person. [29] S 91 = G III 47/28–31.
[30] S 220 = G III 173: *geen ketter sonder letter*. [31] S 93 = G III 49/28–9, S 94 = G III 50/25–6.

since the power of Nature in its entirety is nothing other than the power of God
. . . it follows that whatever man – who is also a part of Nature – acquires for
himself to help preserve his own being, or whatever Nature provides for him . . .
all this is provided for him solely by the divine power, acting either through
human nature [*quatenus per humanam naturam*] or externally to human nature.
Therefore whatever human nature can effect solely by its own power to preserve
its own being can rightly be called God's internal help, and whatever falls to
man's advantage from the power of external causes can rightly be called God's
external help.[32]

Here, as with what was said about revelation at the end of the previous
chapter, any temptation we may feel to decipher what Spinoza must
have really meant could well be our problem, not his. It does not seem
too strange to assume that he meant what he said he meant. God's
choosing to do something is the same as something's happening in accordance with law, which is the same as something just happening. But,
here, the same as must be taken seriously: not, for example, as something
like means the same as,[33] or nothing but.

The place of God in history is not to be seen only in materialist terms,
translated into physical law. We are reminded of this in a strikingly
placed footnote:

Nothing, then, can happen in Nature <note> to contravene her own universal
laws . . . For whatever occurs does so through God's will and eternal decree . . .

[note] Here, by Nature, I do not mean simply matter and its modifications, but
infinite other things besides matter.[34]

The readers of the *Theological-Political Treatise* would have had trouble
in understanding this because the theory about infinite attributes
(Chapter 1, pp. 47–8 in this study) is not explained at all there; but the
point is plain enough. Natural explanation will include what we might
consider the psychological, the sociological and the anthropological.
Out goes any materialist theory of history: surely only Spinoza could
express a point of such massive significance, with such vast ramifications,
in a single Latin footnote.

It is a pointless to consider whether Spinoza's treatment of God's
place in history is better understood in terms of secularising the divine or
in terms of divinising the secular. It is pointless because no contrast exists
in his thinking by which the secular could be characterised. It is also a

---

[32] S 89–90 = G III 46/6–16.
[33] Yovel, *Spinoza and Other Heretics*, p. 190: 'Spinoza's use of the term *God's election* is actually metaphorical and means "successful political existence".'   [34] S 126 = G III 83/9–13 and note.

distraction from the far more difficult challenge presented by his
approach. The assumptions brought from the *Ethics* to history and politics mean that radical standards of explanation are to apply. Just as in the
Ethics, human passions were to be understood in the same way as we are
to understand geometry, so in the *Political Treatise*, human actions are to
be neither praised not blamed, but understood. Human love, hate, anger
and envy are to be seen in the same way as heat, cold, storms or thunder
in the weather, as having causes by which we can try to understand
them.[35] It is relatively fruitless to worry about whether there are, or
should be, different *types* of explanation ('theological', 'natural',
'secular', 'scientific') in the face of Spinoza's claims about the unity
and comprehensiveness of explanation.[36] God's place in history makes
it, like all other fields of knowledge, a branch of theology or natural
science.

HISTORY IN RELIGION

But what about the place of history in religion? Here, Spinoza put
himself in a strange position. The place of history in theology or natural
science – in discovering truths about nature – was nowhere. Historical
traditions or narratives had no value at all in science (presumably with
the obvious exception of historical science). The logic was clear and
inexorable:

Nor can belief in historical narratives, however certain, give us knowledge of
God, nor, consequently, of the love of God. For the love of God arises from the
knowledge of God, a knowledge deriving from general axioms that are certain
and self evident, and so belief in historical narratives is by no means essential to
the attainment of our supreme good.[37]

This can be seen as a declaration of independence for natural science,
freeing it from history. There must also be a dimension relating to
Spinoza's attitude towards Judaism, where it might have been difficult to
understand ritual or the law in anything but historical terms. As Novak
comments: 'It is not to the texts of antiquity . . . that one is to now turn
for truth . . . The best climate for scientific philosophy is the ahistorical
liberal democratic state, where individual intellects are unencumbered

[35] *Political Treatise* I, §4; G III 274/28–35.
[36] A further example of a philosophical instinct that kept him well away from the problems created
by other views: see William and Martha Kneale, *The Development of Logic* (Oxford: Clarendon
Press, 1962), pp. 671–2.   [37] S 105 = G III 61.

by history.'[38] And a fair part of the *Theological-Political Treatise* was taken up with laborious exegesis, designed to show that – contrary to most earlier readings – scripture had never been intended to impart *any* information about physics, astronomy or meteorology (or, at any rate, to show that anything which looked like such information could be understood in some other way).

Philosophy – science – was to rest on the basis of 'universally valid axioms', to be constructed by studying 'Nature alone, whereas faith is based on history and language, and must be derived only from Scripture and revelation'.[39]

In faith or religion, history was by no means absent. This was not only because historical study might be 'profitable in the matter of social relations', but because the practice of religion was to be understood through history.

The grounding of practised religions in history could scarcely be denied. All the religions known to Spinoza had historical origins, and embodied views of their own history.

Naturally, he took Judaism as an example of the relationships between the history of a society and a religion seen by him in terms of laws and ceremonials. One conclusion was that the ceremonial observances specified in the Hebrew Bible 'and indeed the whole Mosaic Law', 'were relevant only to the Hebrew state' from which it followed, in his mind, that much of Judaism should have ceased to exist: 'since the fall of their independent state, Jews are no more bound by the Mosaic Law than they were before their political state came into being'.[40]

And although, as we shall see, he took a different general view about Christianity, he took the reported words of Jesus – 'whosoever shall smite thee on thy right cheek, turn to him the other also' (Matthew 5: 39, AV) – and argued that they could apply 'only in situations where justice is disregarded and at times of oppression, but not in a good commonwealth'. In a just state, justice would apply. Moses, 'concerned to found a good commonwealth', 'demanded an eye for an eye'.[41]

Here we see history coming to the centre of religion. What might be assumed to be a defining element in Judaism, and a characteristic element in Christian ethics, were both placed in the contexts of

[38] 'The Election of Israel: Outline of a Philosophical Analysis', p. 14.
[39] S 226 = G III 179/33–4.
[40] S 119, 115 = G III 76/6–8, 72/26–9. Alan Donagan drew a curiously positive conclusion that 'The moral provisions of the Torah indeed remain valid: but as eternal truths valid for everyone, not as the revealed law of a particular state', *Spinoza*, p. 30. [41] S 146–7 = G III 103.

particular social and historical conditions. (And these two passages alone, both revealing the most extraordinary insensitivity, might have given some thought to commentators who have based their interpretations on the idea that Spinoza was a cunningly cautious writer.)

The unavoidable conclusion seemed to be that religion had to be particular to a time, a place or a society. Within Judaism, such a conclusion would be controversial to different degrees, depending on how it was understood. Spinoza took the widest view: that Jewish law could only apply in a just Hebrew state. And that view can be open to different readings: in today's terms, from the extremely orthodox position that the law cannot apply again until a fully Jewish state exists – either literally, or in some other sense – to an extremely liberal position that the law has to be reinterpreted constantly in the light of changing contexts.

His position was that the appropriate form of explanation for historical religions was history. As we have seen, crucially, that did not mean just materialist history. Particular ceremonies, rituals and moral codes existed for various social, economic or political reasons. They gained their authority or force for similar reasons: solidarity and order were necessary in any society. Apparently, despite what we might think with hindsight, he did not believe that these thoughts undermined the legitimacy or authority of religion. His view was that moral authority is sufficient, and far better than any claim to authority based upon false historical or physical premises.

As with his views on prophecy or revelation, it may be useful to recall the equivalence of God and nature. In saying that historical or moral authority was sufficient in religion, he was not saying that *only* secular authority is available, in contrast with a missing divine authority. Such a contrast could not exist, and the whole picture assumed by it would be wholly wrong. Moral authority, for Spinoza, was natural authority, which was divine authority. The loss of contrast between God and nature, whatever it means, does not mean a disparagement of the natural. (Also, it may be banal but necessary to recall that even if religion is based in history, it remains true – as Spinoza was certainly and proudly aware – that some religions have a lot more history than others.)

Nevertheless, his position leads to two trails that will have to be pursued in the coming chapters First, the obvious implication is that the authority of each religion is contained within the bounds of a society at a particular period. Historically, in terms of post-Reformation religious politics, that might be an interesting thought. Philosophically, it just looks like typical relativism. Yet, equally obviously, Spinoza could not be described as a relativist in his statements about virtue and a right way of life.

Secondly, the cause or reason for adherence to any religion, as he saw it, would be primarily social or historical. In his terms, the *reason why* someone was a Jew or a Muslim or a Mennonite could be sufficiently characterised by birth, upbringing or education in particular circumstances in a particular time and place. The genuine scope for choice in religion, or between religions – in the sense that an individual might want to examine a religious position – seemed restricted. Yet, above all, Spinoza was arguing for religious freedom. How can we deal with that paradox?

PART III

The God of Spinoza

E qui si conviene sapere che li occhi de la sapienza sono le sue
demonstrazioni, con le quali si vede la veritade certissimamente . . .

— Dante, *Convivio*, III, 15

CHAPTER 8

Choosing a religion

The first part of this study focused almost entirely on the philosophy in Spinoza's *Ethics*. The second part was concerned largely with his views on religion in the *Theological-Political Treatise*. Nothing has been said about his personal position in religion: where he stood himself, and his own theological or religious views. Or so it may seem, because hardly any of his biography has been mentioned, and it has been possible to deal with his thinking in objective, depersonalised terms. In fact, the reality is that it is hard to get much closer to Spinoza than by looking at his philosophy. That can be taken negatively, in a feeling that a personality is lacking, in that he effaced any personal character from his writing; or it can be taken more positively, as a sign of how completely he was able to express himself in the most abstract and impersonal of forms – in metaphysics demonstrated in the geometrical manner.

It would be a mistake to think of some parts of his work as any more personal than others, but there are some important elements that have scarcely been considered so far, and these may be important in his attitude to religion. *May be*, because we might imagine that what he would say about the figure of Christ in religion, and about the existence of the mind in eternity, would be philosophically or personally central to him, if only because both of these look like sensitive and vital subjects. The truth is that they are among the many areas where we have to remain uncertain. The figure of Christ was *used* by him in a particular way, which was certainly important to the argument of the *Theological-Political Treatise*, but which does not give an impression of emotional weight. The short passage on eternity in Part v of the *Ethics* was specifically hedged with remarks to the effect that the rest of the argument could be judged without it. (In addition, as we shall see, it has been deemed to be philosophically disastrous, even by some otherwise sympathetic commentators.)

THREE KINDS OF CHOICE

Although we know nothing relevant about Spinoza's biography on this central matter, the question of choice in religion – of a choice between religions, a choice within a religion or a choice to adopt a particular attitude towards religion, or a religion – must have been of importance to him. We can see this in three different ways: personally, intellectually and more narrowly philosophically.

Personally: we know that he was thrown out of his native religious community. He changed his name from a Jewish to a non-Jewish form and refused to rejoin his community for the remainder of his life. As far as is known, he did not live as a Jew. He referred to Jews in the third, not the first, person in his writing. The reasons for his choices are not known, either in terms of his family or personal background or in terms of the central religious attitudes or theological views he felt unable to accept. We have seen in the previous chapters that his opinions expressed in the *Theological-Political Treatise*, as indeed in most of his earlier writings, would have given ample excuse for his excommunication, but the degree of personal feeling connected with them is not known, and the sources of any personal feelings are even more unknown.

Choosing to be or not to be Jewish, and the nature of Jewish identity, are deeply contentious subjects, on which vast amounts have been written in the centuries since Spinoza, and the temptation for some has been irresistible to recruit him to one side or another of a debate. He has been seen both as the primordial traitor, stabbing at the heart of Judaism, and as a founder or originator of a secular Judaism.

This book does not seek to intrude into that debate. Even if Judaism is characterised in the weakest possible terms, not as a set of beliefs, or even as a traditional way of life within the law, some may still think that Spinoza picked out whatever could be regarded as important and then denied it. Even allowing for the robustness of sectarian polemics in the seventeenth century, for a tradition of vigorous critical debate within Judaism and for his extreme philosophical detachment, he did still seem to exhibit an exceptional zeal in trampling on the most delicate subjects. His blunter critics, such as Strauss, have contrasted that treatment of Judaism with an apparently softer line with Christianity; though the horror and incomprehension of Spinoza's Christian correspondents and contemporary readers do not suggest that they found his approach too sympathetic.

His choice to live outside a Jewish community is hard to judge without anachronism. Yovel has explained how the Sephardic Jews of Amsterdam came from a background of double lives and religious compromise in Portugal and Spain.[1] Spinoza's attitude can be seen, as Yovel understands it, as a kind of extension of that existence; or, of course, it can be seen as a complete betrayal. More mundanely, it should be relevant to say that Spinoza was *able* to live as he did – quietly and cautiously, but without sectarian affiliation – in a relatively peaceful and non-persecuting society. His correspondence shows that he knew what persecution meant, but no one has ever suggested that he chose to live as he did to avoid being treated badly as a Jew. That would not have been practical for him in any event, since he was widely viewed by Christians as a Jew, despite his excommunication. We can have absolutely no idea what choices he would have made if he had lived in a more dangerous place or time, or whether his thinking and behaviour might have changed.

Intellectually: he chose to distance himself from many, if not all, of his predecessors and contemporaries. This point was argued in the Introduction, and evidence for it has been added in Parts I and II. Scholars who have worked on earlier thinkers have had no difficulty in finding traces of their influences in Spinoza's works. It may have been less evident that he often mentioned other writers only to indicate dissent, and that he was well able to choose what he wanted and to repudiate what he did not want. Few thinkers can stand at a confluence of so many traditions. From a student's point of view that makes him hard to comprehend: it takes the huge erudition of a Wolfson to pick out only some of the intellectual threads. From Spinoza's own point of view it may be that the diversity of contexts and influences from which he worked gave him a greater detachment. We shall see that, for him, a choice of what to think provided a good analogy for a choice of how to live, or a choice of religion.

Philosophically: he tried to argue a reasoned case for free choice in religion. People should be allowed to decide for themselves on their beliefs, with rather less freedom for their practices. This was the objective of the *Theological-Political Treatise*. By separating 'faith' from 'philosophy' he thought he would be able to show how freedom of judgment might be fully granted to the individual citizen: 'I think I am undertaking no

[1] Yovel, *Spinoza and Other Heretics*, Chapter 3.

ungrateful or unprofitable task in demonstrating that not only can this freedom be granted without endangering piety and the peace of the commonwealth, but also that the peace of the commonwealth and piety depend on this freedom.'[2]

THE 'TRUE' PHILOSOPHY

Before looking at how choice in religion could be possible for Spinoza, we ought to look at the kind of religion, or philosophy, that he seems to have chosen for himself. This takes us to Part v of the *Ethics*, as well as to 'the dogmas of the universal faith' in Chapter xiv of the *Theological-Political Treatise*. A natural supposition is that here we find the views that he chose to hold himself and, we would therefore assume, that he would prefer others to hold.

Part v of the *Ethics* stands at the end of a long chain of reasoning about nature, the mind, people, their emotions and the control of those emotions. It is in two segments. The Preface, propositions 1 to 20 and propositions 41 to 42 concern 'this present life' and what would still be important 'even if we did not know that our mind is eternal'. The central segment – propositions 21 to 40 – concerns 'the mind in so far as it is considered without reference to the existence of the body'.[3] These central passages have always been thought to contain great difficulties. They also seem to suggest a different world from the rest of the work, dealing as they do with the intellectual love of God, intuitive knowledge and eternity.

The general project of Part v is not too obscure in outline. By attaining greater knowledge, the mind will achieve more understanding, becoming more 'active' and less 'passive' towards external influence and the pressure of the emotions. This greater understanding constitutes 'freedom'. Greater knowledge of nature, and greater freedom, will constitute, or lead to, a love of God. But – unexpectedly changing gear at about proposition 21 – something of the human mind is not destroyed with the body. It 'remains', and is eternal: 'we feel and experience that we are eternal'. Then, the highest contentment of the mind is said to come from what is called the third kind of knowledge, a kind of particular intuition. Knowing nature in that way gives rise to 'the intellectual love of God', which is 'eternal'. God is said to love himself with infinite intellectual love. Despite all this, we find in the last two propositions of

[2] S 51 = G iii 7/24–7.   [3] *Ethics* v, 41, 40.

Part v that even if we were not aware of the eternal aspects of our minds, the way of life discovered in the earlier parts of the *Ethics* would still be valid. 'Blessedness is not the reward of virtue, but virtue itself.'

As with much of Spinoza's thought, there seem to be two separate levels of difficulty: the articulation of the system, how (or whether) the technical terminology fits together; and what it is supposed to achieve. The first of these is not our concern in a serious way now. The psychology on which Part v of the *Ethics* rests is constructed intricately in Parts III and IV. In theory, the series of deductions is as strong as its weakest logical link. If the interest in what Spinoza says was limited to its formal validity, the later parts of the *Ethics* would be perilously exposed. We shall come back to some of this in Chapter 10, in looking at what he called 'eternity'.

The point of what he was trying to do is rather more fruitful for investigation. The project offered was one that was supposed to be *practical*. The book was called *Ethica* and the product was not to be wisdom but blessedness: *beatitudo*. At the beginning of Part v, the author carefully distinguished his project – 'the method, or way, leading to freedom' – from what he called 'medicine' or 'logic'. Medicine dealt with 'the science of tending the body' and logic with 'the manner or way in which the intellect should be perfected'. He also distinguished himself pointedly from the stoics who thought that 'the emotions depend absolutely on our will, and that we can have absolute control over them'. The root of all these rejected approaches was a faulty view of the relationship between mind and body, and hence of the respective powers of mind over body and body over mind. Parts III and IV had provided a delicate positioning of the status of the person in nature: not of the mind-as-spirit ruling over the body and not of the mind-as-thought under the sway of the body-as-emotion. As we have seen, one of the most carefully judged and most important assertions in the whole work was Part IV, Proposition 4: 'It is impossible for a man not to be part of Nature.' Much of what followed that assertion depended on its careful balance. We cannot get outside, above or beyond nature, or our nature; but then nature, or our nature, need not get on top of us, either. We need to see that we are part of it, and to see what that means.

The project presented in Part v of the *Ethics* is not offered as optional, as a choice. It is supposed to rest on our nature, how we are: 'The first and only basis of virtue, that is, of the right way of life.'[4] We find this out

---

[4] 41, Demonstration = G II 306/31–2: *Primum, & unicum virtutis, seu rectè vivendi rationis fundamentum.*

by means of philosophical, scientific investigation, not a matter of choice or decision, and certainly not a matter of faith. Understanding is not easy, partly because it is intellectually difficult, and partly because of the negative forces of hope and fear which stand in the way of a clear view.

None of this, of course, is presented in terms of *religion*, though it is the 'true' philosophy.[5] The last mention of religion in the *Ethics*[6] is one which deliberately points back over the top of the thoughts about eternity in Part v to the psychological results of Part iv. Even if we did not know anything about eternity, Spinoza says, the results on human nature in Part iv would still be 'of prime importance to piety and religion'. Here he means piety and religion traced back to the view that 'to act from virtue is to act by the guidance of reason'.[7] The scope for choice, again, is not obvious.

UNIVERSAL RELIGION

The position in the *Theological-Political Treatise* looks very different. We have seen in the previous chapters how historical religions are to be understood in terms of their historical circumstances. The Jewish law was to be understood as applicable to a people living in a particular way at a specific period. A Christian precept – 'if a man strike you on the right cheek, turn to him the left also' – was related to specific political conditions. Everything suggested that religions are to be particular in time and place.

The wider argument of Spinoza's book points in the same direction. Philosophy is to deal with how things are; faith or 'obedience' with the ways in which people have chosen to live, and these will be specific to social and political conditions. The 'freedom' of religion will be a lack of restriction on ceremonies and traditional practices which do not impinge upon others and a freedom to interpret scripture according to individual judgment.

Yet the *Theological-Political Treatise* also contains remarks about 'universal religion' that seem anomalous in such a context. If religions are to be particular to specific societies, how can there be a universal religion, except in the form of some sort of watered-down lowest-common-factor religion? The answer cannot be in terms of some 'essence' of religion,

[5] Letter 76; L 342 = G iv 320/4 = 22. [6] Part v, 41.
[7] Via Part iv, 73, 46, 37, then 36, Demonstration: *Ex virtute agere est ex ductu rationis agere.*

because if religions are supposed to be essentially particular it would be missing the point to formulate an essence for them.

Universal religion appears in differing ways, which may be interconnected.

A consideration of human nature leads us to natural–divine law which applies 'equally to Adam as to any other man, and equally to any man living in a community as to a hermit'. The reward of this divine law is 'the law itself, namely to know God and to love him in true freedom with all our heart and mind'.[8] That sounds identical with the doctrine of the *Ethics*, Part v, though a reader of only the *Theological-Political Treatise* would not recognise how 'knowing God' and 'loving God', for Spinoza, were inseparable. Echoes of the same thinking can be heard in what he selects as the 'teachings of Scripture that are concerned only with philosophic matters': 'There is a God or Being who made all things and who directs and sustains the world' and so on.[9] Here, the basic, universal religion is the philosophy of the *Ethics*.

But later, in Chapter xii of the *Treatise*, we find that divine law is brought into an identity with 'religion universal to the entire human race, or catholic religion'[10] – which might sound like the doctrine of the *Ethics*, until Spinoza adds that it consists not in 'ceremonial observance but in charity and sincerity of heart', citing the diatribe in Isaiah i, against sacrifices, burnt offerings and vain oblations. We see that some specific ethical precepts – if only precepts as uncontentious as a regard for charity and sincerity of heart – are part of a 'true way of life' (*verus vivendi modus*). Here, universal religion looks just like a simple, sincere life.

And later still, in Chapter xiv, the aim seems to be to assemble a set of precepts which will be minimally controversial. These 'dogmas which obedience to God absolutely demands and without which such obedience is absolutely impossible' are a mixture of unsurprising conclusions from the *Ethics*, framed in the religious idiom of the *Treatise*, together with some precepts that are not described as *true*, but as necessary for obedience to the law. These include statements such as that 'God forgives repentant sinners' which seem to be a long way from the mentality of the *Ethics*.[11]

---

[8] S 104–5 = G iii 61/26–8 and S 105 = G iii 62/19–20.   [9] S 120, 212 = G iii 77/25ff, 165/25ff.

[10] S 208–9 = G iii 162/17–19.

[11] S 225 = G iii 178/11–14; although Matheron thinks not, with an argument intended to show how all seven of Spinoza's minimal precepts are rooted in the *Ethics*: *Le Christ et le salut des ignorants*, pp. 103, 111–13. A. C. Fox aims much less clearly to show the same: *Faith and Philosophy* (Nedlands: University of Western Australia Press, 1990).

Still further away, and most problematic of all, was the place given to Jesus, invariably called 'Christ' by Spinoza. This calls for separate discussion in the next chapter. The immediate point, while we are thinking about choice in religion, is that the teaching of Jesus was said to have a universal application, contradicting the conclusion that religions were socially and historically specific. This is an area where Spinoza's readiness to dress his opinions for his Christian readers has been most suspected: 'Paul concludes that, since God is the God of all nations – that is, he is equally gracious to all – and since all mankind were equally under the law and under sin, it was for all nations that God sent his Christ to free all men from the bondage of the law, so that they would no longer act righteously from the law's command but from the unwavering resolution of the heart. Thus Paul's teaching coincides with ours.'[12]

CONSTRAINTS

So the framework for Spinoza's thinking on choice in religion is a confusing one. Religion seems to be both essentially particular and essentially universal: historically particular and philosophically universal. His own religious position does not look much like one that could be said to be *chosen*. In fact, the scope he left for choice would seem to be constrained in a remarkable variety of ways. A short review of those constraints may help to emphasise how unusual his position was, for someone whose declared aim was to advocate religious freedom .

(a) First, of course, *choice* of any kind was a problematic notion for him. Where people believe themselves most to be acting freely, he thought, they are most likely to be in thrall to unknown causes. They are free to the extent that they are able to understand what those causes are.

(b) And in particular, to *choose what to believe* would be even more problematic. If something is known to be true then there can be no choice about believing it.[13] There is no place for choice or decision. The Spinozistic project is to maximise the number of known truths, which is the same as reducing uncertainties. Here, as elsewhere, a geometrical model would be used. Accept the axioms and proofs in geometry, then do not imagine

---

[12] S 97 = G III 54.
[13] See Bernard Williams, 'Deciding to Believe' (1970), in his *Problems of the Self* (Cambridge University Press, 1973). The point is a powerful one which does not depend on any particular theory or understanding of truth.

there can be any choice or decision about whether or not to accept the resulting theorems.

(c) The repudiation of the primacy of the Cartesian ego made the *choosing self* elusive for Spinoza. 'I' can never be identified with 'my' 'inner' consciousness. Although he did distinguish the 'inward worship of God' from 'outward forms of religion', and said that religion consisted in 'honesty and sincerity of heart rather than in outward actions',[14] Part II of the *Ethics* had removed the support that could vindicate such distinctions. An act of faith could hardly be an act of inner assent in the mind. That was not ruled out logically by Spinoza's thinking, but it would have been out of line with his understanding of faith as 'obedience': 'Each man's faith . . . is to be regarded as pious or impious not in respect of its truth or falsity, but as it is conducive to obedience or obstinacy'.[15]

(d) Since the will and the intellect were the same, an *act of will* would be a wholly inappropriate image for a matter of faith, or religious choice, in any event. The equivalence of the will and the intellect made 'choosing to believe' an impossibility. (This is (b) from another direction.)

(e) Nor could a choice in religion, or between religions, be modelled upon a choice of *ends* against means, or of *values* against facts. One well-trodden route has been to argue that we don't or can't choose which facts to believe, but we can choose our values, ends or meanings. As we saw in Chapter 4, a true choice of ends is ruled out by the onslaught on final causes in the Appendix to Part I of the *Ethics*. And a correct way of life – 'virtue' – was to be discovered or understood. It was not to be a matter of choice.

(f) We have seen that 'faith is based on history and language'.[16] Religious practice, including the social enforcement of morality, is to be a matter of tradition or history. All the characteristic features of specific religions are given political, historical, psychological or anthropological explanations, to the extent that *reasons to accept* the elements within a specific tradition could scarcely be said to apply.

(g) Taking the same point from a different angle, the lack of distinction between *cause* and *reason* obscured the scope for persuasion. The *reason why* someone was Jewish or Roman Catholic, as we have seen in the previous chapter, could be, quite sufficiently, a matter of birth and upbringing. Because Spinoza saw religion and religious faith as a matter of piety in practice as much as a question of accurate dogma, the thought of

---

[14] S 280 = G III 229/3–5; S 159 = G III 116/29–30. Fox seems to find the distinction puzzling, *Faith and Philosophy*, p. 169.   [15] S 223 = G III 176/33–5.   [16] S 226 = G III 179/28–9.

arguing someone into, or out of, a religious position would be unusually
anomalous for him. (Perhaps this was an echo of a traditional Jewish disengagement from proselytising.)

Now these constraints seem to paint Spinoza into a corner. He wanted to
advocate freedom of thought and religion, yet the individual appears to
be deprived of any means to make use of such freedom. Religious
choice, and hence religion, could not retreat into the sphere of the personal, along the tracks laid by Pascal, and followed subsequently by
many others: there can be no *reasons* for faith, so any considerations in
favour of faith must be outside reason. Nor, of course, could Spinoza be
attracted by the line of theological thinking to the effect that we cannot
choose God, so God must choose us, though this must have been familiar
enough to him from his Calvinist neighbours. In fact, it may be easy to
forget how far he was from almost all subsequent thinking. A conventional line might be to take the dominance of science as an excuse to
retreat into voluntarism – leaving the act of choice or the agency of the
will as the focus for value. For him, that was ruled out from the start.

THREE DETOURS

There are some threads in his work that we probably need to put aside if
we are to see any sense in his approach to choice in religion. One is the
question of his own personal preference or temperament in religious
terms. His own liking, obviously, was for simplicity, lack of show, inner
conviction and plain virtues. As a matter of temperament, he was in the
archetypal Protestant mould; a fact reinforced by his evident personal
dislike for Roman Catholicism. Although that might not be surprising in
view of his family's presumed history in Spain, Portugal and France, it
should not be relevant, at least logically. It may be tempting to think that
freedom in religion implies minimalist, low-controversy religion. That
may well be what Spinoza thought, and one of the merits of his 'dogmas
of the universal faith' was supposed to be that they were so low-key that
they could 'leave no occasion for controversy in the Church':[17] a view
that was, surely, not only astonishingly optimistic but entirely wrong. If
freedom in religion had any meaning, it must have meant a freedom to
adopt radically differing expressions of piety and observance. In any
event, the idea that 'simplicity' could be a self-evident or uncontentious

---

[17] Matheron calls these 'le *Credo* minimum' (1971), *Le Christ et le salut des ignorants*, p. 98.

notion in religion is debatable. It is easy enough to imagine an argument that nothing could be simpler to explain than transubstantiation, for example,[18] or nothing more rich in meanings than a Quaker silence. The view that 'simpler' religion is less controversial is full of difficulties; and if Spinoza held that view then we can only hope it was not essential to his thinking.

Similarly, we should also put to one side his pragmatic remarks about religious freedom. Anyone who lived after the Thirty Years War might reasonably come to the view that compromise in religious matters might not be a bad idea. There are entirely practical arguments in the *Theological-Political Treatise*, as there are in Locke and Hobbes: it is impossible to control what people think; the sensible route is to limit controversy by keeping opinions as private as possible. Spinoza twice mentions, with clear interest and approval, the fact that Dutch Christians in Japan had to 'refrain from practising any external rites'.[19] He might have said – but it was scarcely necessary – that the desire to make money from Japanese trade could take priority over religious rectitude. More tactfully, the inward piety of the merchants mattered more than their 'external rites'.

These pragmatic and unsophisticated considerations probably had at least as much historical effect as any other arguments, but there is not much to be said about them. The distinctions between thinking privately and speaking publicly, or between communicating opinions and raising sedition,[20] may have had some practical value in the grounding of liberal politics, but they were indefensible in any terms that Spinoza would normally accept himself.

It may seem less evident that we can put aside his elitist views about knowledge. The final pages of the *Ethics* contain a tirade against 'the common belief of the multitude'. The wise man – *sapiens* – is contrasted with the ignorant man – *ignarus* – 'whose only motive force is lust'.[21] The ignorant multitude remain in the sway of hope for rewards and of fear of punishment after death. The wise possess true spiritual contentment. Only a few can attain wisdom. In between the wise and the foolish – it may seem from the *Theological-Political Treatise* – social obedience can be reinforced by the effects of traditional religions on the imagination.

This is a controversial area, only caricatured briefly now,[22] but it is not

---

[18] See G. E. M. Anscombe, 'Transubstantiation', *Collected Philosophical Papers*, vol. III (Oxford: Blackwell, 1981).   [19] S 119 = G III 76, also S 249 = G III 200.   [20] S 293 = G III 241.
[21] *communis vulgi persuasio*, V, 41, Scholium; 42.
[22] Matheron considers it at length: *Le Christ et le salut des ignorants*, Chapter III.

directly relevant to a discussion on religious choice. Perhaps the pious and virtuous, but unreflective, practitioners within a religion should be left undisturbed by criticism or argument, and it may be that any case for religious freedom ought to allow for that.[23] Spinoza did not say that wisdom should be reserved for only a few people; he just thought that only a few will be capable of it, and had a low opinion of the persuasive powers of rational argument. That opinion sank lower in his last years – after the murder of Jan de Witt by a riotous mob – when he wrote, in the *Political Treatise*, that those who persuade themselves that the masses caught up in politics can be induced to live by the precepts of reason are living 'in the golden age of the poets or a dream story'.[24]

Despite that pessimism, there is no thought that knowledge or judgment *should* be rationed. On the contrary, it matters to his views about religious understanding that 'the natural light that is common to all' should be available, rather than 'any supernatural light, nor any external authority'. 'The sovereign right to free opinion belongs to every man even in matters of religion'.[25] The whole theory of the 'natural light' *needs* (if it does not logically depend on) the view that anyone may base their judgments on it.

FREE CHOICE

The way to establish freedom of religion, in his sense, Spinoza said, was to separate 'faith' from 'philosophy'. The whole argument is contained in a few lines at the end of Chapter xiv of the *Theological-Political Treatise*, quoted previously in part. They are worth quoting more fully, if only to illustrate the direction of his thought:

It now remains for me finally to show that between faith and theology on the one side and philosophy on the other there is no relation and no affinity . . . The aim [*scopus*] of philosophy is, quite simply, truth, while the aim of faith, as we have abundantly shown, is nothing other than obedience and piety. Again, philosophy rests on the basis of universally valid axioms [*Philosophiæ fundamenta notiones communes sunt*], and must be constructed by studying Nature alone, whereas faith is based on history and language, and must be derived only from Scripture and revelation . . . So faith allows to every man the utmost freedom to philosophise [*Fides igitur summam unicuique libertatem ad philosophandum concedit*], and he may hold whatever opinions he pleases on any subject whatsoever without imputation of evil. It condemns as heretics and schismatics only those who

---

[23] Kierkegaard is the best-known figure who would disagree violently, for example in the section on 'childish Christianity' in his *Concluding Unscientific Postscript*.   [24] I, §5; G III 275/22–5.
[25] S 160, 159 = G III 117.

teach such beliefs as promote obstinacy, hatred, strife and anger, while it regards as faithful only those who promote justice and charity to the best of their intellectual powers and capacity.[26]

A first reaction to this passage is that Spinoza was being uncharacteristically careless with his terms. On first sight, we might think that an appropriate conclusion would be that faith allows the utmost freedom in religion, not in philosophy, as he says. But the logic is oblique. Faith has nothing to do with the search for truth; so truth may be sought without any bearing on faith. So it is philosophy – research – that is freed.

This passage also shows how the separation between faith and philosophy was a good deal less distinct than it was announced to be. The 'freedom to philosophise' meant a freedom to explore, research and speculate scientifically. It did not mean a freedom to choose between different alternative 'philosophies': Spinoza could not even think in such terms.[27] More importantly, philosophy is given a universality which faith must lack: it is founded in 'common notions'. The crucial implication had been mentioned in passing a few pages earlier, in the form of a constraint. Beliefs need not contain a 'shadow of truth', as we have seen:

provided that he who adheres to them knows not that they are false. If he knew that they were false, he would necessarily be a rebel, for how could it be that one who seeks to love justice and obey God should worship as divine what he knows to be alien to [the] divine nature?[28]

So faith was hemmed in twice. First, it would contain or imply 'nothing other than obedience and piety': not truths about nature. Then if, for some reason, claims about truths should be made or implied, there was an obligation to avoid inconsistency.

A separation of faith and philosophy (for others, but rarely for Spinoza, 'reason') can be a commonplace step. 'Faith' is saved from scientific encroachments by being insulated into a field occupied by value, or the will. That fideist line of thinking contained great weaknesses: a dependence on dichotomies between 'fact' and 'value', a need to say what could influence or determine the will to make choices if any 'factual' support was supposed to be missing. These were to be the weaknesses of Kantian ethics and theology, and Spinoza was a long way from

---

[26] S 226 = G iii 179–80.

[27] Relevant here was his lack of interest in what he saw as speculative theology: 'it matters not what belief a man holds' – on a number of controversial theological topics – provided that a belief does not 'lead to the assumption of greater license to sin, or hinders submission to God': S 225 = G iii 178.   [28] S 223 = G iii 176/20–4.

falling towards them. His basic constraint on 'faith' – to avoid inconsistency – was both minimal and powerful. There was no assumption as to what might constitute a 'factual' claim or statement; only a principle that whatever is held or asserted should not be inconsistent with whatever else is held or asserted 'about divine nature'. And because it was, for him, *divine* nature – 'God or nature' – it was 'faith' that was put at risk of being inconsistent with the divine, not philosophy or science. This is a telling case.

In his metaphysics and politics, right (*jus*) is related to power (*potentia*). And since 'the universal power of Nature as a whole is nothing but the power of all individual things taken together, it follows that each individual thing has the sovereign right to do all that it can do; i.e. the right of the individual is co-extensive with its determinate power'.[29]

The political consequences were pursued along Hobbesian lines in Chapter XVII of the *Theological-Political Treatise*, which aims to devise a theory for the limits to the transfer of individual rights to a sovereign. The consequences for individual choice are more relevant now. An ability to reason is what constitutes a freedom to reason, and: 'A man is free, of course, to the extent that he is guided by reason.'[30]

The thought that *any* application of reasoned or defensible choice might be possible in religion might well be *the* crucial epistemological step. For Spinoza, the freedom we have is the capacity to measure religions, or elements within religions, against what we have to be true. It is not obligatory to measure them in terms of truths that we may have to accept. Instead, we see the stealthy proviso that we should not adhere to anything which we know to be false. This is a maxim to be followed along with a policy to search for truths about nature, and to relate those truths as far as possible in a connected, causal-explanatory system.

THE NEED FOR RELIGION

So where does this leave his attitude towards existing historical religions? One view might be that all existing religions are to be superseded by a philosophical religion of reason, accessible only to those bright enough to understand it. Other 'religions', on such a view, could either fade away or could be watered down into forms suitable for enforcing social conformity. This, in rather less stark terms, is the understanding of Yovel, in *Spinoza and Other Heretics*: we see an Enlightenment figure.

---

[29] S 237 = G III 189/21–5.   [30] S 243, note 33; see also *Political Treatise* II, vii and xi.

But did Spinoza think that the balance between 'faith' and 'philosophy' was a matter of wrong and right understanding, of worse or better understanding, or of less or more understanding? Or, indeed, of different *sorts* of understanding? This seems important. After all, if – to take one Jewish example – he really wanted to 'demolish the entire concept of election',[31] there must have been something badly wrong with this concept, and people would do well to abandon it altogether in favour of something more rational.

As we saw in Part II of this study, though, there is no evidence that Spinoza wanted to argue or persuade sincere believers out of religions in which they lived.[32] Certainly, he was anxious to show that religions should be understood in terms of moral or ceremonial practices rather than as theoretical systems. But he claimed to see his grounding of their force in history and morality as reinforcement, not subversion. (And a basic corollary of the view that religion is grounded in history is that new religions are, at best, not easy to invent; so it is not likely that Spinoza thought he was inventing one himself.)

His repeated view about revelation was not that it was inaccurate or metaphorical, but that it was necessary. The law was of intrinsically religious origin. Although the argument was framed in terms of the necessity of the Jewish covenant, it must have had a more general application: 'prior to revelation nobody can be bound by a divine law of which he cannot be aware. So a state of nature must not be confused with a state of religion; we must conceive it as being without religion and without law'.[33]

Revelation is not disposable. So religion is not disposable. Nor should we see this in cynically reductive terms. Despite Spinoza's admiration for Machiavelli, his view was not that religion is politically useful in maintaining order or control. There is no suggestion that in a perfect state – or a 'state of nature' – religion would not be needed. On the contrary: 'I assert that in a state of nature everyone is bound to live by God's revealed law [*jure revelato*] from the same motive as he is bound to live according to the dictates of sound reason, namely, that to do so is to his greater advantage and necessary for his salvation.'[34]

It is possible to miss the significance of Spinoza's non-reductive approach. If he had thought that religion was, in brief, *nothing but* history,

---

[31] Yovel, *Spinoza and Other Heretics*, p. 190.
[32] The exchange of letters (67, 76) with Burgh might be thought to be an exception; but Spinoza did not hide his disdain for Burgh's zealotry.   [33] S 246 = G III 198/16–20.
[34] S 247 = G III 198–9.

or *nothing but* an embodiment of social control, it might make sense for him to see it as dispensable in an ideally organised society, inhabited by rational people. But in fact he did not think that there could be a society of rational people – because, again, 'it is impossible for a man not to be part of Nature'[35] – and he did not think there could be an ideally organised society. Religions were grounded in how people had been, how they were and how they would be.

This adds up to an untidy set of arguments. Where do they leave religious choice? Considerations about the unavoidable presence of religions in society may not suggest much room for choice; yet it is obvious that at least Spinoza himself felt able to make a religious choice: not to live as part of his native community, bound by Rabbinic law. Was that just a matter of preference? Or did he think that he had discovered a rival truth?

Here, it may be useful to recall that three, not two, sorts of choice by Spinoza were outlined earlier in this chapter. As well as his personal decision not to live in a Jewish community and his philosophical case in favour of religious freedom there was also his intellectual location of himself in relation to his background and his predecessors. It may be that type of intellectual self-location which suggests the best interpretation for his view of religious freedom.

If we are thinking about a real situation of religious choice, the most suitable image is hardly one of a *choice between alternatives*. It is relevant that Spinoza dismissed with derision the typical philosophy textbook free-will 'problem' of a balanced choice between equal alternatives:

The problem: . . . it may be objected that if a man does not act from freedom of will, what would happen if he should be in a state of equilibrium like Buridan's ass? Will he perish of hunger and thirst? If I were to grant this, I would appear to be thinking of an ass or a statue, not of a man. If I deny it, then the man will be determining himself, and consequently will possess the faculty of going and doing whatever he wants.

The reply: I readily grant that a man placed in such a state of equilibrium . . . will die of hunger and thirst. If they ask me whether such a man is not to be reckoned an ass rather than a man, I reply that I do not know, just as I do not know how one should reckon a man who hangs himself, or how one should reckon babies, fools and madmen.[36]

---

[35] *Ethics* IV, 4.   [36] *Ethics* II, 49, Scholium; G II 133 and 135.

Spinoza himself, for example, did not choose, as from a menu, between Cartesianism, Aristotelianism, the orthodoxy of his synagogue and so on. What he must have done was to weigh up what he wanted and what he did not want from a number of sources of which he was quite plainly aware. And he would have been the first to acknowledge that there would have been other influences of which he might have been unaware; but he would have wished to haul those into the daylight as much as he could. The extent to which he did this may be controversial, but the principle that he *did* do it is surely not.

A critical relationship to a past intellectual history may be a better model than a choice 'of' religions. Important choices are seldom much like selecting dishes from a menu or alternative routes on a map. The old joke that if I were going there I would not start from here contains a valuable truth. It is a truism – not an interesting consequence of any form of determinism – that I can't choose where I am (literally) now. I have to start here. Yet the ways in which I could have chosen to get where I am now is something I can research, sometimes with fruitful results as to where I might be next. (And none of this need be denied by any form of determinism or anti-determinism.)

This is one way in which Spinozistic freedom falls between the territories mapped out in some debates about it.[37] Perhaps the process of intellectual self-identification is too familiar to intellectuals for them to recognise it easily, although the thoroughness with which it was carried out by Spinoza is less familiar. His insistence on the causal order in the mental world – in 'nature conceived through the attribute of thought' – is usually read in personal, psychological terms.[38] But it has equal application, and perhaps more interest, in terms of intellectual history and background, and consequent personal choices.

Vast scholarly labours have been devoted to exploring what led Spinoza to the point where he emerged into our sight at the time of his first writings, in about 1660.[39] Yet even someone who thought that *none* of Spinoza's building-blocks were original could still not argue that his views consisted *only* of an unreflecting cocktail of earlier influences.[40]

[37] For example, most famously, between Stuart Hampshire, 'Spinoza and the Idea of Freedom', and Isaiah Berlin, 'From Hope and Fear Set Free', *Proceedings of the Aristotelian Society*, 64, 1964.
[38] As it is read by Hampshire: in terms of freedom of will as applied to physical actions or to moral behaviour.   [39] Popkin, 'Spinoza's Earliest Philosophical Years', is one survey.
[40] Wolfson's 'What is New in Spinoza?' goes as far as it can to dismantle Spinoza into a set of influence but – surprisingly – with no underlying rational that originality and intellectual determinism are at odds with each other: *The Philosophy of Spinoza*, Chapter XXI. Yovel, *Spinoza and Other Heretics*, p. 173, quoted in the Introduction, p. 15, goes even further.

There had to be some weighing of what to retain, to emphasise or to reject. Uncontroversially, to understand one's past and one's influences can be a step towards moving beyond them. There is a sense in which intellectual freedom presupposes some understanding of context and history. Here, *freedom from* the past is not to be distinguished sharply from *freedom to* choose between future alternatives, and we lose useful insights by stressing either at the expense of the other.

These points offer some answer to the thoughts about relativism raised at the end of the previous chapter. In intellectual and also religious terms, metaphors of location seem irresistible. We choose *where to stand*, we choose to *locate* ourselves *within* or *outside* a tradition, or set of traditions; we choose between different *positions*, or between the validations *within* different *fields* of inquiry. Such language is natural enough (it has its *place*) but it is likely to *mislead*: crucially, *towards* a form of relativism. In one *place* are the *areas* occupied by traditional beliefs, legitimised by 'language and history'. Spinoza can choose to *step outside* them by his search for truth and consistency. But then his freedom of choice, *where to stand*, looks diminished, as though his alternative *positions* have been restricted, or as though he has *taken up one position* at the expense of others. (You can't be in two *places* at the same time.)

We might speculate whether intellectual relativism – the alleged challenge posed by the legitimation of separate systems of thought or belief – depends for its persuasiveness entirely on a misleading spatial metaphor. The adoption of spatial metaphor obscures our ability to pick, mix and criticise intellectually, and it ignores the results of reflective understanding. There is no *room* in such language to *locate* the freedom gained from appreciating *where* I may be. To be freed in that way, by *finding where I am*, is neither to be *placed inside* nor *outside* an intellectual *position*: the relativism suggested in the imagery of *areas* is wholly illusory.[41] *You must be somewhere* is a truism, but one of limited applicability. The thought that someone may be *isolated*, or even *nowhere*, if not *within* one or another set of beliefs should have evident failings.

This is why it would be wrong to think of Spinoza's own religious choice as a matter of adopting a personal position alongside, outside or even above other religious positions. (And that misjudgment could be compounded by imagining that he adopted a 'rationalist' position.) 'Faith' and 'philosophy', for him were not really separate, equal or

---

[41] Davidson keeps the imagery even while repudiating a relativistic view: that we might '*take up a stance outside* our own ways of thought': 'The Myth of the Subjective', M. Krausz (ed.), in *Relativism: Interpretation and Confrontation* (University of Notre Dame Press, 1989), p. 160.

symmetrical, and we have seen enough to realise that he could hardly be aligned with those who have worried about 'faith' against 'reason' as alternative channels for religious legitimation. After all, 'reason' was quite sufficient to demonstrate the existence of his God; but that, as far as he was concerned, was not the province of 'faith'.

'TO INCREASE LEARNING IS TO INCREASE HEARTACHE'[42]

'Philosophy' – science – was supposed to be universal in that it was regulated by constraints of consistency. Religions were to be linked to specific contexts. In historical or sociological terms, this might be seen as just an assertion of dominance. Leo Strauss saw it like that. In his 1962 preface to *Spinoza's Critique of Religion*, he concluded that 'the antagonism between Spinoza and Judaism, between unbelief and belief, is ultimately not theoretical but moral'.[43]

But the lack of symmetry between 'faith' and 'philosophy' is not a matter of moral assertion and counter-assertion. For Spinoza it was more a matter of the lack of symmetry between less knowledge and more knowledge: of the fact that what is once known cannot easily become unknown – that what is once realised to be true can be adapted, or can be fitted into what is accepted already, but cannot simply be forgotten. Whether or not it is worthwhile to think about *choices* between traditions (in religion or elsewhere), the existence of choices is itself something that cannot be unlearnt. This kind of asymmetry was caught memorably in an image produced by al-Ghazāli in the eleventh century:

There is certainly no point in trying to return to the level of naive and derivative belief (*taqlīd*) once it has been left, since a condition of being at such a level is that one should not know one is there; when a man comes to know that, the glass of his naive beliefs is broken. This is a breakage which cannot be mended, a breakage not to be repaired by patching or by assembling of fragments. The glass must be melted once again in the furnace for a new start, and out of it another fresh vessel formed.[44]

If *choice* is seen in terms of understanding, what happens if understanding is increased or maximised? Spinoza had to achieve a balance of

---

[42] Ecclesiastes, 1:18 (JPS).

[43] Strauss, *Spinoza's Critique of Religion* (Preface to the English translation), p. 29.

[44] *Deliverance from Error*, in W. Montgomery Watt (ed. and trans.), *The Faith and Practice of al-Ghazāli* (London: George Allen & Unwin, 1953), p. 27. For those who feel that metaphors are inescapable it could be interesting to speculate that if spatial metaphors can be misleading here, temporal ones might be less so: seeing, then taking choices, could be understood as passing irreversibly from past or present to the future, not moving from one location to another.

some delicacy in his approach. A *better* understanding might suggest that
unexamined faith was somehow defective, especially if there was some
thought that a better understanding undermines its legitimacy. This is
how a kindly-looking relativism can sometimes be so corrosive. But in a
note to the *Theological-Political Treatise* he wrote, presumably with sincerity, that: 'it is not reason but revelation that can teach us that it is enough
for blessedness or salvation for us to accept the divine decrees as laws or
commandments, and . . . there is no need to conceive them as eternal
truths'.[45]

So it may be enough – *satis sit* – to live, speaking loosely, *within* a religion. Without any theoretical presuppositions, we can take this to mean
that a charitable, sincere and pious life, ordered as necessary by respect
for traditional values, needs no criticism and no condescension. The
effect of a growth in scientific knowledge was not, as we have seen, a *challenge* to traditional religion, as he saw it. The need was to understand the
claims made, for example in scripture, in ways that would not conflict
with physics or astronomy.[46] So there should be no question of a 'choice'
of views between 'faith' and 'philosophy' or science.

'All men without exception are capable of obedience' (*omnes absolute
obedire possunt*) can be taken as it stands. Anyone is qualified to accept
what Spinoza considers to be faith-linked-to-obedience, since 'he who is
truly obedient necessarily possesses a true and saving faith'.[47] But there is
a reservation. His remark continues: 'while there are only a few – in proportion to the whole of humanity – who acquire a virtuous disposition
under the guidance of reason alone'.[48]

This is to turn from the contents or nature of beliefs and behaviour to
their cause or explanation. Those who possess a 'true and saving faith'
[*vera & salutifera fides*] are not *wrong* or *mistaken* and they do not need to
change their beliefs or their ways of life. The effect of what Spinoza held
to be *more* knowledge was on the understanding of why a true and saving
faith was as it was. That effect was not meant either to subvert its legitimacy and force, or to add to it any extra strength, but to shift its basis.
When we do come to know the 'cause' of the commandments or ordinances of the law 'they cease to be commandments, and we embrace

---

[45] S 307; note 31 to p. 236 = G III 263.
[46] S 79 = G III 36, the example of Joshua asking God to stop the movement of the sun: it would be
'ridiculous' to assume 'that the soldier Joshua was a skilled astronomer'.
[47] S 222 = G III 175/21–2.
[48] *ex solo rationis ductu*; S 236 = G III 188/26–9: this phrase occurs in a central point in the *Ethics*: IV, 36,
Demonstration: 'To act from virtue is to act by the guidance of reason': *ex ductu rationis agere*.

them as eternal truths, not as commandments; that is, obedience forthwith passes into love, which arises from true knowledge by the same
necessity as light arises from the sun. Therefore by the guidance of
reason we can love God, but not obey him.'[49]

This is not a matter of religious choice so much as an understanding
of religion (as one part of nature). No one is obliged to seek such an
understanding. In practice, Spinoza thinks, it is unrealistic to imagine
that many will seek it. Again: 'intellectual or exact knowledge of God is
not a gift shared by all the faithful, as is obedience'.[50] One of the many
reasons why it is unhelpful to see him as a 'rationalist' is that he did not
believe that most people would, could or even should seek to conduct the
investigation, reflection and research required to understand causes in
nature. They were not wrong or mistaken, holding inferior beliefs, but
simply living as they were. There were exceptions. Spinoza must have
believed himself to be one. Another, we shall see, was Jesus.

[49] S 308, note 34 to p. 246 = G III 264.   [50] S 215 = G III 168/28–30.

CHAPTER 9

The figure of Christ

Spinoza's use of the figure of Christ is one of the most puzzling aspects of his work. It might seem less puzzling if he had ever allied himself to a Christian group after leaving his Jewish roots, but he did not, and the signs are that he no more saw himself as a Christian than as a Jew. Yet his remarks about Jesus were almost entirely positive. He made some favourable comparisons between Jesus and Moses, and between what he represented as Christian and Jewish points of view. The general line of his approach – that Jesus spoke uniquely and universally to the whole of humanity, where Moses had delivered the law only for the Jews – has been a routine Christian claim since the time of St Paul; so we need not be surprised that Spinoza's Jewish readers have often been dismayed by what he said.[1] His use of the name 'Christ' and of the Christian title, the 'Old Testament', for the Jewish scriptures, cannot have helped.

Before looking at all this, two preliminary points can be made: first, the personal significance of the subject to Spinoza, and secondly, its importance to his philosophical system. Personally, it does not seem that he had much feeling of reverence or attachment to Jesus as man or as a religious figure. He wrote admiringly and with some respect, but with no great affection, inspiration or warmth. Perhaps that was not too remarkable. He was an extraordinarily cool and detached writer. The warmth that he did show at times was usually negative, in the form of scorn or distaste for what he saw as bigotry or superstition. Readers looking for signs of personal devotion towards Jesus would be disappointed. This chapter is called 'The figure of Christ' because Spinoza *used* Jesus as a figure in his philosophy.[2] Some of those uses, already noted (in Chapter 7), were shockingly insensitive, especially in writing intended to persuade

---

[1] See Strauss, *Spinoza's Critique of Religion*, pp. 18–21, for the views of Strauss and Hermann Cohen.
[2] It is possible to see this in a more positive way, as does Laux. He says that Christ is used in an *exemplary* way, but that this indicates at the same time the 'perfection' and the 'utility' of the exemplar: *Imagination et religion*, pp. 263–4.

Christian readers.[3] There are few signs, despite his philosophical respect, that he had much sympathy or understanding for why anyone might have cared a great deal about Jesus. There are no signs that he cared much himself.[4]

The position is less clear on the importance of Jesus for him philosophically. There is only one mention of Christ in the *Ethics*, and though that comes at a significant point – as we shall see, it seems to be part of a portrait of the free man – it is presented as part of an illustrative *historia* – 'story'[5] – and, as an illustration rather than a theorem, it contributes nothing essential to the logic of the case. Christ is mentioned frequently but unsystematically in the *Theological-Political Treatise*, in many different contexts. Very little is added to the philosophical claims of the *Ethics*, understood narrowly, although some strange anomalies do seem to be created. Spinoza would not have been a lesser philosopher, and his thought would have lost nothing of its interest to philosophers, if Jesus had never been mentioned.

Despite these reservations, there can be no doubt that the subject has to be addressed seriously. It has considerable religious interest, and is baffling in its own right. It alarmed his contemporaries. It provokes questions about Spinoza's sincerity and directness as well as questions – which unfortunately we can never hope to answer – about the sources for his motivation.

Alexandre Matheron opens his classic study of the whole problem by noting Spinoza's distinction between Christ 'according to the flesh' and 'the spirit of Christ'.[6] It should be helpful to deal first with the straightforward and uncontroversial aspects of Spinoza's attitude towards Christ 'according to the flesh': his understanding of the historical Jesus, the historical reality which he accepted.

Spinoza had no doubt that Jesus existed. The written historical record was strong and clear: 'the chief facts of the life of Christ . . . and His Passion were immediately spread abroad throughout the whole Roman

---

[3] The intended readership is mentioned in Letter 30.

[4] On the other hand, there is a possible reading in his letter to Albert Burgh where one text, and the early Dutch translation, has him writing of 'all of us who profess the Christian name' – *omnibus qui Christianum nomen profitemur* – rather than the alternative reading of 'all . . . that profess the name of Christ' – *omnibus, qui Christi nomen profitentur*, Letter 76, L 344 = G IV 322/33 or /16–17; but this might be a rhetorical turn of phrase in that context. In any event, it seems far less striking than his routine use of the third, not first, person in writing of Jews.

[5] *Ethics* IV, 68, Scholium. Curley detects a 'slightly skeptical and ironic' tone in his footnote to the Scholium, Curley, p. 584. Pollock remarks that the extent to which Spinoza was serious 'must be left to every reader's conjecture': *Spinoza, His Life and Philosophy*, p. 269.

[6] *Le Christ et le salut des ignorants*, p. 7. His examples are from Letter 73; L 333 = G IV 308/10: *Christum secundum carnem*, and Letter 43; L 241 = G IV 226/3: *Spiritum Christi habere*.

Empire. It is therefore impossible to believe that, without the connivance of a large part of mankind – which is quite inconceivable – later generations handed down a version of the main outlines of these events different from what they had received.'[7]

In a letter to Henry Oldenburg he was unambiguous about historical facts: 'The passion, death and burial of Christ I accept literally [*literaliter*]', and we can take this as it stands, especially because the letter went on to be entirely frank about what he did *not* accept: 'but his resurrection I understand in an allegorical sense [*allegoricè*]. I do indeed admit that this is related by the Evangelists . . . Nevertheless, without injury to the teaching of the Gospel, they could have been deceived, as was the case with other prophets.'[8]

In an earlier letter he was equally plain in his rejection of the doctrine of the incarnation: 'as to the additional teaching of certain Churches, that God took upon himself human nature, I have expressly indicated that I do not understand what they say. Indeed, to tell the truth, they seem to me to speak no less absurdly than one who might tell me that a circle has taken on the nature of a square.'[9]

The reaction of Oldenburg was orthodox. As Pollock put it wryly, he protested 'exactly as an English Broad Churchman might now [1880] protest if he fell into a similar correspondence with a Dutch theologian of the liberal school, that the literal historical fact of the Resurrection is the indispensable foundation of Christianity'.[10]

It is possible to debate the standards of evidence assumed in these remarks in Spinoza's letters: whether or not, for example, he adopted a more relaxed attitude towards the evidence for the life of Jesus than the critical approach he followed with the Hebrew scriptures.[11] But if there is anything in this, it is a matter of emphasis rather than serious content.

The *Theological-Political Treatise* was less blunt, but not much less clear. A distinction was drawn openly between an instruction or commandment revealed by God in contrast with 'only the teachings of Christ in the Sermon on the Mount'. The chief concern of Christ was 'to teach moral doctrines'.[12]

---

[7] S 212–13 = G III 166.   [8] Letter 78; L 348 = G IV 328.   [9] Letter 73; L 333 = G IV 309.

[10] *Spinoza, His Life and Philosophy*, p. 368.

[11] A point made well by Sylvain Zac: 'When he deals with the New Testament, Spinoza is not always faithful to the golden rule of his method of biblical exegesis which tells us to explain scripture by means of scripture. He falls into the same fault which he ascribes to Maimonides: he explains allegorically and rethinks Christianity in the light of his own philosophy': 'Le problème du Christianisme de Spinoza', *Revue de Synthèse*, 78, 1957, p. 483.

[12] S 198 = G III 152/2–5; S 114 = G III 71/4–5: *nec aliud magis curaverit, quam documenta moralia docere.*

So we see an acceptance of Jesus as a moral teacher who died and who rose allegorically but not literally from the dead. Up to this point the only real interest is historical: to judge how innovative or shocking this might have been in the 1670s. Pollock commented on its 'wonderfully modern character'.

It can seem attractive to recruit Spinoza as an early modernist pioneer, although the point or value of that must be uncertain. The direct creative impact of his opinions about Jesus must have been slight, in comparison with the immense outrage they caused, to the extent that we cannot really think in terms of their 'influence' at all, beyond narrow sectarian circles. As Pollock suggests, though, what may have been shocking in 1670 was more common by the nineteenth century; but not as an immediate result of Spinoza's work.

CHRISTIANITY

If this had been all, there would not be much to say. What we have seen is only what any reader coming to Spinoza might have expected him to say on the basis of the rest of his views and his Jewish upbringing. He could not be *expected*, after all, to admit the particular divinity of Jesus, or to have much regard for the doctrine of the incarnation, or to accept that anyone might be literally brought back from the dead. Oldenburg's bewildered reaction to these opinions seems to overlook not only Spinoza's philosophical views (only dimly grasped) but his Jewish origin.[13]

In fact there is a lot more to say, almost all of it apparently anomalous against the background of the *Ethics*. The treatment of Jesus, and of Christianity, in the *Theological-Political Treatise* is cautious in some ways, but it does not give an immediate impression of insincerity. Spinoza plainly did not wish to become embroiled in scriptural arguments over the gospels and he claimed that his knowledge of Greek was 'insufficient for venturing upon such an undertaking'.[14] That may have been honest enough, but his expertise in textual controversy over the Hebrew scriptures can leave us little doubt that he might have found something to say about the gospels, despite his Greek.[15] So he could be cautious. On the

---

[13] '*Il y a un malentendu profond entre Oldenburg et Spinoza*', writes Sylvain Zac in a laconic understatement: *Spinoza et l'interprétation de l'Écriture*, p. 195. For much of the earlier background see, for example, D. J. Lasker, *Jewish Philosophical Polemics against Christianity in the Middle Ages* (New York: Ktav Publishing House, 1977), particularly Chapter V.   [14] S 196 = G III 150/33–4.

[15] He had an accurate sense of what was controversial in the post-Reformation Christian world, and could not resist some partisan quotations, as in the mischievous use of The Epistle of James, S 222 = G III 175/18–21.

other hand, he did not hesitate to distinguish, in the polemical style of his time, between what he gathered 'from Scripture itself' and 'the doctrines held by some Churches about Christ' – which he claimed not to understand.[16]

He seemed willing to be reasonably frank about Christianity. Jewish critics who have felt that he gave a far harsher treatment to Judaism may not have appreciated how thoroughly he managed to offend his Christian readers. If he really tried to be diplomatically pleasing, he was exceptionally unsuccessful. He claimed, for instance, to be unconvinced that Christian ceremonies, including baptism and the Lord's Supper, were ever instituted by Christ or by the apostles:[17] a view surely guaranteed to outrage almost all shades of opinion outside the most radical sects. And wholly missing from the *Theological-Political Treatise* is any mention of a redemptive rôle for Jesus, or any view of history from a point of view of Christian teleology or eschatology. We see only the vague appearance of the *via salutis*:[18] the way of salvation. His contemporary audience, even with no knowledge of the *Ethics*, would have had no trouble in grasping that what he said about the election of the Jews and the interpretation of Jewish history would apply exactly to Christian views about divine providence and the meaning of history; and this could only be understood as stark heresy.

JUDAISM

A significant part of Spinoza's use of the figure of Christ resembled some traditional, ancient elements in Christian criticism of Judaism: Jesus superseded, abolished or internalised the Jewish law, replacing outward ritual and ceremony with personal moral autonomy. It is not too surprising to find references to St Paul associated with this critique. The general line is not hard to imagine on the basis of the rest of his thinking, but the detail is of some interest.

His treatment of law was discussed in Chapter 2. We cannot tell whether this sprang from a theological motivation, or whether the religious aspect of the subject struck him as a valuable corollary to his argument. In terms of natural, scientific law, external rules 'governing' the existence, action and behaviour of individuals were to be denied. The

[16] S 64–5 = G III 21/13–15. The idea that Christian doctrine could not be understood was an old Jewish defence against inquisitors, here used more combatively.   [17] S 119 = G III 76/8–13.
[18] S 64 = G III 21/12.

actions of nature were to be understood first in terms of causes within nature. This applied equally to personal actions and behaviour:

Paul concludes that, since God is the God of all nations – that is, he is equally gracious to all – and since all mankind were equally under the law and under sin, it was for all nations that God sent his Christ to free all men alike from the bondage of the law, so that no longer would they act righteously from the law's command but from the unwavering resolution of the heart. Thus Paul's teaching coincides exactly with ours.[19]

And again, Christ freed people from bondage to the law 'while nevertheless giving further strength and stability to the law, inscribing it deep in their hearts'. The language has an unmistakably Spinozist ring: 'Christ freed people from bondage to the law' – *a servitute legis liberavit* – must remind us of the titles of Parts IV and V of the *Ethics* – *De Servitute Humanâ* and *De Libertate Humanâ*.[20] In the same way, 'ceremonial observances contribute nothing to blessedness, and . . . those specified in the Old Testament, and indeed the whole Mosaic Law, were relevant only to the Hebrew state'.[21]

<h2 style="text-align:center">UNIQUENESS</h2>

None of this would have been out of line with conventional Christian attitudes towards Judaism. Other characteristics ascribed by Spinoza to Jesus might have looked equally unexceptional on the surface, but they contained elements that might seem surprising to anyone who knew the thinking in the *Ethics*. Jesus was in some ways unique. He had a unique relationship to God. He spoke with unique universality to all nations. He had unique insight into nature. He may have been uniquely 'free'.

These claims must be examined with care. There seem to be obvious problems. After stressing the universality of the 'natural light' as a method of acquiring knowledge, and the transparent intelligibility of nature, how could Spinoza say that one person had any specially privileged insight? Despite Christian claims, all the arguments about the election of the Jews would seem to apply equally to the special position of Jesus.

---

[19] S 97 = G III 54/21–7.

[20] S 108 = G III 65/10–12; for later readers the 'inscribing' might also evoke the inscribed laws in the early *Treatise on the Emendation of the Intellect* §101; G II 37/2.

[21] S 119 = G III 76/5–8: the phrasing is brutally reductionist. The Torah – *tota lex Mosis* – related to nothing but the Hebrew state – *nihil aliud quam Hebræorum imperium . . . spectavisse*. This attitude at times seemed to degenerate into little more than polemical abuse: S 113 = G III 70/9ff.

But – as we saw in Chapter 7 – Spinoza never *denied* the election of the
Jews: he was anxious only to explain his understanding of what it meant.
In exactly the same sense we must understand that 'God sent his Christ.'
There is no unclarity, no ambiguity and there should be no possibility of
misinterpretation about such statements. It was 'through the mind of
Christ . . . that God made revelations to mankind just as he once did
through angels'; 'God revealed himself to Christ'; 'Christ was sent to
teach not only the Jews but the entire human race'; and so on.[22] Those
who look for metaphor, or who worry about non-literal meanings, in the
election of the Jews, should have problems with claims as plain as these.
Yovel, for example, never gets to grips with Spinoza's claims for the
uniqueness of Jesus,[23] such as:

I do not believe that anyone has attained such a degree of perfection [in knowl-
edge] surpassing all others, except Christ.

. . . we may conclude that, with the exception of Christ, God's revelations were
received only with the aid of the imaginative faculty . . .

. . . it must be granted that the authority which Christ gave the disciples was a
unique occurrence [*singulariter*], and cannot be regarded as an example for
others.[24]

The 'sending' of Jesus with unique capacities can, if we wish, be read
along the same lines that Yovel understands the choice of the Jews. In
commonplace terms: it 'means' that Jesus was a uniquely gifted individual. (Presumably in the sense that Wittgenstein wrote of Mozart and
Beethoven as 'the actual sons of God'.[25]) The historical emergence of
Jesus at a time and place was 'really' a natural event. But that is not what
Spinoza said. For him, natural events were divine events.

Part of the uniqueness of Jesus was supposed to be the unique universality of his teaching. We have seen that Spinoza wanted to stress this,
in distinction from what he saw as the geographical, historical and social
particularity of Judaism. Jesus spoke to all nations: 'Christ was sent to
teach not only the Jews but the entire human race.'[26]

[22] S 107–8 = G III 64.
[23] For example *Spinoza and Other Heretics*, pp. 178–9, or in 'The Third Kind of Knowledge as
Alternative Salvation', in Curley and Moreau (eds.), *Spinoza: Issues and Directions*.
[24] S 64 = G III 21/3–5; S 65 = G III 21/23–4; S 285 = G III 234/5–7.
[25] In a letter to Russell, 16 August 1912: Wittgenstein, *Letters to Russell, Keynes and Moore* (Oxford:
Blackwell, 1974), p. 15. An interesting analogy – though not one which would have impressed
Spinoza's original readers – can be found in the claim of Socrates to have been *sent* to torment the
people of Athens like a gadfly: *Apology*, 30–1.
[26] S 97 = G III 54/24; S 107 = G III 64/27–8, *totum humanum genus docendum missus fuerit.*

Once again, a naturalistic reading is available. Matheron gives an intriguing account, relating to the context of the ending of the Jewish state and the universalism of the Roman Empire.[27] But, once again, it might not be wise to assume – and Matheron does not – that this is what Spinoza 'meant', or 'really meant'.

We have seen how Jesus was supposed to have been 'sent' in some negative, anti-Jewish senses as a universal moralist, not as a particular lawgiver. Here, it is not possible to know what axe Spinoza was grinding. Maybe he genuinely wanted an exemplar for the immanence and universality of his understanding of law. Maybe he was mixing together his philosophical and theological idioms along with an animus against Jewish law. Maybe he really wanted to frame his points in personal terms, though we are now firmly with 'the spirit', not with 'Christ according to the flesh'. The living personality of Jesus had no bearing on these arguments.

Spinoza's more positive uses for the figure of Christ present these alternatives to us in a more pressing and difficult way: the general idea of the universalisation of the law is easy enough to grasp, after all, whatever the motives behind it, as is the image of Jesus as a uniquely authoritative moral teacher. These are claims that are to be endorsed or legitimised in terms of moral authority (which a critic might wish to read as *only* moral authority). But they are not the central or the really problematic parts of the picture. The real uniqueness of Jesus, for Spinoza, seems to have been that he was unique in his capacity as a knower, which may have had direct consequences in making him uniquely free.

UNIQUE KNOWLEDGE

It is possible that the information we have on this subject is just too fragmentary to make sense. What Spinoza said was not collected together and was never explained. The most thorough and persuasive treatments[28] rest on perilously few texts.

Christ was supposed to have some special means of knowing. The point was introduced as part of a case intended to prove that 'everything that God revealed to the prophets was revealed either by words, or by appearances, or by a combination of both'. Spinoza was able to convince himself that the only instance in the scriptures where God

---

[27] *Le Christ et le salut des ignorants*, Chapter 1.
[28] Laux, *Imagination et religion*, pp. 258–86, is almost alone in the field, building on the work of Matheron.

'employed a real voice' was in speaking to Moses.[29] Other apparent instances were explained as cases of visionary imagination. In Spinoza's terms it was crucial, of course, that in the normal run of nature 'We may quite clearly understand that God can communicate with man without mediation, for he communicates his essence to our minds without employing corporeal means',[30] and however we read *that*, it is nothing to do with specially privileged, visionary access or illumination; it is *something* to do with 'natural' knowing. But then we get to Christ, in contrast with this and with Moses. With the exception of Christ (*præter Christum*), God's revelations were received by means of imagination – by words or images.[31] The remarkable passage on Christ's form of knowledge is unusually cryptic:

a man who can perceive by pure intuition [*sola mente*] that which is not contained in the basic principles of our cognition and cannot be deduced therefrom must needs possess a mind whose excellence far surpasses the human mind. Therefore I do not believe that anyone has attained such a degree of perfection surpassing all others, except Christ. To him God's ordinances leading men to salvation [*ad salutem*] were revealed not by words or by visions, but directly, so that God manifested himself to the Apostles through the mind of Christ as he once did to Moses through an audible voice. The Voice of Christ can thus be called the Voice of God in the same way as that which Moses heard. In that sense it can also be said that the Wisdom of God – that is, wisdom that is more than human – took on human nature in Christ, and that Christ was the way of salvation . . . if Moses spoke with God face to face as a man may do with his fellow (through the medium of their two bodies), then Christ communed with God mind to mind.[32]

We can ask several questions: given, as we have seen, that Spinoza certainly did not accept the divinity of Christ – or, rather, the *special* divinity, since everything is divine – how could Christ's knowledge be said to surpass the human? And what sort of knowledge was it supposed to be? And what did this unique capacity suggest or imply?

A first comment might be to note the – perhaps – cunning obliqueness of what Spinoza claims. A letter to Oldenburg of 1675 looks as though it might have been written with a copy of this passage from the *Treatise* to hand. Here, the obliqueness comes out more strikingly: 'for salvation it is not altogether necessary to know Christ according to the flesh; but with regard to the eternal son of God, that is, God's eternal wisdom, which has manifested itself in all things and chiefly in the human mind, and

---

[29] S 61 = G III 17/9–23.　　[30] S 64 = G III 20/32–5.　　[31] S 65 = G III 21/23–4.
[32] S 64–5 = G III 20–21.

most of all in Christ Jesus, a very different view must be taken . . . And since . . . this wisdom has been manifested most of all through Jesus Christ, his disciples have preached it, as far as he revealed it to them . . .'[33]

In both this letter and in the *Theological-Political Treatise* the revelation on which Spinoza focuses is the revelation to others – the apostles, mankind – through Christ, not the revelation to Christ himself. God 'manifested himself to the Apostles through the mind of Christ'. Christ speaking then becomes the voice of God. This comes out again, later, when 'it was through the mind of Christ . . . that God made revelations to mankind just as he once did through angels, i.e. through a created voice, visions, etc.'. Christ was not so much a prophet as the mouth of God.[34] Jesus perceived what he did, but the revelation that was passed on to history was not what came to him, but what he revealed to others, or what was revealed in him to others. The point which Spinoza may have been making was partly one of scriptural authority. 'God revealed himself to Christ, or Christ's mind, directly, and not through words and images as in the case of the prophets',[35] to be sure, but what he *said* was adapted to the understanding of those who heard it – 'adapting himself to the character of the people'.[36] Words and images were necessary to explain the mind of Christ, both for himself, and even more so for the apostles. The 'voice of God' or the 'mouth of God' is Jesus speaking his mind. But, for Spinoza, God speaks 'mind to mind', as it were, routinely, to all of us – 'he communicates his essence to our minds without employing corporeal means' – and, as we have seen, whatever that is taken to mean, it is not something non-natural.

The type of knowing available to Christ is not explained at all. A natural reading might be that the 'third type of knowledge' is awarded the highest status, in the *Ethics*. Since Jesus might be assumed to use the highest form of knowledge, he must have been able to use this (always, or more often than the rest of us). Such a view has seemed almost self-evident to many commentators.[37] There are some drawbacks. Spinoza does not clearly stratify levels of knowledge in the *Theological-Political Treatise*, and it is impossible to know whether he had a tidy parallel in mind with the classification in *Ethics*.[38] Then there is the regrettable lack of clarity about the 'third type of knowledge' itself. To say that Jesus employed it is almost to explain the obscure by means of the still more

---

[33] Letter 73; L 333 = G IV 308–9.   [34] *os Dei*; S 107 = G III 64/19–21.
[35] S 107–8 = G III 64/31–3.   [36] *sese ingenio populi accommodavit*; S 108 = G III 65/4.
[37] Matheron has an admirably cautious discussion, *Le Christ et le salut des ignorants*, pp. 251–3.
[38] *Ethics* II, 40, Scholium 2.

obscure. At least, it may be to paper over a problem by covering it with
terminology.

Perception 'by pure intuition'[39] obviously could be Spinoza's highest
form of intuitive knowing. What seems quite certain – because it is quite
explicit – is that Jesus is supposed to have possessed knowledge that was
universal and natural. This is an essential ingredient in the case for the
universality of what he taught, against the particularity of the Jewish law.
As we have seen, 'Christ was sent to teach not only the Jews but the entire
human race. Thus it was not enough for him to have a mind adapted to
the beliefs of the Jews alone; his mind had to be adapted to the beliefs and
doctrines held in common by all mankind, that is, to those axioms that
are universally true',[40] and these axioms or notions look extremely like
the deliverances of Spinozist science or philosophy. Later in the
Theological-Political Treatise we read that the apostles preached religion 'to
all men as a universal law' (*legem catholicam*), and that the 'universal religion' was 'entirely in accord with Nature' (*religio catholica, quæ maxime naturalis est*). And we know from the same work, from the chapter on divine
law that the natural divine law in its entirety 'is in absolute agreement
with the dictates of the natural light'.[41] All this looks as though Christ was
able to act as an exemplar of working philosophical–scientific knowledge.

TRANSCENDENT KNOWLEDGE?

But what are we to make of the suggestion that Christ possessed 'a
degree of perfection surpassing all others' in a capacity for knowing?[42]
The terminology resembles one of the annotations to the *Theological-
Political Treatise* which comments on a remark that the prophets were
'endowed with extraordinary virtue exceeding the normal'. A distinction
is drawn in the annotation between gifts that can be understood 'from
the definition of human nature' and those that cannot. We then get the
sort of oblique logic which exasperates commentators. A giant may be
big, but is still human. Only a few people can still extemporise in verse,
but this is still a human gift: 'But if someone were to possess a quite
different means of perception and quite different grounds of knowledge,
he would assuredly surpass the bounds of human nature.'[43]

---

[39] A rather leading translation of *pura mente percipere*, S 64 = G III 20–21.
[40] S 107 = G III 64/27–31.
[41] S 209 = G III 163/10–15; S 109 = G III 66/11–12: *totam legem divinam naturalem comprehendit, & cum dic-
tamine luminis naturalis absolute convenit.* (Shirley translates *luminis naturalis* as 'the natural light of
reason'.)   [42] S 64 = G III 21/4.   [43] Note 3.

Now this wording suggests strongly that there could not be such a person. The Latin reads: *humanæ naturæ limites transcenderet* – he would transcend the limits of human nature – and it seems beyond imagination that Spinoza could have wanted anyone to match that description. Certainly it would invalidate everything in Part I of the *Ethics*, where the transcendent is completely eradicated. The point of the annotation[44] must be a kind of *reductio ad absurdum* – transcending human nature is not possible, so 'surpassing human nature' must be taken in the sense that could not go beyond the definition of being human.

That looks tidy and painless. Maybe we can work round some of the claims for uniqueness or exclusivity in this way. Where, for example, 'with the exception of Christ, God's revelations were received only with the aid of the imaginative faculty', this could be because Christ perceived with the natural light – 'truly and adequately'[45] – which might have made him unusual or even exceptional, but not super-human.

We should look more closely at the most assertive claim for uniqueness:

a man who can perceive by pure intuition that which is not contained in the basic principles of our cognition and cannot be deduced therefrom must needs possess a mind whose excellence far surpasses the human mind. Therefore [*Quare*] I do not believe that anyone has attained such a degree of perfection surpassing all others, except Christ.[46]

It is possible that 'surpassing the human mind' here can be taken in the sense just discussed in the annotation to the *Theological-Political Treatise*. The Latin text means, literally, 'should be more excellent by far than the human [mind]', and maybe that does not suggest transcendence. On the other hand, Spinoza used the same unusual phrase twice, in a way that looks like some sort of hint or echo: the intuition 'not contained in the basic principles of our cognition' – *quæ in primis nostræ cognitionis fundamentis non continentur* – sounds the same as the 'quite different grounds of knowledge' – *alia . . . cognitionis fundamenta* – in the Note. Which seems to suggest a transcendence of the limits of human nature – which is a problem. Unless there might be some significance in Spinoza's use of *Quare*. Shirley translates this as 'therefore', implying some degree of logical consequence. Curley, in his version, does not translate it at all.[47] Something between the two might be more appropriate. It need not

---

[44] Assuming that it is authentic: there are complicated textual and bibliographic problems about these notes.   [45] S 65 = G III 21/23–4; S 107 = G III 64/18.   [46] S 64 = G III 20–21.

[47] Curley, *A Spinoza Reader* (Princeton University Press, 1994), p. 14.

follow that Jesus possessed a mind that would 'transcend the limits of human nature'. Spinoza is saying, 'from which I do not believe that anyone has attained such a degree of perfection'.

UNIQUE FREEDOM?

If this is the unique form of knowledge possessed by Jesus, we can also see that it may have made him uniquely free. That seems to be the point made in the only relevant reference to him in the *Ethics*. After working through a theory of psychology in Part IV, Spinoza gets to several propositions outlining the character of the free man – 'that is, he who lives solely according to the dictates of reason'[48] – a passage that it seems almost irresistible to see as a self-portrait. In the Scholium to Proposition 68, and quite unexpectedly, we get to the 'story of the first man'. This character is said to have lost his freedom in the manner narrated in Genesis, a freedom, 'which the Patriarchs later regained under the guidance of the spirit of Christ, that is, the idea of God [*ducti Spiritu Christi, hoc est, Dei ideâ*] on which alone it depends that a man should be free and should desire for mankind the good that he desires for himself'.

In a sense, our understanding of this need not be a problem. In brief: by knowing more truths, living under the guidance of reason, internalising the law, the mind becomes more active and more free. The participation of the 'Spirit of Christ', or even the 'idea of God' in such a process need not be seen as more than a realisation in divine terms of something naturally intelligible. Along the same lines we can read the remarks already quoted from a letter to Oldenburg: 'for salvation it is not altogether necessary to know Christ according to the flesh; but with regard to the eternal son of God, that is, God's eternal wisdom, which has manifested itself in all things and chiefly in the human mind, and most of all in [the mind of] Christ Jesus'.[49]

And maybe it is in a similar sense that we can read how Christ by his life and death 'provided an example of surpassing holiness'.[50]

[48] IV, 67, Demonstration.
[49] Letter 73; L 333 = G IV 308/9-13 = /26-30. '<the mind of>' is an addition in one version of the letter. The reference to Christ as 'God's eternal wisdom' can open up avenues of interpretation based on Jewish wisdom literature or, for Christian readers, on the remarks following 1 Corinthians, 1: 24.   [50] *singularis sanctitatis exemplum dedit*; Letter 75; L 338-9 = G IV 314/31.

THE FIGURE OF CHRIST

Or maybe not . . .

The approach in this chapter has been to start with the less surprising, more expected elements within Spinoza's view of Jesus and to work towards the more surprising and unexpected elements. As can be seen, if we try hard enough we can make some of his most puzzling remarks seem quite unalarming. This might create an unfair impression of commonsense ordinariness or normality. Whether or not it is right – as Matheron argues convincingly in *Le Christ et le salut des ignorants* – that what Spinoza says about Jesus in the *Theological-Political Treatise* was honestly consistent with what he said in the *Ethics*, the fact remains that his attitude still seems enigmatic. There remains an elusive feeling that, despite all the explanation, we still can't grasp what he really felt. We can see the trees, but the wood may remain dark.

This is exemplified by the last passages quoted, from Letters 73 and 75. The *historia* in *Ethics* IV, 68, has been passed over as hardly serious by some writers, as we have seen. On the other hand, Henri Laux, in his detailed and impressive study, argues that here we have the picture of Jesus as the ideal free man – the Spinozistic knower. Laux also sees a good deal in the example of holiness in Christ's life and death. We can ask what sort of example that was. He remarks that Christ 'met death in the position of a free man'. And 'by his knowledge of divine truths, by his ethical excellence he became the realisation of something unique; in his passion he pushed steadfastness of the soul and generosity to their perfection'. Spinoza 'paradoxically rediscovered the essence of Christian dogmatics: the language of the cross'.[51] Laux thinks that there is no point in trying to spiritualise or Christianise Spinozism; because it does not 'coincide with Christian dogmatics', it cannot be an orthodoxy. But his reading does find a good deal of Christian significance in Spinoza's few remarks about Jesus.[52]

The problem we have with Spinoza's Jesus is one which is repeated in a more acute way with his views on eternity, to be pursued in the next chapter. We can see what he said, and in some sense we can piece it together consistently with some of the more accessible parts of his philosophical thinking, but what we might call, naively, his *personal view* still seems to be missing.

---

[51] *Imagination et religion*, pp. 275–81, 276, 278, 279.
[52] Much more Christian significance is seen by A. Malet, 'La religion de Spinoza au point de vue chrétien', *Revue de Synthèse*, 99, 1978; a paper followed in discussion by incredulous comments by Robert Misrahi and Sylvain Zac.

This is partly because of his complete silence on his motivation. We might imagine that he wanted to use the figure of Jesus, for some reason, against Judaism. One natural reading is that he did want to adopt or exploit some of the ancient Christian arguments against Judaism – but he did not want to adopt a Christian position himself. (Equally, but less often noted, he might be thought to adopt some conventional Jewish attitudes towards Christian doctrines: that they were unintelligible, for example.) That does not sound at all admirable, and it would be not at all admirable if there were not also a more positive side to his use of the figure of Christ.

His attitude to Jesus has caused great bitterness among Jewish commentators. But there have also been those who can take an extraordinarily different point of view. 'In Christ', writes Robert Misrahi, 'Spinoza admires a Jewish Rabbi extending to the whole of mankind that part of the teaching of the Torah which is purely ethical'.[53] Yet the same few texts can lead another writer to conclude that Spinoza not only believed that his philosophy was not opposed to Christianity, but that it coincided with it, as properly understood.[54]

We have seen that in some ways Spinoza identified Jesus with his own philosophy. Either Jesus was the archetypal Spinozist philosopher[55] – capable of universal natural knowledge – or, as Matheron puts it, he could represent, in a way, in his time what Spinoza represented in his own time. Matheron is able to mount an interesting discussion on the basis of a question such as: 'What would Christ have done if he had lived in Holland at the time of Spinoza?'[56]

We have nothing but some scattered texts from which to form an opinion on why Spinoza wanted to mention Christ. We assume that they must have some connection with each other because he was an unusually systematic writer. His relationship to his native religion seems impenetrable in the absence of any relevant biographical information. But it may be an exaggeration to think that we cannot really understand how he meant to use the figure of Christ, simply because any personal context seems to be lacking. That figure, after all, was constructed fairly solidly.

[53] 'Spinoza and Christian Thought: a Challenge', in Hessing (ed.), *Speculum Spinozanum*, p. 414.
[54] Di Luca, *Critica della Religione in Spinoza*, p. 119.
[55] He was reported indirectly to have said that Christ was the highest philosopher: *Christum ait fuisse summum philosophum.* This was noted by Leibniz from a conversation of Tschirnhaus with Spinoza; so the record is far from authoritative. From G. Friedmann, *Leibniz et Spinoza* (revised from 1945) (Paris: Gallimard, 1962), p. 73.   [56] *Le Christ et le salut des ignorants*, pp. 264–7, p. 264.

Spinoza's identification of God with nature was thoroughgoing, and it presents unusual difficulty in the balance of his portrayal of Jesus. Jesus was a man, but it would tip the balance wrongly to say that he was *nothing but* a man. There are points where we can only conclude that, in the elaborate context of his thought, Spinoza said what he meant and meant what he said: 'The Voice of Christ can . . . be called the Voice of God in the same way as that which Moses heard. In that sense it can also be said that the Wisdom of God – that is, wisdom that is more than human – took on human nature in Christ, and that Christ was the way of salvation.'[57]

Here we find one of his rare expressions of sensitivity to *sense* – 'In that sense it can also be said', *hoc sensu etiam dicere possumus*. Spinoza does not explain what the type of sense is, nor does he mention metaphor. There almost seems to be a refusal to admit any kind of problem about meaning (and still less, of course, about meaningfulness). The meaning of statements such as 'Christ was sent to teach not only the Jews but the entire human race'[58] is not to be extracted by worrying about metaphor or about literal sense; it has to be seen by understanding a wider framework of thought. The 'sending' of Christ has a sense only in the context of elaborate ramifications running through Spinoza's views on the causality of individual modes (explored here in Chapter 2), and the *special* or *unique* sending of Christ has to be seen against a particular understanding of history (explored in Chapter 7). With the figure of Christ, this sort of construction of meanings may have achieved a result in that it would require some very specific critical presuppositions to declare that the result was actually *unintelligible*. The result with eternity, we shall see, might have been more questionable.

[57] s 64 = G III 21/8–12.   [58] S 107 = G III 64/27–8.

CHAPTER IO

Understanding eternity

Proposition 23 of Part v of the *Ethics* says:

The human mind cannot be absolutely destroyed along with the body, but something of it remains, which is eternal.

A demonstration is offered. The scholium to the proposition adds that 'we feel and experience that we are eternal'.

These views seem to form the apex of Spinoza's system, coming almost at the end of the *Ethics* as the apparent culmination of a long series of connected propositions. Although they are not particularly emphasised – Spinoza left his readers to decide what mattered – it would seem strange to imagine that they were not of importance to him.

To commentators, these views form the apex of his system in another way: as a pinnacle of difficulty, or a stumbling-block for the under-standing. Some[1] have just give up on Spinoza at this point, believing that he had extended himself beyond any rational defence or explanation of his position, lapsing into paradox or mysticism. Others have avoided the real problems of interpretation with rhetoric. Even Pollock, normally so lucid, offers no better than this:

Spinoza's eternal life is not a continuance of existence but a manner of exis-tence; something which can be realized here and now as much as at any other time or place; not a future reward of the soul's perfection but the soul's perfec-tion itself. In which, it is almost needless to remind the reader, he agrees with the higher and nobler interpretation of almost all the religious systems of the world.[2]

In addition to the general difficulty in seeing what Spinoza meant, and how it could be fitted into a general understanding of his thinking, there are at least two particular points where his opinion in *Ethics* v, 23

---

[1] Notably Bennett, *A Study of Spinoza's Ethics*, §82, §85.
[2] Pollock, *Spinoza, His Life and Philosophy*, p. 294.

has seemed to conflict with other important views that he expressed: where he has seemed inconsistent as well as, perhaps, unintelligible.

First, most readers of Part II of the *Ethics* have assumed that mind and body must exist together: 'The object of the idea constituting the human mind is the body – i.e. a definite mode of extension actually existing, and nothing else',[3] and so on. That view has often seemed (and often seems to students exasperated by Descartes) to resolve the paradoxes created by an immaterial spirit, affected by and affecting the extended body while retaining a capacity for immortality. Admittedly, although Spinoza may have evaded the problems of body–spirit dualism, he did land himself with the apparently awkward consequence that individual things, not just people, are 'animate, albeit in different degrees'[4] – but otherwise, what he said in Part II of the *Ethics* about the constitution of people looked fairly sensible. So how could something of the mind 'remain' when the body was destroyed? That seems to be in direct conflict with the view that mind and body must go together.

Secondly, his thinking about time was elusive and never collected into a single coherent statement. He followed a conventional enough distinction between endless duration – the experienced passage of time – and timelessness or eternity.[5] The eternal 'does not admit of "when" or "before" or "after"'.[6] A natural reading is that the eternal truths of geometry and philosophy will be timeless, with no 'before' or 'after', in contrast with human experience: eternity 'cannot be explicated through duration or time, even if duration be conceived as without beginning or end'.[7] In the Demonstration to *Ethics* v, 23, we see that 'we do not assign duration to the mind except while the body endures'. Yet we are said to 'feel and experience' that we are eternal. Feeling and experiencing hardly sound relevant to the eternal truths of mathematics or philosophy. And even if they were, what we might call their human relevance would seem to be left as problematic. The type of eternity embodied or expressed by the eternal truth of the theorem of Pythagoras is hardly a type that might offer any consolation, hope or even interest to anybody except a Pythagorean. If eternity is distinguished from experienced duration, how could we experience eternity?

Maybe there is some religious interest in any philosopher who claims

---

[3] *Ethics* II, 13.   [4] *Ethics* II, 13, Scholium = G II 96/28: *omnia, quamvis diversis gradibus, animata . . . sunt.*
[5] In a rare reference to the topic in the *Theological-Political Treatise*, 'the common people, prone to superstition', prize 'the legacy of time above eternity itself', *temporis reliquias supra ipsam æternitatem amat*: S 54–5 = G III 10/22–4.   [6] *Ethics* I, 33, Scholium 2 = G II 75/12–13.
[7] *Ethics* I, Definition 8, Explication, cited at v, 29, Demonstration = G II 46/4–5 and 298/19–20.

to demonstrate that part of the mind is eternal – though, even more than with Spinoza's demonstrations for the existence of God, we are not thinking of proofs to convince the wavering or the unfaithful. It might be imagined that the eternity of the mind was of special personal significance, and that a demonstration of it was a central motive behind his work; but there is not a word of evidence for that view, and no hint of it in his letters or in his mature writings other than the *Ethics*.

As with his remarks about Jesus, these problems might seem to be incidental in terms of his narrowly philosophical interest to us. That is a view that he did something to encourage himself. As we have seen, his passage on eternity in Part v of the *Ethics* appears before two concluding propositions, which tell us that 'even if we did not know that our mind is eternal', the philosophical and moral conclusions of the remainder of the book would still hold. The overt reason for that conclusion is to underline that punishment and reward in an after-life have no part to play in moral philosophy – deep scorn is poured over such an idea – but it does not take a great deal of suspiciousness to say that Spinoza may also have been hedging his conclusions on eternity with a proviso that they were logically optional to his other views. So, philosophically, it might not look too harmful to disregard them.

UNDERSTANDING ETERNITY

There is *some* philosophical, exegetical interest in the removal or explanation of the apparent inconsistencies within Spinoza's work.[8] But the real interest surely comes from the problem of understanding what he was trying to do. This chapter is titled 'Understanding Eternity' for that reason. Suppose – and we are not going to suppose this without reservations – that his views could be made consistent, in that their internal discordances could be removed or explained away. Suppose that his views might be thought to be plausible, in the sense that their demonstrations were no weaker than others that we accept for the sake of comment or exegesis. We can still ask whether he succeeded in making himself *intelligible*: whether the type of eternal existence of the mind which he

---

[8] It is striking that the eternity of the mind is one of the few areas in his work that has received equally valuable attention from Anglo-American writers and from those working in French: see A. Matheron, 'Remarques sur l'immortalité de l'âme chez Spinoza', *Les études philosophiques*, 1972; A. Donagan, 'Spinoza's Proof of Immortality', in Grene (ed.), *Spinoza: A Collection of Critical Essays* and *Spinoza* (New York: Harvester Wheatsheaf, 1988); R. J. Delahunty, *Spinoza* (London: Routledge & Kegan Paul, 1985), Chapter IX; D. Steinberg, 'Spinoza's Theory of the Eternity of the Human Mind', *Canadian Journal of Philosophy*, 11, 1981; Moreau, *Spinoza: L'expérience et l'éternité*, Part III.

hoped to demonstrate, and which he said we experience, is of a type which we find to be of any significant value or interest.

In twentieth-century terms it may seem natural to recast this point into a linguistic sense, as a problem about 'the meaning of religious language'. The meaning of 'eternity' in the *Ethics* might be thought to be exactly the meaning that was constructed or created by Spinoza's apparatus of geometrical proof.[9] And in that event, to ask whether his notion of eternity imparted any significant sense might be thought to fall into the same error as in confusing sense ('What "England" means') with significance ('What England means to me').[10] The meaning of 'eternity' might be thought to have been constructed exhaustively, without remainder, in the context of Spinoza's system, and so it would be an error to imagine that its 'personal significance' could be any wider or deeper, or different from its literal, systematic sense. That might seem especially so in the case of a writer like Spinoza, where precision and intelligibility might matter, and where any aura of unexplained significance might seem badly out of place.

If understanding eternity were no more than understanding how the sense of 'eternity' (rather *æternitas*) was assembled in Spinoza's system, that might be correct. It should be possible to see why that is not so.

We can see it best in the exactly analogous situation created by his use of the figure of Christ, discussed in the previous chapter. One could claim that what he offered in the *Theological-Political Treatise* was, in effect, an elaborate specification of the use of the name 'Christ', whose *meaning* was no more than the collection of uses or applications accepted by Spinoza, and no others. So 'Christ' is used to mean 'uniquely free man', 'supreme knower', 'exemplar of holiness', but not, for instance, 'man who rose corporeally from the dead'. It is hard to know how necessary it is to say that such a reading would be bizarre. The treatment of Christ was not, of course, a form of elaborate stipulative definition of a technical term. It was some form of characterisation that modified or built up a figure already well known to Spinoza's readers. We may think that his Christ was an artificial figure, constructed and deployed for his own

---

[9] 'We need . . . to speak in more detail of how to interpret a text in terms of its immanent meanings – that is, in terms of the meanings immanent in the religious language of whose use the text is a paradigmatic instance': George A. Lindbeck, *The Nature of Doctrine: Religion and Theology in a Postliberal Age* (London: SPCK, 1984), p. 116.

[10] This point is spelled out in R. Trigg, *Reason and Commitment* (Cambridge University Press, 1973), pp. 50–3, and, intimated, in connection with Spinoza, none too distinctly in G. Fløistad, 'Experiential Meaning in Spinoza', in J. G. Van der Bend (ed.), *Spinoza on Knowing, Being and Freedom* (Assen: Van Gorcum, 1974).

philosophical or religious reasons; but the figure was significant enough, beyond its name, to shock Spinoza's contemporaries and to intrigue his commentators. What he said, at least, seemed intelligible.

With eternity he may not have managed that. With the figure of Jesus we saw that there may have been some risk of making the meaning *too* commonsensical to be of interest – if Spinoza *only* wanted to point to Jesus as an exceptionally wise and gifted moral teacher he could have done that in one sentence, without the puzzling penumbra of suggestions of unique freedom and unique capacities for knowing. In a parallel way, if the eternity of the mind is, for example, *only* an acquaintance with eternal truths – from geometry, perhaps – so that the more eternal truths we know, the more 'eternal' our minds are, that might be consistent with his other positions, but it would be too banal to merit interest or attention. We can see why Jonathan Bennett could say:

> Since I gave up medical studies for philosophy I have had thoughts that P, where P is necessary, more often than before the switch, and more often than I would have if I had stayed with medicine. Does my mind have a larger eternal part than it used to? . . . Spinoza should answer 'Yes'.[11]

Although we can understand that Spinoza intended something less immediately graspable than individual personal survival after death, if his views have any interest they should convey something more promising than an eternal contemplation of geometry. Some notion of the eternity of part of the mind may have been constructed by him, but the problem may be in seeing why it should matter or why we should care about it.

The philosophical interest comes from *how, whether* or *how far* he was able to make the eternity of part of the mind intelligible. In an obvious sense it was a technical element in the apparatus of his system, like his infinite modes or *conatus*. If it was no more than that, then explaining its articulation in his system should exhaust its interest, in giving us a full grasp of what it meant.

Of two points, at least, we can be certain: that he must have regarded the eternity of part of the mind as intelligible, and that he must have *wanted* to make it intelligible to his readers. This is worth saying only because we can easily miss the respect in which he differed from almost every other writer on this most difficult of topics: in his refusal to admit any element of mystery or ineffability. If we fail to grasp his meaning, that may be because he failed to convey it successfully, not because he thought it was inexpressible.

[11] *A Study of Spinoza's Ethics*, pp. 362–363.

The philosophical interest goes beyond a narrow one, because what applies to the eternal part of the mind may apply also to an understanding of much of Spinoza's other systematic apparatus. To take the most extreme case, *God* is explained, in a Spinozist sense, in the opening propositions of the *Ethics*, but what do we understand of Spinoza's God as a result? Literally everything, without remainder, or only a series of hints?

'PROOF'

Once again we need to remember that we do not know why Spinoza wrote what he did. An historian of ideas might think that the demonstration of *Ethics* v, 23 would fit nicely in a collection of philosophical proofs of immortality of the soul, starting with those in the *Phædo*. Yet it is very uncertain whether Spinoza can be seen like that. At the end of the *Ethics* he wrote of the belief that the mind is 'eternal or immortal', but only in a context intended to deride eternal punishment or reward. A positive theological context is missing. It would be rash to assume one.[12]

And again, there must be questions about how far a demonstration was meant to 'prove' anything to anyone (and if so, to whom). As much as in the opening propositions of the *Ethics*, with the 'proof' of the existence of God, the Demonstration to v, 23 is one which draws together threads established in other arguments. It is hardly a *persuasive* proof, in the sense of convincing anybody who seriously doubted its conclusion, and it surely cannot have been meant to be one:

In God there is necessarily a conception, or idea, which expresses the essence of the human body [v, 22] and which therefore is necessarily something that pertains to the essence of the human mind [ii, 13]. But we assign to the human mind the kind of duration that can be defined by time only in so far as the mind expresses the actual existence of the body, an existence that is explicated through duration and can be defined by time. That is, we do not assign duration to the mind except while the body endures [ii, 8, Corollary]. However, since that which is conceived by a certain eternal necessity through God's essence is nevertheless a something [v, 22], this something, which pertains to the essence of the mind, will necessarily be eternal.

This would offer nothing by way of hope or consolation to anyone concerned about life after death. In any event, it must be plain that

---

[12] *Ethics* v, 41, Scholium = G ii 307/23. Moreau finds this sole reference to immortality 'very vague and negative': *Spinoza: L'expérience et l'éternité*, p. 535. References in Spinoza's early works do not help us to see what he meant: for example, *Short Treatise*, ii, xxiii and Appendix ii; *Principles of Philosophy* Appendix ii, xii.

Spinoza did not have *that* in mind. To base anything in life on hope for the future would be an error for him. In addition, whatever 'remained', it was not memory – 'The mind can exercise neither imagination nor memory save while the body endures'[13] – so there could be no consciousness of personal continuity.

These negative points should be obvious preliminaries. No one should be surprised that Spinoza's views about the eternity of the mind would be as difficult to reconcile with conventionally religious positions as the rest of his thought.

THERAPY

There is also a less obvious, and more important, way in which his theorising is set apart from considerations about personal survival. This has a wider significance because it is based in a separation of his thinking from psychological speculation, and more widely still in a separation of philosophical or religious thinking from personal therapies. And that is really important, because a reductive understanding of religion as personal therapy or self-improvement has often been read into Spinoza, either as well-meant praise or as criticism.[14]

Stuart Hampshire puts the case most clearly in his comparison of Spinoza with Freud:

The transition from the normal life of passive emotion and confused ideas to the free man's life of active emotion and adequate ideas must be achieved, if at all, by a method in some respects not unlike the methods of modern psychology.

Although Hampshire's discussion is as illuminating as the rest of his work on Spinoza, the point made in his central comparison is a simple one: 'both Spinoza and Freud represent moral problems as essentially clinical problems, which can only be confused by the use of epithets of praise and blame'.[15]

The point is that Spinoza is commending a sort of psychological technique: control through more knowledge or better understanding. Bennett's respectful but critical discussion of Hampshire agrees with that reading, but his objection, in short, is that such a technique *does not work*.[16]

If we read Spinoza in the clinical terms of rationalist, a priori psycho-

---

[13] *Ethics* v, 21, based on ii, 18, Scholium.
[14] There is an analogy with a reductive understanding of historical religion as religious history, discussed in Chapter 7.   [15] *Spinoza*, pp. 141–2.   [16] *A Study of Spinoza's Ethics*, pp. 347–55.

logy, this is surely correct. In those terms (as pointed out in Chapter 5) some of what he says looks thin and implausible. You might seek to refine your mind by thinking the finest thoughts – that is, thoughts about only the finest objects. And that, in blunt empirical terms, is crazy. Do the thinkers of the finest thoughts have the most refined minds? Does self-conscious understanding lead to any improved capacity for mental or personal control? Some may think so, but the evidence is not compelling.

The point worth debating is not whether Spinoza recommends a system of psychological control that works or not, but whether he thinks in those terms at all. The link with what he considers to be religion is direct. What he needs for his own view of 'piety and religion', after all, are the 'precepts of reason' [*rationis præscripta*] derived in Part IV of the *Ethics*.[17] And since Part IV is generally seen as being about psychology, do we not see a reduction of religion to Spinozistic psychotherapy?

That question takes us in a sudden jump from issues of local exegesis to basic principles. It is understandable to read Spinoza in terms of a self-improvement project – think only of a title such as *Treatise on the Emendation of the Intellect*, and of the evident shadows of stoicism. He seems to see religion as the cultivation of personal virtue. As noted earlier, *salus* in his work has a useful equivocation between *health* or *well-being* and *salvation*. What more natural, then, than to think along the lines of Hellenistic character-building exercises,[18] Freudian self-examination or indeed Californian personal enhancement? The identification of religion, or religious development, with psychological technique would be an important reductive step. For a philosopher who can find no place for the spiritual, it might seem to be an inevitable step.

So, before looking at the details of Spinoza's views, we should consider a more general question about what he was trying to achieve. The key to an answer, as with much of his thinking, might lie in a delicacy of balance: here, in two ways, between the divine and the natural, and between the powers of the body and of the mind. A reduction of religion to psychological technique suggests a tilting of both balances, towards the natural against the divine, and towards the mental against the whole person. Spinoza carefully resisted such imbalances elsewhere. A 'natural' process or technique, after all, is divine: 'whatever human

---

[17] *Ethics* V, 41 and Demonstration.
[18] e.g. on stoicism, see Martha Nussbaum, *The Therapy of Desire: Theory and Practice in Hellenistic Ethics* (Princeton University Press, 1994), Chapters 9 and 10; she offers a full discussion of therapeutic arguments and medical imagery in Chapters 1 to 3.

nature can effect solely by its own power to preserve its own being can rightly be called God's internal help'.[19]

And the mind cannot dominate the body. We do not even possess the knowledge to inform ourselves about the true powers of mind or body. There is no reason to think that he abandoned his approach when he reached the end of the *Ethics*, although readings of him as a stoic – or as someone who adopted the precepts of stoicism[20] – suggest just that.

His project is characterised at the beginning of the Preface of Part v:

> I pass on finally to that part of the *Ethics* which concerns the method, or way, leading to freedom. In this part, then, I shall be dealing with the power of reason, pointing out the degree of control reason has over the emotions, and then what is freedom of mind, or blessedness, from which we shall see how much to be preferred is the life of the wise man to the life of the ignorant man. Now we are not concerned here with the manner or way in which the intellect should be perfected, nor yet with the science of tending the body so that it may correctly perform its functions. The latter is the province of medicine, the former of logic. Here then, as I have said, I shall be dealing only with the power of the mind or reason. Above all I shall be showing the degree and nature of its command over the emotions in checking and controlling them. For I have already demonstrated that we do not have absolute command over them.

The exclusion of 'medicine' is not surprising. The distinction from logic, 'the manner or way in which the intellect should be perfected',[21] seems more interesting. Spinoza goes on to criticise the stoics who 'thought that the emotions depend absolutely on our will' and then gets down to an onslaught on the views of Descartes on the link between mind and body. His initial strategic or methodological point may well be obscured by the zeal in that onslaught.

A mirror image for the demonstration of the eternity of part of the mind in *Ethics* v, 23 is the demonstration of finitude – of what is *not* eternal – in Part iv, 4. There, the proposition to be demonstrated is that 'it is impossible for [a] man not to be part of Nature'. Its corollary is that '[a] man is necessarily always subject to passive emotions, and that he follows the common order of Nature, and obeys it'.

This is more than a routine religious sentiment that no one can be perfect. In Part v of the *Ethics*, before arriving at his thinking on eternity,

---

[19] S 89–90 = G iii 46/12–14.

[20] Already discussed in Chapter 5; Wolfson, *The Philosophy of Spinoza*, vol. ii, pp. 261–74, for example, and perhaps understandably in view of Wolfson's concentration on the influences on Spinoza rather than the use made of them.

[21] *Quomodò . . . & quâ viâ debeat intellectus perfici*; G ii 277/12–13. In the *Principles of Philosophy*, logic is seen only as a kind of mental gymnastics: Appendix i, Part i; G i 233/8–13.

Spinoza notes that we can get the 'passive emotions' to 'constitute the least part of the mind'.[22] That may be so, but the crucial point is surely that we cannot be what we are not, and we are not disembodied rationalisers. The demonstration in Part IV makes this plain: 'if it were possible for man to undergo no changes except those which can be understood solely through his own nature, it would follow [III, 4 and 6] that he cannot perish but would always necessarily exist'.[23]

In his earlier work he wrote of 'purifying the intellect'. We may judge how far his view on this may have changed from the fact that then he had expressed himself in baldly finalist, teleological terms which he must have rejected on later reflection.[24] In the *Ethics*, the intellect is the power of the mind: the title of Part V is *De Potentiâ Intellectûs, seu de Libertate Humanâ* – Of the power of the intellect, or of human freedom. The point may be that the intellect may share in the infinite power of God or nature – whatever that means – and so achieve eternity, but equally it is that 'man' as a whole may not. There is no possibility of freeing the whole person from nature. As a project, that would be not only too ambitious but quite inappropriate. 'Absolute control' – *imperium absolutum*[25] – is a delusion.

This should give some of the essential context both for the nature of Spinoza's whole project and for his thinking about eternity. The balance of power in nature, as he sees it, is not a crudely Cartesian one of mind over body (or alternatively, will over intellect). Nor is it a balance which we can aim to redress: both the *aiming* and the *redressing* would be badly out of place in his mature thought. What we can do is to see what is in the interests of the best part of us, and thus to understand how those interests may be cultivated or developed.

---

[22] V, 20, Scholium = G II 294/11. He refers back to V, 14, which does not actually show this at all in any direct way. The suggestion there is that we can achieve a scientific or systematic grasp of the emotions: they can be 'related to the idea of God'.

[23] *non posset perire, sed ut semper necessariò existeret*; IV, 4, Demonstration = G II 213/8–11. The achievement of immortality through perfection of the body was a common seventeenth-century theme, also of interest to Descartes.

[24] *Treatise on the Emendation of the Intellect*, p. 236, §16. There, a footnote (e) even offers the extremely un-Spinozistic thought that 'In the sciences there is only one end, to which all must be directed', *finis . . . est unicus*: G II 9/10–19. In a note to his edition (p. 11) Curley mentions that Spinoza would have found this passage unsatisfactory in later life. Perfecting the intellect is linked with a reduction of a teleological perspective in the *Ethics*: 'the final goal, that is, the highest Desire', IV, Appendix, 4.

[25] *Ethics*, V, Preface = G II 277/19. Wolfgang Bartuschat argues an important metaphysical grounding for this belief. 'Part V of the *Ethics*, which deals with human freedom . . . deals with the power of the finite, and not the infinite intellect': 'The Infinite Intellect and Human Knowledge', trans. C. Schäl, in Yovel (ed.), *Spinoza on Knowledge*, p. 208.

This view has implications for the understanding of religions. As noted in Chapter 5, Spinoza did not think that everyone could or should become Spinozists. Religious practices should not be reasoned away. That stance went beyond a hereditary dislike of proselytism or mere intellectual elitism. The conclusion that we have to live as we are is not a piece of dreary fatalism, but a recognition that people cannot be what they are not. The *imperium* of people is not unlimited: as we have seen, if it were they would be infinite, and hence immortal. (But nature is infinite and we are part of nature, so maybe part of us is unlimited – here, as we shall see, is where problems of intelligibility set in.)

There must also be implications for an understanding of Spinoza's thinking as psychotherapy. He writes of 'remedies' for the emotions, most plainly at the end of the Preface to Part v of the *Ethics:* 'we shall determine solely by the knowledge of the mind the remedies for the emotions – remedies which I believe all men experience but do not accurately observe nor distinctly see – and from this knowledge we shall deduce all that concerns the blessedness of the mind', and it would be pointless to deny his use of an overtly clinical metaphor. But the metaphor becomes misleading when the clinical drifts towards the psychopathological. What we are supposed to appreciate is not only a need for mental adjustment but some kind of redirection – 'supreme contentment of spirit follows from the right way of life'.[26] If the 'remedy' were simply to think more rational thoughts, as Bennett implies (no doubt satirically), of course it would not work. But it cannot be only that. The redirection commended by Spinoza must be, at least, a good deal wider than an inward redirection of attention. For example, we can keep in mind 'our true advantage' and 'the good that follows from mutual friendship and social relations'.[27] *Virtue* will consist of a great deal more than accurate understanding. Spinoza was enough of a Platonist to see the importance of the redirection of attention – the conversion or turning-around of the soul – but also enough of an Aristotelian to feel the importance of practice.

THE DEMONSTRATION

In Spinozist terms, the rational support for a point of view should also be its explanation. We can ask how far the support for a view of eternal exis-

---

[26] *ex rectâ vivendi ratione summa animi acquiescentia oriatur: Ethics* v, 10, Scholium = G ii 288/8–9, referring back to iv, 52.

[27] *Ibid.*; this case is argued well by Pierre Macherey in 'Note sur le rapport de Spinoza à Freud', in his *Avec Spinoza: études sur la doctrine et l'histoire du spinozism* (Paris: Presses Universitaires de France, 1992).

tence serves to explain it, beginning with the technical case in Spinoza's Demonstration to *Ethics* v, 23, and then widening the view to the more general thinking behind it.

The demonstration was quoted above. Although it refers back to a maze of other conclusions, the argumentative strategy is not complicated. Spinoza had to show two things: that there was an eternal aspect to the human mind and that this could 'remain' when the body was destroyed. The first point, while hardly being uncontroversial, only constituted a special case of other conclusions established (to his satisfaction) elsewhere. The second one was much more difficult, given the parallelism of mind and body, and was rooted in one of his most elusive areas of thinking.

The first element needed in his demonstration – that there is an eternal aspect to the human mind – should not be unexpected because, in Spinozist terms, there is an eternal aspect to everything. The technical apparatus hinders rather than helps our understanding: there is a distinction between existence and essence. God's essence is the cause of the essence of the human body, as of all bodies. There must also be an idea which 'expresses the essence' of the body: the mind.[28] Anything conceived through God's essence will be eternal. This sort of scholastic language does not do much to help, and elaborating it further[29] can do even less. The basic idea is one which runs, not too obscurely, through the *Ethics*. For example, in the Scholium to Part ii, 45, more clearly than elsewhere, existence as duration is distinguished from 'the very nature of existence' or 'the very existence of particular things in so far as they are in God'. Existence as duration is determined by the existence of other particular things. But 'the force' by which each thing 'persists in existing follows from the eternal necessity of God's nature'. In Part v,[30] Spinoza refers back to Part ii, 45, providing some further explanation:

We conceive things as actual in two ways: either in so far as we conceive them as related to a fixed time and place, or in so far as we conceive them to be contained in God and to follow from the necessity of [the] divine nature. Now the things that are conceived as true or real in this second way, we conceive under a form of eternity, and their ideas involve the eternal and infinite essence of God.

---

[28] Pierre Macherey points out, usefully, that Spinoza's mention of 'part of' the mind (*ejus aliquid* G ii 295/15) is misleading in that existence and essence are not two distinct parts (or 'somethings', more like the Latin) of things: *Introduction à l'Éthique de Spinoza: La cinquième partie*, p. 129. Spinoza was trapped by his own terminology here: he could not write in terms of 'aspects' or 'conceptions'.

[29] Delahunty gives a full analysis, though one which concludes that Spinoza's proof was 'a botched job': *Spinoza*, pp. 295–300.   [30] v, 29, Scholium.

There is no need to go into any of this, in its general or in its particular applications. In the widest way, we can see that Spinoza's understanding of eternity as existence attaches eternity to substance or nature.[31] In as much as the human mind is seen as part of nature it must be eternal.

That may be adequate as some explanation of how the mind may be eternal, but it gets us nowhere on the second, much more tricky, point of explaining the apparent schism of the eternal part of the mind from the non-eternal body. Here, Spinoza appears to be totally boxed in by his own arguments. Unequivocally, the body is 'destroyed'. As a body, it ends at death.[32] But the mind is supposed to be the 'idea of the body'. The memory and imagination, evidently linked to bodily functions, end with death. But what does not? However we understand his views about time and eternity in general, the assertion in *Ethics* v, 23, sounds irreducibly temporal: 'the human mind cannot be absolutely destroyed along with the body' (such 'destroying' can only take place at some point in time) 'but something of it remains, which is eternal' – and 'remains', again, suggests remaining in time. That surely must be so, even if we pick up the possible hint of an arithmetical remainder.

Errol Harris thinks otherwise. Of 'remaining', he writes, 'there is no need to understand it as otherwise than as meaning that there is some-thing eternal in the human mind besides what ceases to "endure" when the body dies (as we say in arithmetic: $15/6 = 2$, remainder 3). The eter-nity of the "immortal" part of the human mind or soul is thus not a con-tinued duration after the death of the body, but a quality of being'[33] – and perhaps this is right, or at least plausible. But the hint of arithmetic must also create an impression that is more empirical: if you have fifteen apples and divide them into groups of six apples you will have two groups, and three will *remain*. (But maybe even here, one might argue that 'remaining' is only an explanatory metaphor, to assist the comprehension of timeless arithmetic.) Whatever the logic, the rhetoric is that 'remains' (*remanet*), used after 'absolutely destroyed' (*absolutè destrui*), must evoke temporal survival.

---

[31] See Chapter 1, pp. 38–9 above; *Ethics* i, Definition 8. Also Letter 12: a slightly different perspective – 'It is to the existence of Modes alone that we can apply the term Duration; the corresponding term for the existence of Substance is Eternity, that is, the infinite enjoyment of existence or – pardon my Latin – of being' L 102 = G iv 54–5.

[32] Its parts may be disposed in a different way – *Ethics* iv, 39, Scholium – but its direction, *conatus*, as a living body, will be lost. Spinoza certainly did not think that the eternal part of the mind was the 'idea' corresponding to the dust and bones of a dead body.

[33] 'Spinoza's Theory of Human Immortality', in Mandelbaum and Freeman (eds.), *Spinoza: Essays in Interpretation*, p. 250.

The most difficult point is expressed by Spinoza, puzzlingly, in a negative way: 'we assign to the human mind the kind of duration that can be defined by time only in so far as the mind expresses the actual existence[34] of the body, an existence that is explicated through duration and can be defined by time. That is (II, 8, Corollary), we do not assign duration to the mind except while the body endures.'[35]

So there is no duration without the body. The Corollary to *Ethics* II, 8, cited as support here, is one of the most obscure parts in Spinoza's work. It was mentioned in Chapter 2 in connection with possible infinite objects or constructions. The point at issue is the status of objects that do not exist. Simplifying Spinoza's example, an infinite number of rectangles may be constructed in a circle. An infinite number of rectangles cannot 'exist' (idealistically) in a human mind, because it does not have an infinite capacity. We take a dive into heavily technical language: 'as long as individual things do not exist except in so far as they are comprehended in the attributes of God, their being as objects of thought – that is, their ideas – do not exist except in so far as the infinite idea of God exists'.

He goes on, in contrast, to take the non-problematic case of existing finite objects: 'and when individual things are said to exist not only in so far as they are comprehended in the attributes of God but also in so far as they are said to have duration, their ideas also will involve the existence through which they are said to have duration'.

The point is not unclear when left in technical language: infinite possible rectangles plainly do not exist in any actual sense, but if we are to think of them – if they are to be objects of thought – they exist in so far as the infinite idea of God exists.[36] And deciphered into the terms of Spinoza's geometrical example, the technical language seems reasonably retrievable. The 'infinite idea of God', we saw in Chapter 2, was one of his 'infinite modes' which are used *ad hoc* to fit exactly this purpose: of providing some non-subjective basis for infinite possible constructions. A great deal of exegesis has gone into this point,[37] but it

---

[34] A parallel line of argument pursues the distinction between 'actual' and 'formal' existence and essence – see Delahunty, *Spinoza*, pp. 295–300, referring to Donagan.

[35] *Ethics* v, 23, Demonstration = G II 295/20–4. Shirley's translation places the reference to II, 8, Corollary at the end of the sentence.

[36] Spinoza's negative way of putting this – they do not exist except in so far as the infinite idea of God exists – *non existunt, nisi quatenus infinita Dei idea existit*, G II 91/7, is logically equivalent but rhetorically more cautious.

[37] See, for example, Yakira, 'Ideas of Nonexistent Modes', with the copious further references given there.

has a certain commonsense plausibility. There will be actual constructions and there will also be those that are *available* (or excluded), given the
way in which objects and space are constituted.

THE INFINITE IDEA OF GOD

The real difficulty here does not lie in the obscurities or possible inconsistencies of Spinoza's technical exposition. We may accept fully that the
pieces of the puzzle fit together.[38] We may even accept that 'the infinite
idea of God' offers a neat, non-idealistic solution for the ontological
status of non-existent but possible geometrical constructions. We can
even accept some element of analogy from geometrical eternity.
Apparatus may have been devised to cope with the eternal availability of
possible constructions. The basic problem, though, is in the decoding of
the 'infinite idea of God' – not as a technicality, to be dismantled in technical terms – but as anything which gives us some convincing grip on a
notion of the eternity of the mind. We read that 'our mind, in so far as it
understands, is an eternal mode of thinking which is determined by
another eternal mode of thinking, and this again by another, and so on
ad infinitum', and this, as far as it goes, can be read harmlessly, in the
sense that psychological phenomena have psychological explanations,[39]
except that it goes on 'with the result that they all together constitute the
eternal and infinite intellect of God'.[40]

The Corollary to which this Scholium is a note tells us that 'the eternal
part of the mind is the intellect'. The articulation of Spinoza's thinking
should not be in doubt. 'Part' of our minds can form part of the eternal
and infinite intellect of God, in analogy with the way in which there can
be eternal and infinite available constructions in geometry. And the
trouble, obviously, is in the nature of the analogy. There is a non-mysteri-
ous, if not uncontroversial, sense to a notion of infinite available geometrical constructions: we can see roughly what is meant by the assertion
that an infinite number of rectangles may be constructed within any
circle (even if we retain some ontological qualms). But with minds, the

---

[38] Alexandre Matheron assembles the most systematic apologia, ending: 'Indeed, we can regret that
Spinoza included this doctrine of immortality in his system. We can also ask ourselves about the
reasons for this inclusion. But it is a fact, the doctrine is there; and it is in accordance with the
system': 'Remarques sur l'immortalité de l'âme', p. 378.

[39] From *Ethics* II, 9, which is itself a special case, expressed in psychological terms, of the general
argument in I, 28, that all finite individuals are only determined by other finite individuals.

[40] *Ethics* v, 40, Scholium. The 'infinite intellect of God', *Dei æternus, & infinitus intellectus*, is an infinite
mode.

analogy does not seem to work. Mental causality – one mental event being caused or determined by another[41] – can be accepted for the sake of argument. We can, to stretch a point, think of *all* of a person's mental events 'together' as a collection. To go further, we even can assume some world of thoughts, or possible thoughts, comprising everyone's thoughts and possible thoughts.

And this line of demystification takes us to at least two real difficulties. First, it has taken us away from anything which might be not only remotely consoling, but also of any imaginable human interest. So are my thoughts, or some 'part' of them, forever – either atemporally or omnitemporarily – part of eternal nature? That can be taken in various ways – psychologically, as when *my* thoughts exist; objectively, as where *other people's* thoughts exist; conceptually or propositionally, as where we say that *the thoughts of Einstein* have existed – but none of these, shorn of rhetoric, seems worth more than a shrug of the shoulders in a philosophical sense.

Secondly, we can diagnose a more exact source of difficulty. Except as a hopeful analogy, thoughts just do not add up or 'constitute' in the same way as geometrical constructions.[42] We can, if we like, treat *all the thoughts that have been thought and will be thought* as an arbitrary set; but it remains arbitrary. So to be told that my mind is part of the infinite intellect of God[43] is not to be told very much; or at any rate it is not to be told anything very exciting. (A *world of thought* which is only an arbitrary collection of past, present and future ideas may be logically innocuous, but is a good deal less dramatic than a Hegelian *Weltgeist*.[44]) On the other hand, it might be helpful in a negative sense, in what it rules out. Spinoza's God, for example, is *not* thinking any thoughts which are not thought by people. In a letter, we find a statement in wholly impersonal terms, relating to nature rather than God:

As regards the human mind, I maintain that it, too, is a part of Nature; for I hold that in Nature there also exists an infinite power of thinking which, in so far as it is infinite, contains within itself the whole of Nature ideally, and whose thoughts proceed in the same manner as does Nature, which is in fact the object of its thought.[45]

---

[41] As at *Ethics* II, 9.
[42] 'This view of the human mind as but one idea in the infinite intellect of God is at first sight even more bizarre than the human body's alleged containment in larger individuals, reaching up to the universe as a whole': Genevieve Lloyd, *Part of Nature: Self-Knowledge in Spinoza's Ethics* (Ithaca: Cornell University Press, 1994), pp. 16–17. [43] *Ethics* II, 11, Scholium.
[44] Though not on the low-key reading given in Craig, *The Mind of God and the Works of Man*, pp. 179–80. [45] Letter 32 (1665), L 194–5 = G IV 173–4.

The function of the infinite intellect of God is not to think unthought thoughts, in the way that Berkeley's God perceives unperceived percepts.[46] Non-existent possibilities, for Spinoza, are not 'thought' by God, in any recognisable way. They are 'comprehended' or 'involved in' ideas of existing objects. This is not at all clear – some might wish to express the point, with only a dubious gain in clarity, in logical terms of 'entailing' or 'following from'[47] – but we can be reasonably certain that Spinoza was not diluting a hypothesis of existing possible worlds into one of existing possible ideas. Because of this lack of logical detail, idealist readings of his position tend to rely on rhetorical posturing. For example: 'In our essential being . . . we realize our oneness with God, or God is expressing himself in us. And this means that in our clear and adequate consciousness we are eternal: we have attained to the kind of eternity which characterizes human nature. In this sense, our mind – as an adequate, significant thought in the context of God's thinking – is part of the complete intelligence of God.'[48]

INDIVIDUALITY

More to the point, there is a major drawback to any understanding of Spinoza's view of eternity as a merging of part of the mind into a stream of divine consciousness. Although, as we have seen, the eternity of part of the mind implies nothing about the continuity of individual consciousness, it does include some undeniable element of personal identity. My thoughts and memories, in Spinoza's view, will not survive after death; but there will still be something of *me* that will 'remain'. Eternity will not consist in *losing* identity in a *Weltgeist*. The most serious obstacle to idealist readings of Spinoza (as argued in Chapter 1) was the real, separate existence of individuals. With 'ideas', the point is more muted and much less distinct, but we can be sure that Spinoza gave no encouragement to any diminution or loss of individuality in the 'infinite intellect of God'. This must also apply to a loss of individuality in some form of 'transcendence',[49] a notion Spinoza repudiated so strongly else-

[46] The point of similarity is in terminology: both Berkeley and Spinoza use *ideas*, but in wholly different ways: surely a sign that the term was bearing too much weight.
[47] See Yakira, 'Ideas of Nonexistent Modes', pp. 162–9.
[48] Joachim, *A Study of Spinoza's Ethics*, pp. 301–2. A devastating critique of the kind of part-and-whole intimated here was given by G. E. Moore in *Principia Ethica* (Cambridge University Press, 1903), §22.
[49] As in Harris, 'Spinoza's Theory of Human Immortality', p. 261: 'the mind's transcendence of the body's finite limits . . . a transcendence characteristic of idea as such'.

where that he is hardly likely to have embraced it here One commentator has noted that 'most of what Spinoza has to say about individuation in the *Ethics* and elsewhere is expressed in terms of individual bodies'.[50] It is striking that the Demonstration to *Ethics* v, 23, on the eternity of part of the mind, sets off from 'the essence of the human body': 'In God there is necessarily a conception, or idea, which expresses the essence of the human body'. The same approach is repeated in the Scholium: 'As we have said, this idea, which expresses the essence of the body under a form of eternity, is a definite mode of thinking which pertains to the essence of mind, and which is necessarily eternal.' And Spinoza refers back to the preceding Proposition, also rooted in the body: 'there is necessarily in God an idea which expresses the essence of this or that human body under a form of eternity'.

This might seem strange, or unnecessary, in that he could as well have started directly from the mind, not the body. What he seems to be suggesting is that it is the individual's body which is the origin or source of identification. The point is not that the body has an anti-Cartesian epistemological priority over the mind – that we know it first – but that the idea or ideas which make up an individual mind acquire their identity by being ideas of a particular body (rather than of several bodies, or no bodies at all). And it looks as though Spinoza wanted that sort of identity or individuality to 'remain' even when a body had been destroyed. This was imparted in an ornate terminology of actual essences, but the basic thought is a fairly simple one. As Donagan puts it, 'Ultimately, individual human minds differ from one another because the individual bodies whose affections are the objects of their primary constituents are different.'[51] If this was indeed Spinoza's case, it was an interesting one: presumably the thought would be that the body is necessary *at some time* for identity, but not the *continuing* existence of the body. Rather, the appeal would be to something like an identity with the unity of ideas associated with a past body, or a body that had a duration at a particular time.[52] It would be an exaggeration to say that we can find a well-worked-out

[50] Lee Rice, 'Spinoza on Individuation', in Mandelbaum and Freeman (eds.), *Spinoza: Essays in Interpretation*, p. 195. This is also well stressed by Pierre Macherey, *Introduction à l'Éthique de Spinoza: La cinquième partie*, pp. 125–6 and Alexandre Matheron, 'La vie éternelle et le corps selon Spinoza', *Revue philosophique*, 184, 1994. [51] *Spinoza*, pp. 191–2. See also Lloyd, *Part of Nature*, p. 135.
[52] This could be seen, critically, as getting the benefit of the powerful considerations given by Bernard Williams for the necessity of the body in questions of personal identity while evading the necessity for bodily continuity ('Personal Identity and Individuation' and 'Bodily Continuity and Personal Identity', both in *Problems of the Self*). Amihud Gilead gives an extremely abstract treatment in 'Spinoza's *Principium Individuationis* and Personal Identity', *International Studies in Philosophy*, vol. 15/1, 1983.

defence for this view in the *Ethics*. The view is probably there,[53] but a solid defence for it is not.

What is clear and certain is that Spinoza attached the highest importance to individual knowledge: 'The more we understand particular things, the more we understand God.'[54] And it is hard to read this in any way except as meaning that a knowledge of the individual detail of nature is what matters. In theological terms, the way to God is not by losing the identity of the self in generalities or abstractions: it is by discovering specific, concrete knowledge. But this should not be taken as an ideology of empirical facts. Spinoza was not a proto-positivist.

He stresses the superior power of what he has called 'intuitive' knowledge, or 'knowledge of the third kind'. This forms a specific connection between a knowledge of individuals and eternity. A general proof that everything depends on God, for example: 'although legitimate and exempt from any shadow of doubt, does not so strike the mind [*non ità tamen Mentem nostram afficit*] as when it is inferred from the essence of each particular thing which we assert to be dependent on God'.[55] An intuitive grasp of individual truths – not a general, mystical view of nature – is what brings us nearest to eternity.

EXPERIENCE

This takes us to the experience of eternity: the remark that 'we feel and experience that we are eternal', which has caused such enormous exegetical difficulty.[56]

It is worth seeing that Spinoza does not need to *prove* anything about our 'experience' of eternity, nor does this experience appear as a conclusion from any proof offered by him. The assertion that 'we feel and experience that we are eternal' is offered as a *datum*, not as a theorem or an hypothesis.[57] Its support is left undetermined. One explanation for this might be that the demonstrated eternity of part of the mind somehow *made possible* a feeling and experience.

This might be taken loosely, as offering a theoretical substructure for a

---

[53] Donagan refers to *Ethics* II, 17, Scholium = G II 105/30–106/9.

[54] *Ethics* V, 24: *Quò magis res singulares intelligimus, eò magis Deum intelligimus.*

[55] *Ethics* V, 36, Scholium = G II 303/16–25.

[56] 'une formule particulièrement frappante, qui a fait couler beaucoup d'encre ... Cette formule a l'allure stylistique d'un véritable oxymore, associant des éléments qui paraissent incompatibles ...' Macherey, *Introduction à l'Éthique de Spinoza: La cinquième partie*, p. 131; or, in contrast, 'a strikingly figurative expression, which may seem out of place in the austere surroundings of the *Ethics*', Parkinson (ed.), *Ethics*, p. 284, n. 171.

[57] And it is 'we' who feel and experience, not a Cartesian 'I': more on this shortly.

kind of experience reported along similar lines from many different sources, some of them mystical. The thinking might be that many writers have reported intimations of immortality, often in language far removed from precise logic, but here is what enables such feelings to have some sense: the mind has some element of eternity, after all, and it has ways of knowing which allow direct glimpses of eternal truths.

Such a vague account does have two advantages.

First, it does allow for a kind of intuition which has proved extremely difficult to accommodate within critical theories of knowledge – but without providing any general legitimation or endorsement. Remarkable intuitions or insights – mathematical, musical, personal or religious – may after all occur, and any account of human experience which excludes them may be defective.

Secondly, it may indicate, if only in outline, how Spinoza bridged the gap between what we experience in duration and what we know in eternity. Experience must be in time, at a particular time. So experience of eternity is, as Macherey puts it, a veritable oxymoron. But Spinoza does not offer experience of eternity as any kind of proof of eternity. He says that 'we' have the feeling and experience. The surrounding propositions and demonstrations indicate ways in which such experience can be understood.

This reading seems to be supported by the order of thought in the Scholium to *Ethics* v, 23:

it is impossible that we should remember that we existed before the body . . . Nevertheless, we feel and experience that we are eternal. For the mind senses those things that it conceives by its understanding just as much as those which it has in its memory. Logical proofs are the eyes of the mind, whereby it sees and observes things. So although we have no recollection of having existed before the body, we nevertheless sense that our mind, in so far as it involves the essence of the body under a form of eternity, is eternal, and that this aspect of its existence [*æternam esse, & hanc ejus existentiam*] cannot be defined by time . . .

So, in grasping or knowing individual 'eternal' truths, we have an experience of eternity. This suggests a kind of Kantian argument: that the metaphysical structure of essence and existence makes the experience possible.[58] Because some aspect of our minds is eternal we are able to have access to eternal knowledge. But in contrast with what we would

[58] Diane Steinberg argues a stronger case, 'that Spinoza came to hold that a part of the mind is eternal in order to account for the mind's ability to have adequate knowledge and knowledge under the form of eternity': 'Spinoza's Theory of the Eternity of the Human Mind', p. 65. This applies to the second – scientific – as well as the third – intuitive – form of knowledge.

expect in a Kantian transcendental argument – *a* makes *b* possible, *b* is a condition for *a* – there is no sign of a counter-argument running in the opposite direction: because we are able to have access to eternal knowledge some aspect of our minds is eternal. Spinoza never argues from experience. It may be evidence, but it is not support or proof.

Maybe this gives what we might call an *enabling mechanism* for an experience of eternity, and may even give some shadow of intelligibility to Spinoza's views, but there seem to be two important objections.

First, even if we want to accept that there is any point in describing some truths as 'eternally true', it appears to be an unbearably *ad hoc* approach to say that we need an eternal apparatus to register eternal truths. Couldn't we start from an opposite angle and say how remarkable it is that wholly mortal minds are able to encompass eternal truths?

Secondly, there remains the difficulty that a grasp of many eternal truths would appear to the prosaic critic to offer only an unpromising, unconsoling form of eternity. Even if we take a more generous view of this than Bennett, awkward factual questions can come up. 'Through the greatness of the universe which philosophy contemplates, the mind is also rendered great' sounds splendid,[59] but seems to be valid only in some circular sense: that a great mind is one that has great thoughts. Can I really become more eternal by acquiring more eternal truths? Even if we allow that the apparatus is plausible, how plausible is the project?

A response to the first of these objections would require a long detour through Spinoza's theories about knowledge, but the basic outline is straightforward. To the question: how are we able to know necessary – that is, eternal – truths? the answer given by Spinoza, as by Descartes, was that we share in a divine perspective: part of our minds must share a divine eternity. But the crucial difference, which removes the unsatisfactorily *ad hoc* quality from Spinoza's answer, is that for him the divine perspective, or the divine mind, is entirely immanent. We do share in the divine mind by knowing necessary truths, but no shares are left over for God alone. An increase in human knowledge or understanding is also an increase in the 'infinite intellect of God'. It is possible to argue that 'man possesses knowledge of objects only under the condition that he is part of the infinite intellect',[60] in the sense only that knowledge is supposed to be indefinitely expandable.

But if something along these lines is right, it seems to make the second

[59] From the Spinozistic closing words of Russell's *Problems of Philosophy*.
[60] Bartuschat, 'The Infinite Intellect and Human Knowledge', p. 206.

difficulty more, not less acute. If the divine perspective is[61] the perspective of human understanding of necessary or eternal truth, it sounds intolerably banal to say that we become more eternal as we acquire more necessary or eternal truths. Bennett's jibe that he would have become more eternal by acquiring more necessary propositions would be reinforced.

But the point – of course – must be that it is not just *any* necessary or eternal truths that we acquire. Spinoza never says this explicitly, but his sense is surely not that we can undergo some kind of empirical treatment to acquire eternity by deciding to obtain as many truths as possible: $1 + 1 = 2, 1 + 2 = 3, 1 + 3 = 4$ . . . What he has in mind is an orderly and systematic understanding of nature. That will, for the physical world, mean mathematical physics, and for the human and moral world – 'those things that can lead us as it were by the hand to the knowledge of the human mind and its utmost blessedness'[62] – it will mean the understanding of nature elucidated in the *Ethics* – and then 'in so far as we rightly understand these matters, the endeavour of the better part of us is in harmony with the order of the whole of Nature'.[63]

It should be possible to be more specific than that, but the particular detail has to be speculative. The general picture appears reasonably certain: in understanding how nature is, how we are part in it, we acquire a view which is less bound by duration and more derived from a perspective of eternity.

But this can still sound trite, especially if it goes no further than thoughts of the empirical effectiveness of a psychological therapy. 'A free man thinks of death least of all things, and his wisdom is a meditation of life, not of death'[64] – does this *work* in the doctor's waiting-room? There may be some suspicion that such blunt objections can be raised against even the most carefully shaded interpretations:

The Spinozistic mind aspires to understand itself as an integral part in a total unified articulation of the world, sustained by the necessary being of substance. It is the mind's recognition that it has such a place in a systematically unified order of thought that sustains the Spinozistic reconciliation to finitude. What is supposed to reconcile us to death is the perception of the mind as part of a systematically interconnected totality of thought, a unified 'idea'.[65]

---

[61] Just *is*, not *is nothing but*: the point is not a reductive one. Again, for Spinoza, the divine perspective can be a human one but the human one can also be divine.

[62] *Ethics* II, prefatory paragraph. The physical alternative is sketched in the sections between Part II, Propositions 13 and 14.   [63] *Ethics*, IV, final lines.   [64] *Ethics*, IV, 67.

[65] Lloyd, *Part of Nature*, p. 137.

A reading with more ramifications – and therefore one which goes well beyond a suspect psychotherapeutic prescription – is suggested by Pierre-François Moreau – *J'éprouve ma finitude, donc mon éternité*[66] – I experience my finitude and thus my eternity. He latches on to the point of Spinoza's remark that 'we' feel and experience that we are eternal. The claim is not that we feel and experience that eternal truths exist. The feeling and experiencing, he thinks, is not the knowing of a necessity, but an awareness of our contrasting finitude which accompanies such knowing.[67] Descartes, he says, regarded the finite as a reasonable starting-point in his thinking; but for Spinoza, finitude would not start from our limitations: on the contrary, the thinking is reversed and the finite is grounded in the infinite.[68] We understand our feeling of finitude only through a wider understanding of infinite (and eternal) nature. Moreau's reading does not suggest that our experience *demonstrates* anything about eternity, directly or indirectly, and that must be correct. But it can set us off on a quest for an eternity 'at the same time promised and given, that is to say the path which will lead us towards knowledge and beatitude'.[69]

The famous final words of the *Ethics* warn us that all things excellent are as difficult as they are rare. 'What is so rarely discovered is bound to be hard.' It is not a truism to tie together the difficulty of understanding Spinoza's thinking on eternity and the difficulty, which he underlines himself, in his philosophy. Some may experience eternity. Anyone *could* have such experience. But to understand what eternity is, we need to understand God or nature, which is not easy, and not for everyone.

---

[66] *L'expérience et l'éternité*, p. 548; *éprouve* helpfully suggests proving and realising as well as experiencing.
[67] *Ibid.*, pp. 547, 543.   [68] *Ibid.*, p. 546.   [69] *Ibid.*, p. 549.

CHAPTER 11

Why Spinoza?

Spinoza has an unusual historical position. For practical purposes we can disregard his direct historical influence. What took place at his meetings with Leibniz in 1676, and the subsequent effects on the work of Leibniz, can only be guessed.[1] There were no other noticeable effects on other important philosophers in the seventeenth century. The emergence of Spinozism in the German Romantic movement has its own interest,[2] but it has little to do with the true force of Spinoza's case.

The explanation for this lack of direct influence is not at all obscure. The *Theological-Political Treatise*, like any shocking book, sold extremely well. It engendered a torrent of refutations and denunciations. A personal influence remained significant in Protestant groups in the Netherlands, but otherwise for a century Spinoza and his work were unmentionable except in terms of abuse or ridicule. And it has to be said that he himself did not do much to prevent this. Despite the rhetorical tone of the *Theological-Political Treatise*, he was no propagandist and even less of a diplomat. Almost all his writing was difficult, with minimal exposition and with virtually no attempt to please or reassure the reader.

Alan Donagan remarked that two of the best commentators, Sir Frederick Pollock and Edwin Curley, 'rescue Spinoza for the twentieth century by restoring him to the seventeenth'.[3] The varnish applied by nineteenth-century idealism has been thoroughly stripped from the portrait. Curley has also done a good deal to destroy a stereotype of Spinoza as a 'rationalist' in any meaningful sense in relation to knowledge.[4] The preceding chapters of this study have aimed to obliterate any image of Spinoza as a religious rationalist, or as a precursor to eighteenth-century

---

[1] See G. Friedmann, *Leibniz et Spinoza*.
[2] See, for example, D. Bell, *Spinoza in Germany from 1670 to the Age of Goethe* (London: Institute of Germanic Studies, 1984).   [3] Donagan, *Spinoza*, p. xiii.
[4] Curley, 'Experience in Spinoza's Theory of Knowledge'.

Enlightenment deism. His interest is far greater than as an influence in a
chronological sequence.

   He does have a position in the history of philosophy, though it is a
strange one, as the proponent of views which had no real effects in their
time because they were overshadowed by the influence of Descartes and
his successors. But these were also views which retained a great deal
more interest when that influence started to weaken. This is a sort of
might-have-been effect, which can make Spinoza seem startlingly
modern. (Though an attempt to recruit him as a modern, or even postmodern, figure can be even more anachronistic than trying to enlist him
as a herald of the Enlightenment.) The effect was mentioned at the end
of Chapter 3, and most obviously in relation to his repudiation of the
method of doubt. He was the last major figure until Frege in the Western
canon to give a subsidiary place to epistemology. A less evident area is his
thoroughgoing immanentism, seen in Chapter 2 with his attitude
towards laws. We should explore these points in more detail.

LEGITIMATION

As seen in Chapter 3, he just refused to accept any challenge from
Cartesian doubt. He did not accept an approach to philosophy from the
self-conscious self. He did not believe that knowledge had to be dismantled and then reassembled from a subjective point of view. There is
no need to return to his reasons. We saw that, at least, they went beyond
mere dogmatism. From the perspective of religion, the main interest is in
his refusal to give priority to a need for a critical theory of knowledge.

   And this had radical effects on his approach. The vindication or
justification of religion against a real or imagined philosophical critique
was no part of his project. The existence of God was demonstrated by
means designed to exhibit the articulations between God, nature, substance and other elements in the system. The practice of religions was
never understood in a way that required a justification of defensible
premises.

   This cleared the ground for a historical approach to religions. Because
there was no question of a need for a philosophical, epistemological
legitimation, the fact that 'faith is based on history and language'[5] was
not in any way a sign of weakness or deficiency. It was a recognition that
human practice is based on human history. Spinoza could have added

---

[5] S 226 = G III 179/33-4.

that a search for any other legitimation or endorsement would be misguided, and sure to end in deadlock.

The same attitude applied in his approach to issues within religions. We saw that his treatments of the election of the Jews (in Chapter 7) and of revelation (Chapter 6) were essentially non-critical in an epistemological sense. Nowhere did he seek to deny, for example, that the Jews had been 'chosen', or to argue that they had not. His approach was to report that Jewish election was widely believed and to discover what might be the origins and contents of the belief. Similarly, he did not seek to deny that there have been many reports of divine revelation, and he did not try to apply an epistemological criterion to undermine or devalue it.

This made systematic sense. He saw no basis for a Cartesian deconstruction of beliefs and practices. Cartesian suspension of belief was an untenable pretence. The need to produce philosophical 'evidence', 'proof' or vindication for beliefs or practices was itself philosophically weaker than the beliefs and practices that might seem to require vindication. (This alone should be enough to indicate how far he was from the attitudes of the Enlightenment.) 'Faith is based on history and language' does not mean that religious practice is justified or legitimised by history and language, if that suggests that legitimation is *needed*, in the sense that some challenge of doubt has been accepted. The assertion is a blunter one: that faith is a matter of history and language. (From this, there are implications against the sort of relativism which can insist that distinct traditions validate or legitimise distinct forms of religion.)

Spinoza said very little about language or meaning. His writing suggests that he had no more need for a critical theory of meaningfulness than for a critical theory of knowledge. Whatever his approach to assertions such as that 'God chose the Jews' or 'Christ was sent' to teach the entire human race, it was certainly *not* one of claiming that they lacked meaning, or that their meaning needed to be understood in some specific, 'religious' sense. In fact, there is no support to be found in any of his work for the existence of any special category of religious meaning or religious language. He provides explanations for his understanding of (for example) revelation or eternity; but it would be misleading to present these as explanations of the meanings of *revelatio* or *æternitas*.

In a post-positivist era it may be unnecessary to say this. The point is only worth stressing to see how distant Spinoza was from the subject that came be known as the philosophy of religion: a subject that had first an epistemological base and then a rooting in the philosophy of language. In Spinoza there is no support at all for an approach that could claim to

assess religious beliefs or practices in terms of their epistemological value
or their meaningfulness. Getting outside a religion at all, to address it
without presuppositions, as we saw in Chapter 8, was a project to be
undertaken only at some cost.

IMMANENTISM

Spinoza's thoroughgoing immanentism had implications as drastic as his
refusal to engage in critical epistemology. In Chapters 1 and 2 it was
argued that his views can be read as radically non-theoretical. The
identification of a necessarily existing God with substance or nature, far
from being a grand-scale metaphysical theory, can be seen as a complete
removal of ontology from theology. The question does God exist?
cannot be asked usefully, not because it is meaningless in a positivist
sense, but because it is brought into equivalence with the question: does
anything that exists, exist? To argue or defend the existence of God as an
object would be to misunderstand the nature of God's existence in the
most serious way.

The distinction between this position of Spinoza and pantheism was
discussed in Chapter 1. That remains one of the most difficult areas in
his work, resting as it does on his thought about infinity, which was never
expressed in helpfully clear terms.[6] At the most general level, though, the
distinction should be simple. In so far as pantheism has ever been
asserted, it must be a view about what exists, which is said to be somehow
equivalent to God. Spinoza distinguishes between what exists – nature
or God – and the ways in which it is conceived to exist – the attributes of
thought, extension and the other infinite unknown attributes. He distinguishes, too, between what exists in the sense that it could not not exist
– nature – and individual things whose causes or explanations for existence could be (at least partly) specified. Because of both the contrast
between substance and attributes and between substance and individuals (or 'modes') it would be crass to make a pantheist identification of
God with particular individuals.

The separation of physical ontology – general questions about what
exists and how – from theology may be a comparatively obvious effect of
Spinoza's immanentism, and one which, perhaps, has immediate interest mainly for a theologian.[7] The effects of his views about laws and,

[6] Letters 12 and 81, and *Ethics* 1, 15 are the central texts.
[7] Jean-Luc Marion, for example, develops an idea of God without 'being', in *Dieu sans l'être* (Paris: Fayard, 1982).

more generally, about necessity, strike more centrally within the philosophy of logic. *How God acts* was explored in Chapter 2. Spinoza's key idea – never disputed by any commentator – was that the reason for existence and action in nature cannot be external to it, simply enough because nothing is external to nature. Nature is its own explanation which is to say that no explanation for it is to be sought – and the explanation for anything else must be sought within it.

It is the ramifications of this view, not the general outline, which have caused a lot of trouble. Writers who have stressed the immanentism in his thinking have seen nothing strange about going on to say that individual statements are made necessarily true by logical laws or that individual events happen because of the necessity of the laws of nature. And yet Spinoza went to the most pedantic lengths to emphasise that 'every individual thing, i.e. anything whatever which is finite and has a determinate existence'[8] must have an infinite series of finite determinants. The necessity of nature cannot reside in the force of any set of laws or rules applying to it: where would that force come from? Not 'logic': where would *that* come from? In fact, for Spinoza, necessity was identified with nature and nature was identified with law. God neither 'made things happen' nor laid down the rules that make things happen.[9] Things happen in nature. That is how it is.

For philosophers, the consequences in logic must be more intriguing (even though this, as a topic in itself, was even less interesting to Spinoza than language). The Cartesian story of a God superintending or underwriting the truth of necessary truths must have struck him as preposterous. He worked without the theological restraints that were to create such difficulty in this area for Leibniz. The logical corollary of immanentism must have been, again, a no-theory theory. What must be so can have reasons which we can state. Within nature, the reason why anything is so will be the same as the reason why it must be so. To ask why *everything* must be as it is – this is the Leibnizian danger-zone of asking about God's freedom of choice – is blocked by the fact that

---

[8] *Ethics* I, 28: '*Quodcunque singulare, sive quævis res, quæ finita est, & determinatam habet existentiam . . .*', G II 69/2–3.

[9] Guttmann, *Philosophies of Judaism*, p. 272: 'The activity of God is no more than another locution for the mathematical–causal law governing existence.' This makes three misleading suggestions in one sentence: 'no more than' suggests a reduction of the divine to the natural; 'another locution' suggests that Spinoza was saying something about meanings; 'governing' suggests that laws govern. A more suggestive view is given by Albert Friedlander, writing of the Jewish Law in Lévinas: 'The Law . . . is more the ontological structure, the nature of being itself, which relates us to others': *Riders Toward theDawn* (London: Constable, 1993), p. 193.

nature itself has no 'external' explanation, because 'external' has no application.

This is an impressive view, which has not received a due amount of attention. The effect on religious thinking is not to separate mathematics and physics from theology, but to identify mathematical and physical questions with divine questions. The study of nature – following a common seventeenth-century theme – is equivalent to the study of God. As we have seen, some of the corollaries – for example, in connection with miracles or with the reading of scriptural narratives – could be subversive.

The liberation of theology from ontology, mathematics and from physical theory might seem to be entirely welcome. In Spinoza's terms, there could be no need for a 'religious' account of what exists, what sorts of things exist, why or how, and no need for a religious account of why mathematics and physical theory might be true. But we must be careful. Theology, in a sense, was physics. It was not nothing but physics. As noted in Chapter 1, despite the undeniable identification of God with nature or substance, Spinoza hardly used 'nature' or 'substance' in the *Ethics* after making the essential metaphysical connections in Part 1. He wrote about God, even where his points would have been far more intelligible and more plausible if he had switched to *nature*.[10] We shall return to the vital question of *balance* between nature and God later in this chapter.

RATIONALISM?

So far, even though Spinoza's approach seems to deprive the philosophy of religion of much of its traditional subject-matter, one might imagine that theology and religion themselves remain reasonably unaffected. Cosmological theorising might appear to be placed safely in the hands of cosmologists, rather than theologians. Religious meanings might seem to be liberated from philosophical criticism.

These impressions are misleading. It is almost worthless to describe Spinoza as a rationalist. But he did adhere rigorously to two intellectual values which – while of course not absent from previous religious thought – owed little to specifically religious support or endorsement; in short, consistency and persistent curiosity.

---

[10] *Ethics* II, 2, 20, 32, 47; V, 16, 24, 30 are some examples. Notable exceptions, expressed in terms of nature, appear at IV, Axiom and 4.

The need to avoid inconsistency comes out explicitly in a passage already quoted several times:

faith requires not so much true dogmas as pious dogmas, that is, such as move the heart to obedience; and this is so even if many of those beliefs contain not a shadow of truth, provided that he who adheres to them knows not that they are false. If he knew that they were false, he would necessarily be a rebel, for how could it be that one who seeks to love justice and obey God should worship as divine what he knows to be alien to the divine nature?[11]

These remarks continue by noting that 'men may err from simplicity of mind, and . . . Scripture condemns only obstinacy, not ignorance'; but nevertheless, the avoidance of paradox or inconsistency has become an intellectual duty. Applied in Part I of the *Ethics* to the conventional apparatus of philosophical theology, this duty, unhindered by any other religious loyalties, had the effects that we have seen. If you want God to be without limit and you want to make consistent sense of the inheritance of *substance* and *cause* then you may face Spinoza's conclusions. Maybe a social theorist might say that this attitude is itself a consequence of monotheism, but it was a consequence that had not been so ruthlessly apparent to many of Spinoza's predecessors.

Curiosity as an intellectual value may seem less prominent. It appears most plainly in the case against teleology and (more widely) in an attitude towards the intelligibility of nature. The problem with teleological explanation seemed to be that it had an end – it put an end to inquiry, killing curiosity. We saw in Chapter 4 the punning argument from the Preface to Part IV of the *Ethics*, where God the infinite – *end*less – being (*infinitum Ens*) has no *end* to his acting (*finem habet nullum*).[12] We should go on looking for causes – not stop in the 'sanctuary of ignorance' – because nature is constituted so that every causal chain or network is endless. Equally, mystery and paradox were to be eschewed in even the most intractable theological topics, such as eternity and infinity. This can appear – as it does appear in Spinoza's early work[13] – as Enlightenment dogma. But, as argued at the end of Chapter 3, it was not. Spinoza exposed the logic of an assumption that nature, or parts of nature, can *not* be understood. Nature was not transparent because of the X-ray intensity of the light of human reason, but because an assumption that nature could be unintelligible could not itself be made intelligible. His

---

[11] Or, just as well, 'to divine nature'; S 223 = G III 176/18–24.   [12] G II 206–7.
[13] As in the opening pages of the *Treatise on the Emendation of the Intellect*, where we are no distance from the enthusiasm of a simple Cartesian *Search for Truth by means of the Natural Light*.

254 The God of Spinoza

confidence in the interpretive, manipulative and predictive powers of human reason was far weaker than in some later empiricist writers. All of this was a long way from doctrinaire rationalism, a principle of sufficient reason or from some principle of plenitude which might have come to underwrite Enlightenment quests for certainty in the subsequent century.

A crucial notion in a grasp of Spinoza's thinking about God and religion is one of balance. One of his greatest achievements must surely be to have shown how it might be possible to attain a non-reductive view in theological cosmology, religious history and in religious psychology. It is not difficult to assume that the formulation 'God or nature' must have been meant reductively – perhaps not in a simplistic, crude way, but where it might be understood that by God, Spinoza really meant nature (or, of course, that by nature he really meant God). But there is no evidence that he really meant this, or anything like it, and there are ample signs that he went to great pains to achieve an equilibrium between the divine and the natural in physics, in history and in religious psychology.

First, in physics we have seen how 'it is the same thing whether we say that all things happen according to Nature's laws or that they are regulated by God's decree and direction'.[14]

The metaphysics of Part I of the *Ethics* is strengthened, not weakened, by melting together the conventional characteristics of God and of nature, not by tilting the balance in one direction or the other.[15] In the *Theological-Political Treatise*, divine law gains in universality by being natural law and natural law gains its force and legitimacy by being divine.

Then, in religious history, we find a refusal to interpret the religious into terms of the 'natural', to the extent that these terms lose any contrast with each other. In Chapter 7 we could see how an attempt to naturalise or secularise the history of the Jews could not be supported from Spinoza's writing. Rather the reverse, in fact. He was clear that we

---

[14] S 89 = G III 46/4–6: *Sive . . . dicamus omnia secundum leges naturæ fieri, sive ex Dei decreto & directione ordinari, idem dicimus.*
[15] Grace Jantzen suggests that a combination of a non-reductive approach towards God with a view of the universe as 'God's body' can be theologically fertile, and even that 'transcendence is compatible with a divine embodiment': *God's World, God's Body* (London: Darton, Longman and Todd, 1984), p. 127.

need to understand how it was that God chose the Jews, just as, elsewhere, he tried to show how it was that Jesus was sent uniquely by God.

In religious psychology, the balances between the mind and the body and between God and nature allowed Spinoza to present a non-reductive account. Religion is not psychological therapy.

In a specific religious context, the knowledge of Jesus was both divine knowledge and human knowledge, because all knowledge is to some extent like that. Like all of us, Jesus was to be human, but not nothing but human.

In all these fields, the temptation to tip the balance is almost irresistible, particularly if we think about Spinoza's historical location. We can imagine a tidy narrative in which he represents the point in the seventeenth century where the roller-coaster of theology reaches a peak before plunging into a trough of science: for an instant we can judge things both in terms of religion and science. That may be unfair, in seeing Spinoza as being of transitional interest. It is more unfair in seeing his thought as a stage on a continuum that went anywhere directly, least of all to a smooth slide through the history of modern science. His attitudes to Cartesian doubt and to natural law were both seriously out of line with preceding and with subsequent thinking. As with Berkeley, we can see his work as a building-block in an attempted ideology for modern science. The problem is that the continuing route to modern science happened to go on through subjectivist epistemology and a propositional understanding of scientific laws (in a philosophical reading of scientific history, if not in practice) and Spinoza repudiated both.

It may sound dull to stress the element of careful balance in his thought, but in fact this is a crucial issue of interpretation. Spinoza-as-rationalist is the philosopher who wanted to reduce God to nature, religious history to sociology, revelation to fantasy and to submit the will to the power of the intellect. Spinoza the God-intoxicated man – the 'holy, rejected Spinoza . . . full of religion, full of the Holy Spirit'[16] – would have wanted to make nature divine, see God's work in history and play up the importance of intuitive knowledge, the intellectual love of God and our experience of the mind's eternity. He did not want to take either or both of these courses, or some tepid compromise between them. The minimalist compression in the central metaphysics of his system –

---

[16] Friedrich Schleiermacher, *On Religion, Speeches to its Cultured Despisers* (1799), trans. J. Oman (New York: Harper Torchbooks, 1958), p. 40.

discussed here in Chapters 1 and 2 – allowed him to hold together polarities that might be expected to fly apart: substance and attribute, substance and mode, infinite and finite, law and nature. This opened the possibility of non-reductive accounts of religious history and revelation and for an account of the 'natural' which did not beg questions of contrast with the divine.

SCIENCE

Even though Spinoza's work may have had little immediate influence, there should be no doubt that it does represent a turning-point in the relations between religion and the natural sciences. It cannot be unfair to see it as carrying forward a seventeenth-century project of making science possible. Much of his thought provides an ideology or a metaphysical base for the development of physical science. Bernard Williams has suggested that a remaining 'piece of philosophy' after the work of Descartes which 'would constitute almost all of philosophy' and which might have 'absolute status' might be one 'which makes clear why natural science can be absolute knowledge of how things are'.[17] Central aspects of Spinoza's work acted as a licence for research into 'how things are'. For him, science is not made possible because we are able to share an external, absolute God's-eye view of nature. We have seen how much of his thought revolves around the idea that nature could not be unintelligible. Again, related to that is the principle that causes can always be sought, essential to his case against teleology, which in turn has its grounding in the endless interconnection of causes in the 'infinite idea of God'. A God's-eye view becomes not an unattainable ideal but an understanding we cannot fail to attain if we are to know how things are.

Some aspects of his approach do offer a way in which a religious life could be pursued without conflict with the physical sciences. Yet he hardly fits at all into any story of a smooth progression between a 'religious' and a 'scientific' view. That is largely because he made a strong distinction between theological–scientific–natural subject-matter on the one side and religious practice on another. There is no conflict at all in his thought between cosmological theology and 'science', because these subjects, for him, would be not continuously connected, as they were for Descartes, but identical. His contrast was between known truths about

---

[17] Williams, *Descartes*, p. 302; to be fair, the quotation goes on in a way that certainly could not apply to Spinoza: 'while social science, common perceptual experience and so forth, cannot (with the result that we cannot even agree how much other knowledge we have)'.

the existence and working of things – including people – and historical human practice. And that viewpoint was still more unusual because, as we saw in Chapter 8, he could not have followed a voluntarist path towards a choice of values or meanings in an unchosen world of scientific facts.

'Science' against 'religion' could not be some sort of relativist legitimation problem for him. Although his thinking cut away much of the conventional subject-matter of later philosophy of religion, he did assume an important distinction between the practice and the understanding of religion. Practice, following an historical context, was unavoidable in society and for nearly all individuals. In no sense did he want conventional religious observance or ritual to change, reform or disappear. It was *necessary* in a sense that went beyond a Machiavellian need to retain social order. The understanding of religion was a different matter. The understanding of anything had to be not inconsistent with what was known already. A correct understanding, we must assume, for those who could attain it, would lead to knowledge; not to obedience to the law but to what he called the love of God: 'for by virtue of reason we can neither accept divine commandments as divine while not knowing their cause, nor can we conceive God as a ruler enacting laws'.[18]

RELIGION

The importance of Spinoza's work on religion can be seen more usefully as like the work of a scientist in the development of the sciences than like a philosopher in past philosophy. In some areas that must be self-evident. For example, nothing has been said in this study on his biblical criticism because we can only say that his method and conclusions – with appropriate scholarly reservations – were broadly right and that the body of biblical knowledge was permanently altered. That would be an unusually rash claim to make about any contribution to philosophy, rather than to the study of ancient texts. Philosophical argument is rarely, if ever, conclusive or irreversible. But there may have been ways in which Spinoza's approach left religion different, far more than did the epistemologically based onslaughts in the two subsequent centuries, and despite the fact that his best work was little read and less understood. After the publication of the *Theological-Political Treatise* it became impossible to believe that the whole Pentateuch was composed by Moses alone.

---

[18] *Theological-Political Treatise*, Note 34.

Some of Spinoza's fundamental methodological principles presented an irreversible challenge more widely. We have seen how the persistent use of curiosity and consistency can – at least – provoke difficult debate. What, for example, are the serious consequences of a thought that anything might be, in some important way, *not* intelligible? A casual admiration for paradox is all very well, but what would it imply for our understanding of the world if taken consistently? If we want to make use of a concept of causality, is the whole of nature, and God, to be included in it?

The 'personal beliefs' of Spinoza may seem to remain as unclear as they were at the beginning of this study. His use of the figure of Christ and his experience of eternity may create a tantalising impression that much more can be said. His attitudes towards Judaism and Christianity might seem more intelligible if we knew the feelings behind them. But, in different ways, he removed both theological beliefs and religious practice from anything resembling a domain for personal choice. What exists and what happens, who we are and how we behave, are to be subjects for research. How we are to act, to pray or worship and to treat each other can be a matter for how and where we are born, raised and educated. We do not *have* to seek knowledge or understanding about what exists and how to act, but if we *do* seek it consistently we may obtain an illumination that might enable us to act from free understanding, not obedience: 'obedience forthwith passes into love, which arises from true knowledge by the same necessity as light arises from the sun'.[19]

So where did Spinoza leave religion?

At many points in this study he may seem to have had more in common with the twentieth century than with his own time, or with the intervening centuries. His resolution of the tensions between religious understanding and the growth of scientific knowledge may seem more radically satisfying than the more circumspect compromises attempted since the nineteenth century. Here, he can look thoroughly modern.[20] Yet the foundation for his approach – an identification of the existence and action of God with nature and its actions – may have little appeal today, when the subtleties that distinguish it from crude pantheism are more likely to arouse impatience than admiration. His lack of interest in an epistemological approach to religion can make him look postmodern. Not for him the debates about the 'evidence' for religion, about the rival

---

[19] *Ibid.*   [20] *Studia Spinozana* 9 (1993) includes papers discussing 'Spinoza and Modernity'.

merits of 'faith' and 'reason' or about the 'meaningfulness' of 'religious language', which for so long provided a curriculum for the philosophy of religion, if not a litany of genuine concerns for any seriously religious person. Yet he was a long way from postmodern relativism. He maintained an entirely un-postmodern attachment to truth and consistency. He was ready to acknowledge the continuation of disparate religious practices, not because they were equally validated, but because they were existing, naturally historical activities, where validation was no more appropriate than for disparities in geography or in climate. His aim was not to replace God with an ideology or narrative of science; but nor did he try to evade the challenge created by claims in the new natural sciences.

In two ways his attitude to religion has scarcely been recognised or absorbed.

The route opened by Pascal towards irrationalism and – more importantly – into voluntarism was blocked from the outset by Spinoza. For him, there was no world of the personal inner will, a home for values and meanings, into which religion could retreat away from the cold outer world of rational, impersonal facts. That whole set of dichotomies, and the epistemology on which they were based, was never accepted by him. This was not because, as a 'rationalist', he wanted to subsume the personal into the external, or to subjugate meanings and values to positive facts. In current terminology we could say it was because he refused to accept the possibility of unconnected, discontinuous forms of description. We are to understand ourselves in the same way as we understand lines, planes and bodies,[21] not because we are *nothing but* lines, planes and bodies, but because ways of understanding cannot be disconnected from each other. And that position is not dogma, but an appreciation that enclaves of unintelligibility are barren rather than fertile, like enclaves of inconsistency.

The other element in his thought which remains undigested is the balance between the divine and the natural, mentioned many times in this study and sketched in summary in this final chapter. A recognition or acceptance of God and religion as natural is one of the hardest thoughts to keep in focus, because it can only be seen at the same time as an acceptance of nature as divine. (It is a desire to divide the natural from the divine and to read either in terms of the other that is the real anachronism in reading Spinoza.)

---

[21] *Ethics* III, Preface.

We began with the many contexts within which Spinoza constructed his philosophy, and the balance he created between them. Equally significant is the balance between the harsh logic at the opening of the *Ethics* and the experience of eternity at the end. We may feel that we are missing something that would enable us to decide that Spinoza started his thinking with a thirst for natural, 'scientific' understanding or, alternatively, from some intuitive experience of divine love. In fact we are missing nothing. He left the manuscript of the *Ethics* in his desk, to be published by his friends after his death. The text of the *Ethics* tells us all we need to know about his views on the balance between the love of God and the understanding of nature, between the natural and the divine. There is no 'personal philosophy'. Almost all of what we need to know about Spinoza as a person can be learnt from his confidence in the value of his book and from his trust in his friends.

Bibliography

Details are not given for references to standard philosophical works where any edition may be used.

Akkerman, F., 'Spinoza's tekort aan woorden: Humanistische aspecten van zijn schrijverschap' (I) and 'Pauvreté ou richesse du latin de Spinoza' (II), *Studies in the Posthumous Works of Spinoza* (Meppel: Krips Repro, 1980).

'Le caractère rhétorique du *Traité théologico-politique*', *Spinoza entre Lumière et Romantisme*, Les Cahiers de Fontenay, 1985.

Alquié, F., *Le rationalisme de Spinoza*, 2nd edn (Paris: Presses Universitaires de France, 1991).

Anscombe, G. E. M., 'Causality and Determination', *Collected Philosophical Papers*, vol. II (Oxford: Blackwell, 1981).

'Transubstantiation', *Collected Philosophical Papers*, vol. III (Oxford: Blackwell, 1981).

Aquinas, *Summa Theologiæ*, Blackfriars edn, T. Gilby (general ed.) (London: Eyre & Spottiswoode).

Arnauld, A. and Nicole, P., in P. Clair and F. Girbal (eds.), *La logique, ou l'art de penser* (The *Port-Royal Logic*), (Paris: Vrin, 1981).

Ayers, M., 'Analytical Philosophy and the History of Philosophy', J. Rée, M. Ayers and A. Westoby (eds.) in *Philosophy and its Past*, (Hassocks: Harvester, 1978).

Barnes, J., 'Parmenides and the Eleatic One', *Archiv für Geschichte der Philosophie*, 61, 1979.

Bartuschat, W., 'The Infinite Intellect and Human Knowledge', C. Schäl, (trans.), in Yovel (ed.), *Spinoza on Knowledge*.

Bedjai, M., 'Métaphysique, éthique et politique dans l'œuvre du Docteur Franciscus van den Enden', *Studia Spinozana*, 6, 1990.

Bell, D., *Spinoza in Germany from 1670 to the Age of Goethe* (London: Institute of Germanic Studies, 1984).

Bennett, J. F., *A Study of Spinoza's Ethics* (Cambridge University Press, 1984).

'Spinoza and Teleology: A Reply to Curley', in Curley and Moreau (eds.), *Spinoza: Issues and Directions*.

'Spinoza's Metaphysics', in Garrett (ed.), *Cambridge Companion*.

Berlin, I., 'From Hope and Fear Set Free', *Proceedings of the Aristotelian Society*, 64, 1964.

Beyssade, J.–M., 'The Idea of God and the Proofs of his Existence', in J. G. Cottingham (ed.), *The Cambridge Companion to Descartes* (Cambridge University Press, 1996).

Blackwell, K., *The Spinozistic Ethics of Bertrand Russell* (London: George Allen & Unwin, 1985).

Blair, R. G., 'Spinoza's Account of Imagination', in Grene (ed.), *Spinoza: A Collection of Critical Essays*.

Bolton, M. B., 'Spinoza on Cartesian Doubt', *Noûs*, 19, 1985.

Brann, H. W., 'Spinoza and the Kabbalah', in Hessing (ed.), *Speculum Spinozanum*.

Brykman, G., *La Judéité de Spinoza* (Paris: Vrin, 1972).
  'De l'insoumission des Hébreux selon Spinoza', *Revue de l'enseignement philosophique*, 2, 1984.

Buckley, M. J., *At the Origins of Modern Atheism* (New Haven: Yale University Press, 1987).

Caton, H., *The Origin of Subjectivity* (New Haven: Yale University Press, 1973).

Clark, M., *Nietzsche on Truth and Philosophy* (Cambridge University Press, 1990).

Cohen, H., *Religion of Reason, out of the Sources of Judaism* (1919), S. Kaplan (trans.) (New York: Ungar, 1972).

Cottingham, J. G., 'The Intellect, the Will and the Passions: Spinoza's Critique of Descartes', *Journal of the History of Philosophy*, 26, 1988.

Cover, J. A. and Kulstad, M. (eds.), *Central Themes in Early Modern Philosophy* (Indianapolis: Hackett, 1990).

Craig, E., *The Mind of God and the Works of Man* (Oxford: Clarendon Press, 1987).

Curley, E. M., *Spinoza's Metaphysics: An Essay in Interpretation* (Cambridge: Harvard University Press, 1969).
  Behind the Geometrical Method: A Reading of Spinoza's Ethics (Princeton University Press, 1988).
  A Spinoza Reader (Princeton University Press, 1994).
  'Experience in Spinoza's Theory of Knowledge', in Grene (ed.), *Spinoza: A Collection of Critical Essays*.
  'Spinoza as an Expositor of Descartes', in Hessing (ed.), *Speculum Spinozanum*.
  'Spinoza on Miracles', in E. Giancotti Boscherini (ed.), *Proceedings of the First Italian International Congress on Spinoza*, (Naples: Bibliopolis, 1985).
  'On Bennett's Spinoza: The Issue of Teleology', in Curley and Moreau (eds.), *Spinoza: Issues and Directions*.
  'Notes on a Neglected Masterpiece (II): The Theological-Political Treatise as a Prolegomenon to the Ethics', in Cover and Kulstad (eds.), *Central Themes in Early Modern Philosophy*.
  'On Bennett's Interpretation of Spinoza's Monism', in Yovel (ed.), *God and Nature*.
  'Donagan's Spinoza', *Ethics*, 104, 1993.

Curley, E. M. and Moreau, P.–F. (eds.), *Spinoza: Issues and Directions* (Leiden: Brill, 1990).

Dante, *Convivio*, ed. M. Simonelli, (Bologna: Pàtron, 1990).

Davidson, D., 'Causal Relations' (1967), in *Essays on Actions and Events* (Oxford: Clarendon Press, 1982).

'On the Very Idea of a Conceptual Scheme' (1974), in *Inquiries into Truth and Interpretation* (Oxford: Clarendon Press, 1984).

'Reply to P. F. Strawson', in B. Vermazen and M. Hintikka (eds.), *Essays on Davidson* (Oxford: Clarendon Press, 1985).

'The Myth of the Subjective', in M. Krausz (ed.), *Relativism: Interpretation and Confrontation*, (University of Notre Dame Press, 1989).

Davidson, H. A., *Proofs for Eternity, Creation and the Existence of God in Medieval Islamic and Jewish Philosophy* (Oxford University Press, 1987).

De Deugd, C., *The Significance of Spinoza's First Kind of Knowledge* (Assen: Van Gorcum, 1966).

Delahunty, R. J., *Spinoza* (London: Routledge & Kegan Paul, 1985).

Derrida, J., *La dissémination* (Paris: Seuil, 1972).

Di Luca, G., *Critica della Religione in Spinoza* (L'Aquila: Japadre, 1982).

Donagan, A., *Spinoza* (New York: Harvester Wheatsheaf, 1988).

'Spinoza's Proof of Immortality', in Grene (ed.), *Spinoza: A Collection of Critical Essays*.

'Spinoza's Dualism', in R. Kennington (ed.), *The Philosophy of Baruch Spinoza*, (Washington: Catholic University Press, 1980).

'Spinoza's Theology', in Garrett (ed.), *Cambridge Companion*.

Donagan, A., Perovich, A. N. and Wedin, M. V. (eds.), *Human Nature and Human Knowledge* (Dordrecht: Reidel, 1986).

Doney, W., 'Spinoza on Philosophical Scepticism', in Mandelbaum and Freeman (eds.), *Spinoza: Essays in Interpretation*.

Fløistad, G., 'Experiential Meaning in Spinoza', in J. G. Van der Bend (ed.), *Spinoza on Knowing, Being and Freedom*, (Assen: Van Gorcum, 1974).

Force, J. E. and Popkin, R. H. (eds.), *The Books of Nature and Scripture* (Dordrecht: Kluwer, 1994).

Fox, A. C., *Faith and Philosophy* (Nedlands: University of Western Australia Press, 1990).

Frankfurt, H. G., 'Descartes' Validation of Reason', *American Philosophical Quarterly*, 2, 1965.

'Two Motivations for Rationalism: Descartes and Spinoza', in Donagan, Perovich and Wedin (eds.), *Human Nature and Human Knowledge*.

Frege, G., *The Foundations of Arithmetic* (1884), J. L. Austin (trans.) (Oxford: Blackwell, 1968).

Friedlander, A. H., *Leo Baeck: Teacher of Theresienstadt* (London: Routledge & Kegan Paul, 1973).

Riders Towards the Dawn (London: Constable, 1993).

Friedman, J., 'How the Finite Follows from the Infinite in Spinoza's Metaphysical System', *Synthèse*, 69, 1986.

Friedmann, G., *Leibniz et Spinoza* (revised from 1945) (Paris: Gallimard, 1962).

Freudenthal, J., *Spinoza* (Stuttgart: Frommanns, 1904).

Funkenstein, A., 'Comment on R. Popkin's Paper', in Force and Popkin (eds.), *The Books of Nature and Scripture*.

264 *Bibliography*

Garrett, D., 'Truth and Ideas of Imagination in the *Tractatus de Intellectus Emendatione*', *Studia Spinozana*, 2, 1986.
'Spinoza's Necessitarianism', in Yovel (ed.), *God and Nature*.
(ed.), *The Cambridge Companion to Spinoza* (Cambridge University Press, 1996).
Gaukroger, S., *Cartesian Logic* (Oxford: Clarendon Press, 1989).
Descartes: An Intellectual Biography (Oxford: Clarendon Press, 1995).
Gellner, E., *Legitimation of Belief* (Cambridge University Press, 1974).
Gewirth, A., 'The Cartesian Circle', *The Philosophical Review*, 50, 1941.
al-Ghazāli, *Deliverance from Error*, in W. Montgomery Watt (ed. and trans.), *The Faith and Practice of al-Ghazāli*, (London: George Allen & Unwin, 1953).
Gilead A., 'Spinoza's *Principium Individuationis* and Personal Identity', *International Studies in Philosophy*, vol. 15/1, 1983.
'The Indispensability of the First Kind of Knowledge', in Yovel (ed.), *Spinoza on Knowledge*.
Grene, M. (ed.), *Spinoza: A Collection of Critical Essays* (Garden City: Anchor, 1973).
Grene, M. and Nails, D. (eds.), *Spinoza and the Sciences* (Dordrecht: Reidel, 1986).
Gueroult, M., *Spinoza I: Dieu* (Paris: Aubier-Montaigne, 1968).
Guttmann, J., *Philosophies of Judaism*, D. W. Silverman (trans.) (London: Routledge & Kegan Paul, 1964).
Hampshire, S., *Spinoza* (Harmondsworth: Penguin, 1951).
'Spinoza and the Idea of Freedom'. *Proceedings of the British Academy* (1960), in Grene (ed.), *Spinoza: A Collection of Critical Essays*.
Harris, E. E., 'Spinoza's Theory of Human Immortality', in Mandelbaum and Freeman (eds.), *Spinoza: Essays in Interpretation*.
'Finite and Infinite in Spinoza's System', in Hessing (ed.), *Speculum Spinozanum*.
Haserot, F. S., 'Spinoza's Definition of Attribute' (1953), in Kashap, S. P. (ed.), *Studies in Spinoza* (Berkeley: University of California Press, 1972).
Hawking, S., *A Brief History of Time* (New York: Bantam, 1990).
Heidegger, M., *Identity and Difference* (1957), J. Stambaugh (trans.) (New York: Harper Torchbooks, 1974).
Hessing, S. (ed.), *Speculum Spinozanum* (London: Routledge & Kegan Paul, 1977).
Hubbeling, H. G., *Spinoza's Methodology* (Assen: Van Gorcum, 1967).
Hughes, G. J., *The Nature of God* (London: Routledge, 1995).
Ishiguro, H., 'Contingent Truths and Possible Worlds' (1979), in R. S. Woolhouse (ed.), *Leibniz: Metaphysics and Philosophy of Science* (Oxford University Press, 1981).
Israel, J., *The Dutch Republic: Its Rise, Greatness, and Fall 1477–1806* (Oxford: Clarendon Press, 1995).
James, S., 'Spinoza the Stoic', in Sorell, T. (ed.), *The Rise of Modern Philosophy* (Oxford: Clarendon Press, 1993).
Jantzen, G. M., *God's World, God's Body* (London: Darton, Longman and Todd, 1984).
Jarrett, C. E., 'The Logical Structure of Spinoza's Ethics, Part I', *Synthèse*, 37, 1978.
Joachim, H. H., *A Study of Spinoza's Ethics* (Oxford: Clarendon Press, 1901).

Kasher, A. and Biderman S., 'Why was Baruch de Spinoza Excommunicated?', in D. S. Katz and J. I. Israel (eds.), *Sceptics, Millenarians and Jews* (Leiden: Brill, 1990).

Kneale, W. and M., *The Development of Logic* (Oxford: Clarendon Press, 1962).

Lachiéze-Rey, P., *Les origines cartésiennes du Dieu de Spinoza* (Paris: Vrin, 1950).

Lasker, D. J., *Jewish Philosophical Polemics against Christianity in the Middle Ages* (New York: Ktav Publishing House, 1977).

Laux, H., *Imagination et religion chez Spinoza* (Paris: Vrin, 1993).

Lévinas, E., 'Monothéisme et langage' (1959), in *Difficile liberté* (Paris: Albin Michel, 1963).

'Réponse au Professeur McKeon', in *Spinoza: His Thought and Work* (Jerusalem: Israel Academy of Sciences and Humanities, 1983).

'Ethics of the Infinite', interview (1981) in R. Kearney (ed.), *States of Mind*, (Manchester University Press, 1995).

Levine, M. P., *Pantheism* (London: Routledge, 1994).

Lindbeck, G. A., *The Nature of Doctrine: Religion and Theology in a Postliberal Age* (London: SPCK).

Lloyd, G., *Part of Nature: Self-Knowledge in Spinoza's Ethics* (Ithaca: Cornell University Press, 1994).

Lovejoy, A. O., *The Great Chain of Being* (Cambridge: Harvard University Press, 1936).

McDowell, J., *Mind and World* (Cambridge: Harvard University Press, 1994).

Macherey, P., 'Note sur le rapport de Spinoza à Freud', in his *Avec Spinoza: études sur la doctrine et l'histoire du spinozism* (Paris: Presses Universitaires de France, 1992).

Introduction à l'Éthique de Spinoza: La cinquième partie, les voies de la liberté (Paris: Presses Universitaires de France, 1994).

McTaggart, J. McT. E., *The Nature of Existence*, vol. 1 (Cambridge University Press, 1921).

Maimonides, *The Guide for the Perplexed*, M. Friedländer (trans.) (New York: Dover, 1956).

Malcolm, N., entry on Spinoza in J. H. Burns (ed.), *The Cambridge History of Political Thought 1450–1700* (Cambridge University Press, 1991).

Malet, A., 'La religion de Spinoza au point de vue chrétien'. *Revue de Synthèse*, 99, 1978 (with comments by Misrahi, R. and Zac, S).

Mandelbaum M. and Freeman, E. (eds.), *Spinoza: Essays in Interpretation* (La Salle: Open Court, 1975).

Marion, J.-L., *Dieu sans l'être* (Paris: Fayard, 1982).

'The Essential Incoherence of Descartes' Definition of Divinity', F. P. Van de Pitte (trans.), in A. Oksenberg Rorty (ed.), *Essays on Descartes' Meditations* (University of California Press, 1986).

Mason, R., 'Spinoza on the Causality of Individuals', *Journal of the History of Philosophy*, 24, 1986.

'Spinoza on Modality', *The Philosophical Quarterly*, 36, 1986.

'Logical Possibility', *Metaphilosophy*, 19, 1988.

'Explaining Necessity', *Metaphilosophy*, 21, 1990.

'Ignoring the Demon? Spinoza's Way with Doubt', *Journal of the History of Philosophy*, 31, 1993.

'Spinoza on Religious Choice', *Philosophy*, 69, 1994.

'How Things Happen: Divine-natural Law in Spinoza'. *Studia Leibnitiana*, XXVIII/I, 1996.

Matheron, A., *Le Christ et le salut des ignorants chez Spinoza* (Paris: Aubier-Montaigne, 1971).

Individu et communauté chez Spinoza (revised from 1969) (Paris: Editions de Minuit, 1988).

'Remarques sur l'immortalité de l'âme chez Spinoza', *Les études philosophiques*, 1972.

'La vie éternelle et le corps selon Spinoza', *Revue philosophique*, 184, 1994.

Méchoulan, H., 'Le herem à Amsterdam et «l'excommunication» de Spinoza', *Cahiers Spinoza*, 3, 1980.

Meinsma, K. O., *Spinoza et son cercle* (revised H. Méchoulan, *et al.* and translated from 1896 edition) S. Roosenburg and J. –P. Osier (eds.) (Paris: Vrin, 1983).

Mellor, D. H., *The Facts of Causation* (London: Routledge, 1995).

Mignini, F., 'Per la datazione e l'interpretazione del *Tractatus de Intellectus Emendatione* di B. Spinoza', *La Cultura*, 17, 1979.

Milbank, J., *Theology and Social Theory* (Oxford: Blackwell, 1990).

Misrahi, R., 'Spinoza and Christian Thought: a Challenge', in Hessing (ed.), *Speculum Spinozanum*.

Moore, G. E., *Principia Ethica* (Cambridge University Press, 1903).

Moreau, P.–F., *Spinoza: L'expérience et l'éternité* (Paris: Presses Universitaires de France, 1994).

Murdoch, I., *Metaphysics as a Guide to Morals* (London: Chatto & Windus, 1992).

Nietzsche, F., *Beyond Good and Evil* (1886), R. J. Hollingdale (trans.) (Harmondsworth: Penguin, 1990).

Novak, D., *The Election of Israel* (Cambridge University Press, 1995).

'The Election of Israel: Outline of a Philosophical Analysis', in D. H. Frank, (ed.), *A People Apart: Chosenness and Ritual in Jewish Philosophical Thought* (Albany: SUNY Press, 1993).

Nussbaum, M. C., *The Therapy of Desire: Theory and Practice in Hellenistic Ethics* (Princeton University Press, 1994).

Oppenheimer, J. R., Speech to the Association of Los Alamos Scientists, November 2, 1945. In A. K. Smith and C. Weiner (eds.), *Robert Oppenheimer: Letters and Recollections* (Stanford University Press, 1995).

Orcibal, J., 'Les Jansénistes face à Spinoza', *Revue de Littérature Comparée*, 23, 1949.

Parkinson, G. H. R., *The Renaissance and Seventeenth-century Rationalism* (*Routledge History of Philosophy*, vol. IV) (London: Routledge, 1993).

Spinoza's Theory of Knowledge (Oxford: Clarendon Press, 1954).

'Spinoza on Miracles and Natural Law', *Revue Internationale de Philosophie*, 31, 1977.

Introduction and Notes to Spinoza, *Ethics*, revised ed. (London: Dent, 1993).

Pollock, F., *Spinoza, His Life and Philosophy* (London: Kegan Paul, 1880).
   The History of Scepticism from Erasmus to Spinoza (revised from 1960) (Berkeley: University of California Press, 1979).
Popkin, R. H., *Isaac La Peyrère* (Leiden: Brill, 1987).
   'The Religious Background of Seventeenth Century Philosophy', *Journal of the History of Philosophy*, 25, 1987.
   'Spinoza's Earliest Philosophical Years, 1655–61', *Studia Spinozana*, 4, 1988.
   'Spinoza and Bible Scholarship', in Force and Popkin (eds.), *The Books of Nature and Scripture*, also in Garrett (ed.), *Cambridge Companion*.
Popkin, R. H. and Signer, M. A. (eds.), *Spinoza's Earliest Publication? 'A Loving Salutation' by Margaret Fell* (Assen: Van Gorcum, 1987).
Rey, J.–F., 'Lévinas et Spinoza', in O. Bloch (ed.), *Spinoza au XXe siècle* (Paris: Presses Universitaires de France, 1993).
Rice, L. C., 'Spinoza on Individuation', in Mandelbaum and Freeman (eds.), *Spinoza: Essays in Interpretation*.
Rorty, R., *Essays on Heidegger and Others* (Cambridge University Press, 1991).
Roth, L., *Spinoza* (London: Benn, 1929).
Ruben, D.–H., *Explaining Explanation* (London: Routledge, 1990).
Savan, D., 'Spinoza: Scientist and Theorist of Scientific Method', in Grene and Nails (eds.), *Spinoza and the Sciences*.
Schleiermacher, F., *On Religion, Speeches to its Cultured Despisers* (1799), J. Oman (trans.) (New York: Harper Torchbooks, 1958).
Schlesinger, G. N., *The Intelligibility of Nature* (Aberdeen: Aberdeen University Press, 1985).
Schmitt, C. B., 'The Rediscovery of Ancient Skepticism in Modern Times' (revised from 1972), in M. Burnyeat (ed.), *The Skeptical Tradition* (Berkeley: University of California Press, 1983).
Siebrand, H. J., *Spinoza and the Netherlanders* (Assen: Van Gorcum, 1988).
Skinner, Q., 'Meaning and Understanding in the History of Ideas' (1969), in J. Tully (ed.), *Meaning and Context* (Cambridge: Polity Press, 1988).
Stead, C., *Philosophy in Christian Antiquity* (Cambridge University Press, 1994).
Steenbakkers, P., *Spinoza's Ethica from Manuscript to Print* (Assen: Van Gorcum, 1994).
Steinberg, D., 'Spinoza's Theory of the Eternity of the Human Mind', *Canadian Journal of Philosophy*, 11, 1981.
Strauss, L., *Spinoza's Critique of Religion*, E. M. Sinclair (trans.) (revised from 1930) (New York: Schocken, 1965).
   'How to Study Spinoza's Theologico-Political Treatise', in *Persecution and the Art of Writing* (New York: Free Press, 1948).
Traherne, T., *Centuries* (1670?), *Poems, and Thanksgivings*, H. M. Margoliouth (ed.) (Oxford: Clarendon Press, 1958).
Trigg, R., *Reason and Commitment* (Cambridge University Press, 1973).
Unger, P., *Ignorance* (Oxford: Clarendon Press, 1975).
Van Bunge, W., 'On the Early Dutch Reception of the *Tractatus Theologico-Politicus*', *Studia Spinozana*, 5, 1989.

Watson, R. A., *The Downfall of Cartesianism, 1673–1712* (The Hague: Nijhoff, 1966).

Watt, A. J., 'Spinoza's Use of Religious Language', *The New Scholasticism*, 46, 1972.

Williams, B., *Problems of the Self* (Cambridge University Press, 1973).

Descartes (Harmondsworth: Penguin, 1978).

'Personal Identity and Individuation' (1956), in Williams, *Problems of the Self.*

'Bodily Continuity and Personal Identity' (1960), in Williams, *Problems of the Self.*

'Deciding to Believe'(1970), in Williams, *Problems of the Self.*

Wittgenstein, L., *Letters to Russell, Keynes and Moore* (Oxford: Blackwell, 1974).

Wolfson, H. A., *The Philosophy of Spinoza* (reprint from 2 vols., 1934) (Cambridge: Harvard University Press, 1983).

Yakira, E., 'Ideas of Nonexistent Modes: *Ethics* II Proposition 8, its Corollary and Scholium' in Yovel (ed.), *Spinoza on Knowledge and the Human Mind.*

Yovel, Y., *Spinoza and Other Heretics*, vol. 1 (Princeton University Press, 1989).

(ed.), *God and Nature: Spinoza's Metaphysics* (Leiden: Brill, 1991).

(ed.), *Spinoza on Knowledge and the Human Mind* (Leiden: Brill, 1994).

'The Infinite Mode and Natural Laws in Spinoza', in Yovel (ed.), *God and Nature: Spinoza's Metaphysics.*

Zac, S., *Spinoza et L'interprétation de l'Écriture* (Paris: Presses Universitaires de France, 1965).

'Le problème du Christianisme de Spinoza', *Revue de Synthèse*, 78, 1957.

Index